"Every young actor anticipating a fulfilling life in the theater can benefit mightily from this book. There's lots of wisdom and helpful, practical advice here. It's up-to-date and comprehensive. The variety of perspectives helps to clarify the daunting, maybe overwhelming, prospect of entering this oh-so-demanding yet oh-so-rewarding field. A welcome addition to the PERFORM series. Thank you, Anna and Chris!"

—Eric Forsythe, Head of Directing, University of Iowa Theatre, IA, USA

"The most comprehensive and impressive collection of useful real-world advice about thoughtfully pursuing a career in the theater I have read in a very long time. If you are looking for one book that will improve your prospects and positively change your theatrical future, this is it."

—Guy Roberts, CEO & Artistic Director,
Prague Shakespeare Company, Czech Republic

"Required reading for any business class on acting. An invaluable book for anyone looking to peer into the real world of the working actor. Easy to read, with a wide array of working artists talking about how to live and breathe acting. This book could radically change your career. I wish someone had handed this to me 20 years ago!"

—Richard Robichaux, Head of Acting, Penn State University, PA, USA

PERFORM

Acting for the Stage

Acting for the Stage is a highly accessible guide to the business of theater acting, written for those interested in pursuing acting as a profession. This book is a collection of essays by and interviews with talented artists and businesspeople who have built successful careers in the theater; it's a goldmine of career advice that might take years to find on your own. Herein, the myths around professional acting are dispelled, and the mysteries revealed. *Acting for the Stage* illuminates practical strategies to help you build a life as a theater professional and find financial rewards and creative fulfillment in the process.

- Contains essays by and interviews with working stage actors, acting coaches, directors, writers, and agents.
- Features discussions on selecting a graduate school program, choosing acting classes and workshops, making the most out of your showcase, landing an agent, networking and promoting yourself, and the business of casting.
- Covers issues of money management, balancing the highs and lows of the profession, finding work to nourish your acting career, and building your creative team and support network.

PERFORM: Succeeding as a Creative Professional

The PERFORM series aims to offer engaging, uplifting, and expert support for up-and-coming artists. The series explores success in the arts, how we define success in artistic professions, and how we can prepare the next generation of artists to achieve their career goals and pay their bills.

The books in this series include practical advice, narratives, and insider secrets from industry professionals. Each book will include essays by and interviews with successful working artists and other professionals who represent, hire, or collaborate with these artists.

Ultimately, the goal of this series is simple: to illuminate how to make a living—and a *life*—as an artist.

Volumes in the series:

Acting for the Stage, edited by Anna Weinstein and Chris Qualls

Directing for the Screen, edited by Anna Weinstein

Writing for the Screen, edited by Anna Weinstein

PERFORM

Succeeding as a Creative Professional

Acting for the Stage

EDITED BY ANNA WEINSTEIN AND
CHRIS QUALLS

Routledge
Taylor & Francis Group

NEW YORK AND LONDON

First published 2017
by Routledge
711 Third Avenue, New York, NY 10017

and by Routledge
2 Park Square, Milton Park, Abingdon, Oxon OX14 4RN

Routledge is an imprint of the Taylor & Francis Group, an informa business

Library of Congress Cataloging in Publication Data
Names: Weinstein, Anna, 1972- author. | Qualls, Chris editor.
Title: Acting for the stage / edited by Anna Weinstein and Chris Qualls.
Description: New York : Routledge, Taylor & Francis Group, 2017. |
Series: Perform | Includes bibliographical references and index.
Identifiers: LCCN 2016031512| ISBN 9781138945203
(hbk : alk. paper) | ISBN 9781138945159 (pbk : alk. paper) |
ISBN 9781315671567 (ebk : alk. paper)
Subjects: LCSH: Acting—Vocational guidance.
Classification: LCC PN2055 .A15 2017 | DDC 792.02/8—dc23

ISBN: 978-1-138-94520-3 (hbk)
ISBN: 978-1-138-94515-9 (pbk)
ISBN: 978-1-315-67156-7 (ebk)

Typeset in Adobe Garamond and Avenir
by Keystroke, Neville Lodge, Tettenhall, Wolverhampton

For our children, Abraham and Gabriel

CONTENTS

ACKNOWLEDGMENTS

We owe many thank yous for this book. First, we are a deeply grateful to the contributors who jumped on board to participate in this project. It was a true pleasure to reconnect with old friends, make new friends and colleagues, and spend time with some of the theater professionals we most admire. They took time out of their busy schedules to share their perspective and expertise, which is among the most generous of gifts. We must also acknowledge the many photographers who graciously allowed us to include their work in this book.

Thank you sincerely to our friends, colleagues, and mentors who supported this project from the outset—those who lent an ear, served as reviewers, or provided initial encouragement. Thanks especially to Tom Aulino, Trai Cartwright, Lisa Channer, Lee Michael Cohn, Jay Paul Deratany, Chuck Erven, Mark Futterman, Connie Haneline, Andy Hawtrey, Jim Jennewein, Kevin Jones, Jordan Lund, Joshua Malkin, A.K. Murtadha, Allison Phillips, Bill Rabkin, Robert I. Rubinsky, Andrea Stewart, Deanne Stillman, and Jeff Wood.

To our students at Auburn University, thank you for providing perspective and inspiration. To our colleagues and mentors in Auburn University's Departments of Theatre and Media Studies, thank you for the support at various stages of this project and throughout the past decade.

Thank you to Emily McCloskey, Stacey Walker, Elliana Arons, Meredith Darnell, and John Makowski at Focal Press | Routledge. Emily and Stacey initially saw the possibility in this series and advocated for it from the beginning. Elliana supported the early stages of development, and Meredith shepherded the manuscript through development. We are grateful to Katherine Hemmings for her expertise in taking the book through the production process and to Helen Baxter who was especially attentive and thorough in her copyediting. Thank you also to Nicci Leamon, who has been transcribing interviews for years now, to Susan

Cochran for her last-minute transcriptions, and to Ande Nichols, Jill Nusbaum, and Geneva Willis for their truly excellent editorial support.

To our parents, thank you for encouraging us to pursue the arts, and to our siblings, thank you for applauding us along the way. Finally, we thank our children, who have been endlessly patient and encouraging these past few years and have also offered unique insight at crucial moments during the making of this book and series. You're our inspiration, boys. We hope you will continue to pursue your dreams with tenacity, enthusiasm, and confidence.

INTRODUCTION

Where should you move to after graduation? Where can you find additional training? How can you prepare a showcase if your school doesn't have one? What is your best chance of finding an agent? How can you get better at auditioning? What is it like to be part of a national tour? How can you get work in corporate entertainment? How can you use your acting talents and skills to do more than just entertain?

You'll find answers to all of these questions in this book. The conversations and essays in the pages that follow will address the most common concerns actors have, as well as little known secrets about the business and topics that are often considered taboo—for instance, can you "take a break" from acting, or does that make you *less than* your actor friends?

If you're an actor, you've no doubt questioned your career choice on any number of occasions. And you might now be looking at the graphic below that scarily denotes the cyclical nature of the acting business and wonder again whether your decision to embark on this career was a wise one. Is this really a business you want to pursue with passion and conviction?

You get started, you stick with it, you achieve success, you keep pushing for more success, and then you start all over again. The implication is that you'll lose your success somewhere along the way—that the need to begin again is due to a fall.

There will be some stumbles in this career, certainly. But that would be true in any career, in any industry. Sure, an actor's career is admittedly less stable than many other professions, but the fact that there's risk involved isn't itself unique to acting.

Besides, you're accustomed to risk. You risk putting yourself out there, opening yourself to judgment every day. That's your job. You dare to entertain. And with that dare, you invite the possibility of a standing ovation on a good night and people leaving the theater early on a bad night.

You know this by now. You can't achieve great success without risking great failure. As John F. Kennedy said, "only those who dare to fail greatly can ever achieve greatly."[1]

The cyclical nature of the acting business isn't something you cycle through once or twice in a lifetime. As a working actor, you'll move through this process weekly or daily if you're auditioning regularly. You'll become accustomed to throwing out your sides (script pages) after every audition. You'll begin again regularly and repeatedly, and with time you'll become used to this process. Before you know it, engaging in the *business* of acting will be as second nature as engaging in the *craft* of acting.

How to Use This Book

This book is about the business of acting. There are other books that reinforce craft, the tasks associated with developing your skills and talents as an actor. But this book is specifically about the work involved with becoming a professional actor.

You don't have to read it cover to cover. It won't benefit you necessarily to read the essays and interviews in order—although there's certainly nothing wrong with that approach. But the book is structured so that you can pick and choose what to read when, at the pace that works best for you. Flip through the pages and browse the interviewee introductions and contributor bios. This will give you a glimpse of the personalities, successes, and individual perspectives on building a life in the theater.

What you'll find in this book is insider insight into the day-to-day life of an actor. What is it like to be a struggling actor? What is it like to be a working actor? What is it like to be one of the most celebrated and successful actors in the world?

You'll hear from a range of actors, directors, agents, acting coaches, professors, vocal trainers, and artistic directors in this book. You'll read stories about people who started their own theaters, or worked their way from Off-Broadway to Broadway to film or television. You'll read about overcoming physical challenges, emotional challenges, and financial challenges. You'll learn how theater can support your efforts to achieve a greater good while at the same time bringing you immeasurable personal reward.

You'll find out what traditional agents are looking for, as well as booking agents for corporate acting gigs. You'll get perspectives from agents in England and Canada, from acting coaches and directors in Los Angeles, New York, Boston, North Carolina, and Pennsylvania. You'll hear words of wisdom from Ellen Burstyn and her five decades' acting in theater, film, and television in New York and Los Angeles. You'll get the opinion of a working theater actor in Berlin, and a 100-year-old stage actor in India.

The range of advice, wisdom, and stories you'll read in this book is meant to give you perspective. The essays and interviews are grouped thematically, exploring the broad ideas of "Getting Started," "Sticking It Out," "Finding Success," "Getting Ahead," and "Starting Again." These groupings, however, do not indicate that what you'll find in each chapter is a logically ordered list of how-to advice. You won't!

Some interviews include topical questions and responses about how to approach specific goals and situations as a theater actor, and others take a broader exploratory approach, with the interviewees sharing personal narratives or opinions about some of the more intangible aspects of the career. The same is true of the essays. You'll find a range of scope, from direct advice to calls to action to interview snippets with multiple working actors.

The key is this: Don't look for advice alone. Look for insights. Look for new ways of approaching challenging aspects of the career. Look for information about the realities of the business. Above all else, look for a deeper understanding of how to celebrate the *pursuit of* success as well as the *result of* success.

Note

1 "Day of Affirmation Address, University of Capetown, Capetown, South Africa, June 6, 1966," John F. Kennedy Presidential Library and Museum, accessed May 1, 2016, http://www.jfklibrary.org/Research/Research-Aids/Ready-Reference/RFK-Speeches/Day-of-Affirmation-Address-as-delivered.aspx.

CHAPTER 1

GETTING STARTED

"Great people do things before they're ready. They do things before they know they can do it. Doing what you're afraid of, getting out of your comfort zone, taking risks like that—that is what life is."

Amy Poehler

Taking the first step in any endeavor is always the most challenging—and also the easiest to put off. "I'll start tomorrow. Next month. After I pay off the credit cards. After I feel a little more accomplished."

It can be intimidating to proclaim to be a professional when so far all you have is amateur experience. Even if you have worked professionally, chances are you know actors who have worked more than you. Are they more professional? More worthy of success?

As you know from your experience auditioning, you won't do yourself any favors comparing yourself to your competition. Now is the time to focus on *you*.

You know about the craft of acting. You've been honing your craft for years, and you're well aware that you'll be working on that for the rest of your life. The business of acting, though, that's something entirely different. The business of acting for a living—and more importantly, the business of making a *life* as an actor—isn't as Wild West as it might sound. There are some truths about working as an actor, and that's where we'll start with this chapter.

You're about to begin your professional career as an actor. What do you need to learn to set yourself up for success?

Who Knew?

According to the U.S. Department of Labor's Bureau of Labor Statistics, the job outlook for actors is encouraging. Employment for actors is projected to grow by ten percent from 2014 to 2024, which is faster than the average for all professions.[1]

Here's what we're going to address in this first chapter:

- Why you should act big, buttery, and bold, even for the camera
- How to prepare for an interview as well as for an audition
- What an agent is looking for in a new client and appropriate etiquette for reaching out to agents
- Why it's important to embrace your age and type but not limit yourself to type
- The importance of ongoing training
- What you need to know about auditioning for Shakespeare
- What directors and casting directors do and don't want to see in a Shakespeare audition
- Expectations and what it's like to work in a resident theater
- Why casting agents are your new best friends
- What it means to move toward your goals and not away from your frustrations

Where you choose to begin your acting career is entirely up to you, and it *is* possible to make an informed decision about next steps. In fact, there are criteria you can use to make this decision.

Let's begin there. You're about to graduate from school . . . now what?

MOVING TOWARD YOUR DREAM

Big Buttery Acting and Developing Business Relationships

▶ An Interview With Richard Robichaux

Richard Robichaux's theater credits include the Shakespeare Theatre in Washington, DC, Yale Repertory Theatre, the Mark Taper Forum, Syracuse Stage, among others. He received his MFA from Rutgers University where he studied under William Esper and Maggie Flanigan.

Richard Robichaux
Photo by Mark Bennington

Robichaux has had leading, guest starring, and recurring roles on ABC, NBC, CBS, Showtime, Comedy Central, the Lifetime Channel, as well as the Sundance Film Festival and Tribeca Film Festival. He can be seen in Richard Linklater's film *Boyhood* (2014), and as Lloyd Hornbuckle opposite Jack Black and Shirley MacLaine in Linklater's film *Bernie* (2011).

Robichaux has worked with top training programs such as the Juilliard School, Yale School of Drama, and University of Texas at Austin. He is currently Head of Acting in the MFA program at Penn State University.

In 2012, Robichaux delivered the keynote address at the Southeastern Theatre Conference. Other keynote addresses include the Texas Thespian Festival, Florida Association for Theatre Education, Heartland Film Festival, and the Educational Theater Association's National Teacher Conference in San Diego. Robichaux has been featured in *Southern Theatre* magazine and *Dramatics Magazine*.

Can you tell me how you prepare students for the business of acting in your program?

The first year at Penn State, my students learn process, which builds a foundation. It's separate from product, and it's separate from the industry. It comes from the self, from where you stand. Then slowly but surely we start to move away from that. Getting an authentic point of view is the most powerful thing for an actor in the beginning—this is what we're working on.

Then in the third year, I have a camera in the classroom almost every day just so they're comfortable with it. And we have serious conversations about the business of television, film, and theater—and conversations about money. Are the best actors working? No. Are there good actors working? Yes. If we're going to be responsible, we have to deal with that question. When I was in school, I had excellent teachers who had never been on a set themselves. So the bridge between the classroom and the casting office wasn't a walking bridge, but the Grand Canyon. What I try to do is make that bridge as small as possible.

How do you go about doing that, bridging that gap?

I'll tell you this way: The MFAs study with me in a place called Room 6. I say, "If we figure out the theory of acting in Room 6, it doesn't benefit anyone. We're preparing for outside Room 6." This isn't hermetically sealed acting theory. It has to move outside, and it has to be practical. The theory can't be enough. So we do mock agent meetings. We do all sorts of things. What I don't want my students to feel after graduation is out of place, because once you feel out of place, you are.

How can you address that problem practically?

Every Monday, for instance, there's a quiz. I ask what the number one movie at the box office was, who cast it, who was in it, and why it's important that it was number one. They have to know that information but also know why it's a big deal. When you come to set on Monday in LA, that's all anybody is talking about. So every Monday, I bring my MFA students my Arts and Leisure sections from the *New York Times* as required reading. They read it, and then we discuss. They become living, curious, working artists who understand why things get made—and they learn about collaboration. They get to think about context outside of a studio where they do scenes by dead white men over and over again.

That's interesting about the white male playwrights. Do you make an effort to diversify your program at Penn State?

Our program is one of the most diverse in the United States. The public theater in New York loves to use our actors for their emerging writer series. We have a relationship with the Classical Theatre of Harlem. We just brought in Dominique Morisseau to do a commissioned work for our students, called "Blood at the Root," which is now in New York at the National Black Theatre. We have Hansol Jung coming in next year to do our commissioned work. That to me is what the twenty-first century is about. This is what the world looks like right now, in the day to day and in television and film. I want my students to know that because it's empowering.

So in terms of teaching students to act for film and television as compared to theater, how do you differentiate?

Here's what I tell my students: I tell them I want their acting big, fat, rich, and buttery. I want them to be big. Underplaying a part is just as bad as overplaying. The moment must be played, and the actor must have confidence. Only an acting technique derived by a director or a playwright would tell actors to do less. Audiences have proved that isn't what they want. Say what you will about ham, but everybody loves it. You can't eat it all the time but, yeah, I see Kevin Spacey chewing the scenery in *House of Cards*, and I say, sign me up. If my actors can begin to express themselves fully and live through something with no apologies, it's really empowering for them.

Many film and television actors aren't rich and buttery, though. Is this in the training?

I think there's fear. So many programs don't talk honestly about acting for the camera. What you end up getting are actors being still and quiet. I tell my actors that when casting directors say "less," they're really saying "more." It needs to be more real. Don't take something away, just dig deeper. They're so afraid of the camera, of doing too much and being "a theater actor" that they forget everything that made them want to be an actor—all of that big, fat, buttery acting that we're talking about.

Actors are told not to act, but that's a cheesy, disingenuous slogan. I don't think it's a serious response to the art and craft of acting. Of course it's acting. Of course it is, so then let's seriously talk about it rather than throw around these bumper stickers and one-liners about acting.

Could it also be the idea that minimalism is what people want for film and television?

Yes, first-year students get caught up in scenes being "too dramatic." But you can't imagine the circumstances that television has right now. I coach an actor on *The Walking Dead*, and the circumstances he has to go through are outrageous. He has to think, my sister was just eaten by a zombie because there's an apocalypse. And then he has to do that on the tightrope of a live set where time and money are everything. He has to live through it so that this unbelievable circumstance can for a moment or two be believable to me and you sitting in our house. We need to believe that zombies exist. That's a huge responsibility for the actor, and it must be taken seriously.

> "Here's what I tell my students: I tell them I want their acting big, fat, rich, and buttery. Underplaying a part is just as bad as overplaying."

Is there any acting—any types of role—that the actor shouldn't take seriously?

Sure, there's a lot of acting that's just what I call "hotel art." They don't build museums for hotel art. Its whole purpose is to *not* be seen. There are some roles that you don't need to research and backstory. If it's an under-five in a TV show and you're supposed to work at Best Buy, then you're a supporting player who, of course, should play it as close to your own nature. And let's be honest—it doesn't require a lot of craft. There's a time and place for crafting. I've done roles where it required an immense amount of concentration and craft, and I've also done roles that I could have done with my eyes closed. It was hotel art.

I'm curious about the decision actors have to make about where to move after school. Do you recommend New York or LA? Chicago or Minneapolis? How do actors make a decision that's practical and also most likely to set themselves up for success?

One thing I do in my business class is I make everyone present why they should move to New York. Everyone has to tell me why New York is the place for them. They have to find an apartment, a job, and a studio where they'll study. And they have to tell me why those things will work. I make them do a budget. Through this, I'm trying to get them to see the possibilities, to truly imagine how it would be. The next week, they do the exact same thing but for LA, and they have to tell me why New York is *not* the place for them.

I'm trying to help them see that they have to make decisions based on their pros list, not their cons list—so they're running *toward* something rather than *from* something. I think for so many of us, the scarcity and lack of work chased us into the big cities like New York and LA, but there are opportunities everywhere. Take Atlanta—television there is booming. I want people to go to a city because they actually want to live and work there. I think that sets them up for much more success, and it's much more empowering.

My wife and I left LA to move to Austin, and I remember my agent saying, "I can't believe you're leaving LA." And I very clearly said to him, "I'm not leaving LA. I'm going to Austin." I want to live. I'm the boss of me, and I'm going to live in Austin. Six months later, I was living in Austin, sitting across the table from Shirley MacLaine, Jack Black, and Rick Linklater about to shoot *Bernie*.

I was going to ask you about that. Was that a turning point in your career, when you took control in that way?
I'd never felt more power than when I thought, "I'm the boss of me." It's silly, but it occurred to me that I can do whatever I want.

It confuses them at first, but I tell my students in their third year, "I want you to know that I don't care what you do after this. That if you call me in ten years and say you still read poetry, go to the theater, and you're happy, then I'll be thrilled." I think so many times actors end up living their career to please their mentors or their parents, and then they find that it's difficult to be happy where they are. That breaks my heart for them. I think so often how blessed I am to talk about art all day.

So that's what I do. I make them think about and talk about this idea of "Where do you want to live?" And I do the same thing for grad school. If they want to do grad school, I say, "Give me five grad schools and tell me why each one is the right grad school and no other grad school is right for you." Then I ask them, "Here are these five grad schools you say you want to go to. Now if the name brand of the university had nothing to do with it, where would you want to live?" There's a relief when you can release yourself from the brand name pressure that I think a lot of mentors put on you.

Can an actor in the United States train specifically to have a career in the theater? Is that possible or practical? Or should you be training and preparing for any type of acting work?

A relatively new problem is that the bulk of the MFA programs swelled at the same time as the regional theater system. There were lots of theaters doing classic American repertory where it had ten or twelve people in it, or they were doing Shakespeare or Chekhov. Then the downturn started to happen in the 1980s and 1990s, and the LORT system did as well. So a lot of those programs started to winnow out a bit, and the plays that were really successful, the ones producers liked, had two people in them. They had one set. Theaters started hurting, and there was less work for theater actors.

New York has also never properly paid actors wages Off-Broadway. You want to stay in New York so that you can get a review in the *New York Times*, but actually, going to the Milwaukee Repertory Theater would allow you to make more money. So, financially, this doesn't work. Even if you had a really successful year as an actor, that also means you would never be home. And for those of us who decided to have families, it just proved untenable. After grad school, I did very well my first year. I booked a lot of plays, and I did lots of regional theater, but I was still broke.

You were in New York?

Yes, I was living in New York. I did two or three plays my first year, but I remember the day I got the check from my first national commercial. It was a commercial that took one day to shoot, not three months, and I didn't have to leave my apartment. One day, and I made as much on that commercial as I'd made the previous year. You have a moment where you come to terms with that.

And it influenced your choices?

It did. I started auditioning for TV. I remember when I booked my first TV job—it was great but very difficult, and I realized how undertrained and how underprepared I was. One of my favorite stories is my first camera audition at CBS. I was just out of Rutgers, and I remember the casting director leaned in from around the camera and said, "Slate." And I said, "No, it's Richard."

I didn't get that part that day. And that's why I believe in not just the *theory of acting*, but *acting for a living*. I'd much rather you make the mistake with me than at CBS. I'm hard and demanding because I want my students to go to CBS and think, "Well, this is easy. At least Richard isn't in the room."

You're training them to expect the career to be difficult—to be prepared for the challenge?

Yes, that's part of the training. You have to be prepared. It doesn't matter if actors are students or if they have agents—they should never be complacent or arrogant. They need to build a habit of excellence, and it starts in school. No one just beginning their training has any talent. What you have is *potential.* Talent is *potential* activated repeatedly. What I mean is, if when you graduate you are good over and over again, the people around you, those you work with and for, will refer to you as *talented.* This will be based solely on the repetition of your excellent work. You see, I can take a great photograph occasionally. This doesn't make me a photographer, because I can't do it repeatedly under a variety of circumstances. Talent must be manifested. It's not enough to just say you have it; I need to see it.

> "I believe in not just the *theory of acting,* but *acting for a living.* I'd much rather you make the mistake with me than at CBS."

That's an interesting way to look at it.

I think this word *talent* is overused. If you're still in school and you haven't worked yet, then so far, none of that talent has been tested by the industry. You have *potential,* and now it's time to activate it. What happens is most actors just don't. They wait for somebody else to activate it.

I can see that, but I can also see how tough it could be to activate it. How do you know where to begin? You move to the new city you've chosen, and then what?

Once they move to their new location, one of the things I tell my students is that we must localize joy. We often see joy at a distance by thinking, "Once I move here or once I have this job, then I'll have joy." Localizing means that before the student leaves wherever they are, they should look around and think, "Oh, actually, there's the SAG/AFTRA branch right here in my city." They should do mixers or workshops. They should begin to get themselves acquainted. If they've never been an extra, I think they should do it so they can see what it's like to actually be on set. They start to see how hard it is, the reality of the business.

Then, when they decide to move, they should spend the first six months taking care of their lives. Your job needs to be first. Your apartment needs to be first. Your friends, family, and connections all need to be first. Then, you can start networking with likeminded artists at a local studio where you want to study. Then you look at the theaters in town and get involved in any way you can. Maybe you're not ready to act for the Alliance Theatre, but you can offer your services to the casting director as a reader, or as a reader for new works. Being an artist is about offering services. You should first ask how you can serve the community, not what you can take from it.

We all know how challenging the business is. How can aspiring actors assess whether they have the emotional capacity to deal with these challenges?
What I don't like is when people tell students that if they can do anything else, do it. I think it's cruel. I'm very smart, and I make no apologies about it. I could have done anything else besides acting, but I chose not to. I don't think it's helpful when people say that. Again, that's running away from pain rather than running toward pleasure.

Wanting to be an actor doesn't make anyone special. It actually makes you incredibly common. What we're lacking in is people who want to *act*. That's very different. Do you want to be an actor or are you actually interested in acting? You have to ask yourself that question. I think in our society where people are famous, where we have celebrities, people are interested in the byproduct of acting rather than the actual doing of it.

You have to crave it. It's like the fire is in the firewood. It's in there. It's embedded in it, and it has to crave the friction that will create it—and that life is what we do. As a teacher, I feel like I'm a firestarter. I say, "Okay, I'm going to help create some of the friction needed to release the fire in you."

It has to be embedded in you. You have to be very honest with yourself. As an acting teacher, I say that I can't teach acting but I can train an actor. What that means is that I require an actor first. That can't be taught. If it could, I wouldn't waste my time recruiting and watching auditions.

So when you're auditioning students for your MFA program, what are you looking for in an audition? What makes someone stand out for you?
The thing I look for is mysterious and personal, but it's a point of view. It has to come through their aliveness. This is a person who has an aliveness to them. So

often, I see people who are uncomfortable or who have fear. They find it hard to even smile, and I think, "Why are you doing this to yourself?" They're forcing something to happen. There's this idea that anybody can act, but it's not true. I'm auditioning right now for our MFA program, and I saw about seventy-five people this morning. I called back one young woman.

What did you see in this woman?
She walked in with confidence. She took up space. She had a charm quotient. Her monologue wasn't great, but when I'm thinking about an MFA program, I'm thinking about what this person is going to look like after three years with us. I'm not interested in how you acted before you met me, but you have to have something I can work with. There was something there with this woman. The other people who auditioned, they wanted to be actors, but they aren't. I'm going to talk to this woman one on one to see if it'll work out.

> "No one just beginning their training has any talent. What you have is *potential*. Talent is *potential* activated repeatedly."

So you're going to meet with her. What are you looking for from her in the interview?
I'm looking for people who are curious about the world, who have a point of view about the world. They're bright. It isn't about grades, but there's a brightness to them. In the interview process, they're the actor in the room, so I expect them to help lead the conversation. Even though I'm interviewing, this should be a conversation. I can't tell you how many people just give one-word answers.

Couldn't they just be nervous?
Sure, they could be nervous, but the basis of this job is performing at a high level under high stress, so I have a low tolerance for that. The other thing is that if I am casting a lead in a play, what I'm looking for is a leader. If you're not a leader in your classroom, you shouldn't be surprised that you're not a lead in the school play. I need someone who'll be able to do the interviews and junkets, to be a leader in the room where you have forty journalists asking you the same question over and over again.

What would you say to an aspiring actor who is uncomfortable in interviews? Someone who is good on stage but not so good in the one on one?

The thing to do is to practice. A lot of my students say, "I don't know how to do an interview." So that's why we do mock interviews at our school all over campus. We don't just do it in Room 6. So if you're going to audition for grad school or if you're going to an interview, then you need to practice in front of friends. You need to practice in your living room. You need to practice in different places, just like you would practice a performance.

We control so little in this business, which means that actors must control everything they can. I can control my preparation. I can control my physical health, what clothes I'm wearing, that I get to audition on time. Everything I can control I must. That way, after an audition or after an interview, I can say, "Well, there's nothing else I could have done. I did my job." Acting takes preparation and discipline.

At CBS, when you didn't know how to slate, did you think to yourself, "This will never happen again"? Do you make a conscious effort to learn from your mistakes?

Absolutely. But what's also important is that I didn't crumble. I made a joke, and Mikie—the casting director who I still love—she made a joke with me, and then I gave a great audition. She didn't cast me that day, because I was too green to be on set, obviously. But she cast me later. The main thing is I survived.

And you also developed a relationship with her, obviously. Can you address those kinds of relationship that actors will develop in the business? How to do that organically when in fact they really do want something—like being cast?

Some relationships are friendly, and some are very businesslike. But I've always had good friends who are directors, producers, and casting directors, and I'm friends with them because I like them and their work. So we're colleagues and friends. You have to stay genuine with yourself and with others. If you feel like you're networking, then you probably are. You have to be able to say, "Am I being overly nice? Am I being disingenuous? Is that the authentic me?" My students know about this, because on the first day with me, they know that I expect authenticity in their work, and I expect authenticity with them as people. I'm demanding of them to be as good as they actually are, and they trust me.

In the end, though, it's not about charm. It's about the work. Your work should speak for itself.

HOW TO BREAK IN

An Agent's Perspective

▶ An Interview With Kay Hilton

Kay Hilton

Photo by Sandi Hodgkinson

Kay Hilton's KMC Agencies has been open since 1996. She has offices in London and Manchester, and represents her actors and dancers in theater, film, and television across the UK and internationally. As often as she's able, Hilton makes university visits to speak with aspiring actors about joining the industry. Her advice is always the same: to conduct your career as a business, stay positive, and be open to the endless possibilities that come your way.

When you visit with students on campuses, what types of thing do you teach them to prepare for the business world?

It sounds really basic, but things like preparing your CV properly and getting the right headshot, how you approach a producer or agent, audition technique—your tools when you go for an audition. They're so basic that they tend to be overlooked.

As an agent, when actors come to you and are auditioning, how do they first approach you?

It used to be via letter or phone call, but now it's email. So they may go onto our website and use the contact form, or they may know of us and email us directly. They generally send a cover letter, CV, headshots, and show reels if they have them. From that information, we would decide whether we're going to see them. Sometimes they're in a performance and they say, "Here's my CV. Would you like to come out and see me?" We would do that or audition them, really, depending on the situation.

So what is it about the information that an actor might send you via email that would attract you to follow up with that actor?

A good headshot. If they're students or they're just coming into the business, they're not going to have a massive amount of disposable income. Nonprofessional shots are okay initially, but not if it's clearly been snapped by your phone or something. If you can't get the basics together properly, then you're not going to be a professional person to work with. So we're looking for them to be organized and professional from that very first point of contact. The CV has got to have something that's worth looking at. Students or graduates would invite us to a showcase. We'd go see it based on their talent, a particular look, and whether there was space for them on the books.

What do you mean by a particular look?

It depends what's popular at the time but also who's already on our books. If we've got, say, two blonde 20- to 25-year-old girls at 5'8", then we're not going to be taking a third one on unless there is too much work for the two we've already got. We tend not to take more than two of any one type. Even within the categories, you split again. You might have somebody who looks really young, or alternative, or heavier. There are always categories within ages. When we look at our board, we don't want to see the same character over and over again.

What's next in terms of what would make an actor shine in comparison to the competition?

They form an impression even when they're first writing to you. It's that X-factor thing you can't put your finger on. Sometimes there's something on the CV that makes you think, "Hmm, yeah, I'd quite like to see that person." We tend to acknowledge people who are organized enough to send a proper cover letter. CV credits are important, whether they've done college work or if they've worked hard to do things outside of their college productions, things like that.

So when you go to the showcase, can you describe what you're looking for in a performance?

It's whoever draws you in—an engaging performance, somebody who's clearly confident in what they're doing so nerves aren't getting the better of them. Nerves are huge, and, unfortunately, you have to get them under control. But you can be as confident as you like, and without skill, you're not going to get representation or a job.

When you say *skill*, that sounds different than talent. Is there a difference?
Yes, because people who have a natural talent could still enhance that with some technique.

Is that something that you come across, somebody who has talent but not skill?
Definitely. Nine times out of ten you would take that person on because they'll pick up the technique along the way. We have done it a couple of times, and sometimes it works, and sometimes it goes horribly wrong. In that scenario, they've got to have the work ethic. They've got to be willing to put in the extra hours to get the technique there.

> "I tend to remind actors who are just getting started to simply do the work, as they would in any business field. Do the work and be open to new opportunities. So much of our success lies in our outlook."

So if you see them in the showcase, and you can see that they're really talented but don't have the skills, what's the next step?
We would probably speak to them after the showcase. In the UK, that's what happens. They all come off stage and chat with whoever is there. We would invite anybody we were particularly interested in for an interview. We would also audition them sometimes, because when you see a showcase, you see something that's been rehearsed and prepared. An audition mirrors what would happen in a professional audition.

Can you tell me what that looks like, the professional audition?
There's two ways, television and films. They would initially go in with a monologue or a piece, or they may have been sent scripts from the company to go through when they get there. Sometimes there is somebody reading without any

emotion who is very difficult to act with. Sometimes they'll bring in somebody who's auditioning for the other part so there's two of you auditioning. That sometimes works, sometimes doesn't.

But from our point of view, we would just bring them in and ask them to prepare a couple of contrasting pieces. So we might ask for a Shakespeare piece and a comedy piece. Sometimes casting directors ask for a poem or a verse or something similar.

What about the stage auditions? When you send people out for a stage audition, how does that typically work?
They would be asked to prepare a monologue or a piece of their own choice, or a couple of contrasting pieces, depending on the job. This goes back to what we said originally, having the right tools and the right things in your bag, really. You've got to have a variety of monologues and pieces that you could pull out for different types of audition.

How long are those monologues?
Always less than two minutes. We say anywhere between about ninety seconds and two minutes, because anything longer and you're bored.

At the audition stage, what should an actor be prepared to do when it comes to taking direction or trying something again in a different way?
Most auditions, if they like you, they'll give you direction during the audition. If you've done it one way and they want you to do it in a different way, then they'll ask you to do it. A lot of it is to see if you pick up direction. This is where the training comes in, because it's being able to understand what the director wants you to do. If they get direction and then do it exactly the same, we'd be unlikely to offer them representation at that stage. They're being asked to do it in a different way for a reason.

Do you find that actors are resisting on purpose, or are they unable to be self-reflective?
We've had both of those, and there are some who think they're right and theirs is the only way. They're the people you probably won't work with. And some people aren't aware of what they're doing, and when you point it out they say, "I didn't realize I was doing that," and then they try to put it right.

My advice is to be open to constructive feedback and self-reflection. Actors need to understand that if they want to work for a particular director, they're going to have to do it the way he wants.

What kind of advice would you have for the young person who was the star in his or her school and is now struggling to succeed, struggling with self-confidence after graduating?

I think what they probably need to appreciate is that unless somebody spots them and thinks, "That's the person I want to make my lead in my new film," then they'll be going into ensemble roles or small roles. So those ensemble roles or very small roles, they're not looking for somebody who wants to be a superstar. They're looking for somebody who can fit into the group that they're working with. I think that's probably the best bet. They could be the next Elizabeth Taylor, but they've also got to know they can fit in. I think it's a matter of taking away that sort of diva basis a little bit.

One of the first times I ever saw James McAvoy act, he was in a production called *Shameless*. It's a UK drama and not on the biggest channel, so quite small ratings. It grew in popularity. He had a reasonably good role early in the series, but for all intents and purposes here in the UK, he was really no big deal. But then, whatever it was about him, somebody saw it, and now he's Mr. Hollywood, isn't he? I think if you've got that star quality or you've got what people want, then people will see it anyway without you forcing it down their throats. I suppose the way to look at it is that you don't need to court success to be a good, strong, successful actor.

> "My advice is to be open to constructive feedback and self-reflection. Actors need to understand that if they want to work for a particular director, they're going to have to do it the way he wants."

When I think of the actresses coming out of the UK, like Helen Mirren and Judi Dench, and Maggie Smith, we know their names. With some actors, there might be this desire to achieve that level of stardom as opposed to just saying my goal here is to be a working actor, to make a living as an actor.

One seems to overtake the other. The people you just mentioned, they still do theater. You can still find them on stage in the West End. You know they're grounded. They're not saying, well no, I'm not going to do theater because I'm a big star now. It's like you say, they're doing their job.

What is your advice to those actors who haven't been able to get an agent yet? That's most often the goal for actors, because it's hard to get professional work without an agent.

The need for agents has created more agents, and what happens now is a little bit of a lottery for people coming out of college, because it's like, "Well, I can't get the agent I want. Am I better off on my own, or am I better off with just any agent?" And my advice there would be that you're better off on your own than with a bad agent, because they can do more harm than you could do by working on your own, if you see what I mean.

What is the harm they can do?

For one, if you sign with an agent who doesn't do his job, then you're really out of luck. Say for instance, you're sitting on somebody's books for twelve months, and you're unable to get work with other people because you signed with this agent, but they're not doing anything on your behalf. So, you spend a year not being seen, not having your face on casting directors' desks, things like that.

Then you've got the other side, where maybe they would be inviting you to take any jobs just so they can get commission, which a lot of people do. They don't care really where your career is going as long they're getting paid. In the early stages, any experience is good for your CV, but you really want to find an agent who understands where you want to go. You might not always agree. And the agent might say, "You're limiting yourself. You need to open yourself up—look at this and this in addition to this."

But it's about the relationship you have with them. For us, we have a check-in policy, so we speak to our guys every single week, irrespective of whether there's any work in. We tell them what's coming in, what they've gone up for, who's likely to bring them in, who *is* bringing them in, what the casting details are, so we have that regular contact.

> "You're better off on your own than with a bad agent, because they can do more harm than you could do by working on your own."

What kind of self-care do you recommend to young actors to be emotionally available but also be able to function like a professional in the business world?

I think the best advice that we give to people starting out is to treat yourself as a business. It's no different than if you have a job in an office. You go to the office at nine o'clock, you work until five, and you come home. And you get paid for that, and in exchange for that pay you're expected to do certain things. And I think that new actors starting out need to approach it like that. They are their business, and they promote and manage themselves, which is hard and emotional. But you have to detach yourself from it, because you're going to go for a lot of auditions and a lot of those auditions aren't going to result in you being offered the job.

They have to learn not to take that personally, which is really difficult. They need to understand that they're presenting a character, and that's their business. When they go home and they're going out with their friends, their friends like them, and they want to see them again because that's them. It's no different than any other job insofar as it's not personal. That's probably the biggest thing they have to learn, because they're going to get more rejection than job offers. So yes, it's just being able to cope. You're going into an industry in which you're judged on your looks and the way you act, and you've got to accept that's not always going to be what people want. So there are going to be occasions when they say, "No, you're not what we're looking for," and in the end, all that means is that you're not what they're looking for. Nothing more.

An actor who's experienced and has trained and has skill and talent, when it's a no, they know that it can just be because they've got the wrong color hair, or the wrong color eyes, or they weren't quite tall enough. I think it's hard to understand that initially.

Can you address learning to not be hurt by the ninety-nine nos for every one yes?

Everyone's experiencing that no, no, no. Especially at the early stages, we give them the support and encouragement that they need. We reaffirm that it's not personal, that they're talented. Initially, as an agent, you send them out across the board for things, and it might take a couple of months to help them find their niche, where they fit best. So they may get a lot more rejection in that initial period than they would do, say, in the later part of their representation.

How does the management of an actor's career change as the actor ages into different characters types?

It tends to work differently with different people. For some people, it's a plus. We've got one girl who has just had a baby, and she is late 20s, early 30s. Now, that's a category that there's a lot of people in, a lot more roles. So that's a good thing for her. But guys can get more vain and a bit more stubborn than women. We've got guys who we're putting them up for 45-year-old roles, and they're ringing you up, disgusted, wanting a character who's 36. You're thinking, there's no way in the world you're going to pass for 36, but they don't see that. The women are a lot more accepting of this fact that they need to go for the older roles.

What happens when you've signed an actor who isn't getting work? Do you keep working with that actor to help him get work?

We don't take on hundreds of people, so we do have to have the majority of people working most of the time. The way we try to address it is we look at what we're sending them up for. We bring them in, talk to them on the phone, have a look at their CV, we think okay, can we tweak this, can we take stuff out, is there anything that we missed? Can we reset it, format it? We look at the headshots. Is that representing you properly, do we need to get more headshots in? And I look at everything that we're doing, what we're sending them up for, who's seen them, why people aren't bringing them. We do a general overview of CVs, headshots, and the way we approach a casting director, which will be a good few weeks' work. Oftentimes those small tweaks are enough just to give it a bit of a kick, and then they go on and start to get work.

Any advice for the actor who's really struggling to break in? It's been however long and they haven't found the success yet?

I do find that this can sometimes be a perception—that perhaps someone else looking in on this actor might see something different, might actually see success. Changing the point of view can be helpful. But I tend to remind actors who are just getting started to simply do the work, as they would in any business field. Do the work and be open to new opportunities. So much of our success lies in our outlook.

TRAINING AND RESPECTING THE WORK

A Director's Perspective

▶ An Interview With David Hammond

David Hammond is a former resident director for the American Conservatory Theater (ACT) and the Yale Repertory Theatre and former Artistic Director of PlayMakers Repertory Company. He has directed productions for New York's Roundabout Theatre Company and Montevideo's Comedia Nacional, Teatro El Galpon, Teatro Alianza, and Teatro Telon Rojo. He has staged operas for the San Francisco Opera, the Aspen Music Festival, the Carmel Bach Festival, and the Opera Company of North Carolina. A Shakespeare specialist, he has conducted workshops or coached Shakespeare texts for the Actors Theatre of Louisville, the American Shakespeare Festival, the Denver Center Theatre Company, and the Atlantic Theatre Company.

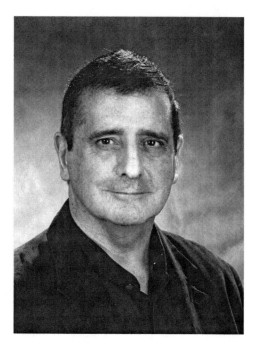

David Hammond
Photo by Julie Knight

He has taught at the Juilliard School, the Yale School of Drama, the American Conservatory Theater Advanced Training Program, the University of North Carolina at Chapel Hill, the New York University Graduate Acting Program, and the American Repertory Theater/Moscow Art Theater School Institute for Advanced Theater Training at Harvard University. In Montevideo, Uruguay, he has taught for Escuela de Expression Teatral Anglo Ombu, Escuela Multidisciplinaria de Arte Dramatico, Institucion Teatral El Galpon, Federacion Uruguaya de Teatros Independentes, Escuela del Cine, and Escuela del Actor.

Hammond joined the faculty of Guilford College in 2007. He is a BA Magna cum Laude graduate of Harvard College and an MFA graduate of Carnegie Mellon University.

What would you say is most important for someone to understand about making a career as an actor?
I started teaching in 1972, and I've seen tremendous talent, many who were truly committed. But that's nothing without resilience. Resilience is key. And you have to know yourself. You have to know your instincts and how they work in acting. What is it that I bring? That's what you ask yourself. You have to understand how it fits into creating a character so that you have your truth.

How would you describe "success" for actors?
Here's what I would call a success. I remember a student many years ago who wasn't from a very sophisticated background and had a rather naive idea of what theater was. This was at ACT, which was a classical conservatory that trained people for classical repertory theater. This young woman wanted to act in soap operas. She could have cared less about playing Juliet, but she went to class and worked hard, and she eventually became a soap opera star and won a lot of Emmys. And she deserved them, every one.

For me, she's a total success. She knew what she wanted, and she went for it. And I'm not belittling soap operas. For her, doing those stories for that audience was meaningful, and she did them very well. Everyone who has worked with her always remarks on what a pro she is, that she knows that business cold and helps everyone. So I would call her a successful artist, not only because she knew what she wanted but also because she loves the craft. She always brought everything she had to offer.

A love of the craft and a willingness to do the work.
A willingness and a *desire* to do the work. You have to respect whatever you're doing. Whether it's a commercial or Broadway, you have to bring your complete self to it and give it your best. Early in your career, you need to know what you want the peak to be and then find the base of that pyramid. Any commercial, any voiceover, any audition—it's all a chance to do excellent work, and you have to approach it with full preparation.

I'll sometimes do a showcase with actors who want to work with me. And it's interesting to see the ones who go to the rehearsals and give it everything they have, and the ones who inform you that they're going to miss the next night because of x, y, and z. That's a terrible habit to start. And these are professionals, not students. You have to be committed and start to build that habit of excellence early on in your training.

When people don't have that commitment, do you think it's self-doubt? Laziness?

It's ego and a lack of respect for the craft of acting. You have to have it, just like Uta Hagen said. Acting deserves respect, and you don't cheat on it. People think it's all about externals, about a good face and body. Well, that's a different profession. There are plenty of people doing extra work who are pretty. There are people who get cast because they're pretty—but I'm sorry, they're not actors. Even if they become very successful selling pretty, they're not actors.

When I was teaching at Yale, I had two young men who graduated, and we got together about a year later. One of them had been on a full-year contract at a major regional theater, and he had played major parts through the year. He was based in New York. The other one had done six episodes of a television show. He was based in LA and had also done a couple of commercials.

The one who was doing theater was lamenting about how little money he made compared to the other. The one in LA was lamenting about how he felt he was just selling himself. I told them that there's nothing wrong with either path—that there were good reasons behind their choices, but they *chose* these paths. You have to stand behind your choices and have respect for them. If you want to try a different path, then go for it. Don't just wish for things to happen. Don't stay in professions you don't respect. Why would anybody hire you if you don't respect what they're asking you to do.

That's the resilience. If you're in LA and you can't get an audition, get yourself into a showcase and invite some casting directors. Evaluate, reevaluate, make another decision, and commit to it and take responsibility for it—that's essential. Don't hide in the corner and feel sorry for yourself. Don't take a television salary and be condescending to your colleagues or go to a regional theater and tell everybody that you used to be on *WKRP in Cincinnati* and you don't have to do this crap, that you don't have to rehearse eight hours a day. No. Commit. Commit, evaluate, reevaluate, make another choice, stand behind it, and move on.

> "Any commercial, any voiceover, any audition—
> it's all a chance to do excellent work, and you
> have to approach it with full preparation."

So if you're looking at an actor, what would you say is a good sign of commitment?

I would say that step one is training, which means having a good teacher and good classes. It doesn't have to be an MFA program. The MFA opens up possibilities, but there are always good studio programs, like the HB [Herbert Berghof] program and the Larry Singer Studio in New York. Don't just do one class on a three-day weekend. Really commit to a program for a few years.

HB has a program that you can take mostly in the evenings, so you can get yourself to New York and do it. Rather than stay somewhere and have a subsistence job and dream about the theater, you can have a subsistence job in New York or New Jersey and go to a good studio and commit to it. But that takes resilience, time, and the actor saying that acting is *the* most important thing.

You say don't do just one class on a three-day weekend, but could that be a good place to start?

Maybe, but that's not being a committed actor. A weekend class or a six-week class doesn't cut it. Real training is day in and day out commitment to growth. You can ignore it and go in on just your looks, but that's not going to last, and that's not acting. That's selling yourself. Now take Sandra Bullock in *The Blind Side*. That's a knockout, Oscar performance. The preparation for that performance is seeping through her pores. That woman walked onto that set having done all the work you would do on a Chekhov play, and she owns it. When I think of Vivien Leigh at her best, it's the same thing.

I don't think you need to go to a top-tier school, but it's got to be real, and you've got to commit to the real training. If you want a long-lasting career, at some point, you have to know what you're doing. It can't just be luck, and it can't just be that you're the type they're looking for. If you go to a good program, you'll learn to recognize your so-called type—the way you're perceived by others, what initial impression your instrument makes—and you'll learn how to bring more than that. You'll be able to work from your inner personal truth and surprise people. You never want to just play to your perceived "type."

If a commitment to training is the first step, can you describe what it is that actors will get from this type of training? What should they expect to learn? Or what skills will they need to have to work in the business?
Step one is learning the difference between presenting an interpretation that you have decided from reading the play and actually stepping into the circumstances. You should come in with a complete history that you have made real and alive to yourself. Be present in the place and circumstances with the other actor. And then, between the two of you, have a moment-to-moment reality happening, which the director then shapes into the interpretation of the production, or the interpretation of the film.

Step two is having control of your attention. You have to be able to put your attention on the stimuli that are necessary to achieve the work, and that means training your concentration, which is a steady two- to three-year process. You can't be up there sort of in the moment and at the same time sort of thinking of what you planned the night before. You have to be totally in the moment, which means having the training to be able to stay there.

You have to have physical and vocal training to be able to be relaxed in the moment and respond to physical stimuli, to be able to respond spontaneously with your full voice, your full instrument, not confined to limitations from your daily habits. You should be able to have circumstances influence your physicality and your voice. If you're Linda Loman in *Death of a Salesman* and you're putting dinner on the table in the kitchen, your body has to be able to become the body that's done this for forty years. Those are physical realities that you have to be able to respond to, and that means letting go of your habitual physical realities and focuses.

That takes time and is parallel to the imaginative work. Then there's play analysis, which is not what you're taught in undergraduate school. It's lovely to say the super objective is x and the objective in the scene is y, but you've got to discover those things on your feet in rehearsal from hours and hours of given circumstance work and personal work that you do at home. It takes time. Most people have no idea how deep given circumstance work is and how much time it takes, how detailed it has to be.

What do your best students have that the others don't? What makes some students particularly exciting to work with?

The students who are most exciting to me are the ones who first do the work and who then create something that I would never have thought of. What comes out of them is original and from themselves and right for the circumstances. They don't *choose* to play it a certain way. Instead, they choose the placement of their attention. That choice makes all the difference.

And there are students who do it a lot, and then there are students to whom occasionally it happens, which means it's in there. There are students to whom it happens occasionally and you say, "Gorgeous, you're doing it," and then they come back in the next scene and it's only half as well prepared. They don't make the connection that the reason that thing happened is because they've lined up all the stuff to make it happen. And then you think, "Well, maybe you don't really want to do it." Believe it or not there are people with the ability to do stunning work, but they don't want to do it.

Why do those people not want to do it? Do you have a sense of that?

It's never the same thing. It's very rarely that they're afraid. They really may just not be interested. For me, that's mindboggling. I think, if I had the gift that you've got, I would chase it to the end of the world. It's different for everyone. Some people really want it, and some people simply don't. Those who don't want it won't grow and won't last. If they don't always do the work and really want to pursue it, then they shouldn't.

Auditions and nerves? Any advice?

Well, get a grip *[laughs]*. You have to think of the audition as the chance to present work that you have thoroughly prepared and can exist in. You go in and do a professional job and offer them something they either can or can't use for the project. It's not about rejection. You can't walk in needing approval. If you do, you're not a professional. No one's going to hire an actor who needs approval. If I'm directing a play, I will try to be nice to you. I will try to be encouraging to you. But if you have a hungry need for me to demonstrate constantly my approval, it keeps me from watching you properly. You're interfering with my concentration.

I say to people, ask yourself this: What if I were about to have a brain operation and the surgeon leaned over and said, "This always makes me really hysterically nervous." I would run like hell. I expect my brain surgeon to be able to concentrate on the tiny area of my body that he's working on. I would have no sympathy if he said, "I really, really try, and I really want to save your life, but I'm very nervous." Likewise, I have no sympathy for the actor, because that's part of the job.

So for those who are really frightened of the audition process, what would you tell them?

They might not be actors. If what you're looking for in acting is approval, you may be a very creative person who is very theatrically intelligent, but you may be a director, or you may be a writer. It's possible that you're not suited to acting. I think one is not quite facing the truth when saying, "I am just too scared." That's very self-flattering. That's a comfortable thing to say. Rather than saying that, the person should admit to being anxious about approval and realize that acting maybe isn't for them. You should confront that head on. You'll hear people say, "I was always so terrified when I auditioned, and actors are so brave." No, actors are skilled people with concentration. They may be personally very shy people, but that's different.

> "I say to people, ask yourself this: What if I were about to have a brain operation and the surgeon leaned over and said, 'This always makes me really hysterically nervous.' I would run like hell."

The average person might think the actor is somebody who has an ego, somebody who enjoys attention. But it's interesting to think that successful actors are just doing their job.

I believe that with all my heart. When actors have egos, it's outside their creativity. Actors will get upset if they get inappropriate billing, because they've invested their life in it. If their name gets left off the program, they may get angry, and that's okay. That's ego, but it's ego about your career.

The really good actor doesn't have an ego at stake in the moment of doing the actual work. They may be shy in situations outside of their acting, like at an award ceremony, for example, because they feel like they're exposed. Eventually they learn to treat the awards as part of the job. Same with interviews. It's part of the job. The actor in these situations is simply the ambassador for the work. The interview isn't about being judged.

If someone tells an aspiring actor, "Don't put yourself through this. You don't have what it takes," but then someone else tells this actor that he's pretty terrific and has a chance, how does he know if he really has the talent?

The criteria there are wrong. You shouldn't talk about *it*. The criteria should be whether you're prepared and whether you take the challenge seriously. I don't think someone can say whether someone has *it*. I think if somebody says that, you walk away. But you can ask yourself, "Are you really interested in this? Why are you doing this? Do you like exploring all parts of your experience and another world and making the two meld?" Well, that's the actor. If you don't like that, maybe there's something else you can do. I think asking why you're doing it is a legitimate question. Or you can say that people are going to see you as a difficult type, so you're going to have to overcome that. Those are both legitimate.

What's an example of a difficult type?

Very often when an actor asks the question, he's typing himself. There's no such thing as, for instance, an Asian male type. You're an Asian male and you're an actor, and if you have the qualities of a leading man, you're a leading man who happens to be Asian. Now, you may be seen when you walk in the door as limited to a type, but you don't come in and act just the type. If somebody says you could be a young sinister drug lord without any education, they also should be able to say that you could be a young successful doctor or lawyer.

We know this is a major problem—that's a given. But there are more casting directors now who will call in an Asian American or African American actor for the doctor, the lawyer, the teacher. There are more who will investigate casting interracially. There aren't enough, and it's still a continuing problem, but the actor must not add to the so-called "limitation." Don't add to people's limited perception—expand it.

Final advice for the aspiring actor?

Respect the work, that's really my best advice. If you've tried or you try again and find that you can't respect it—that you're not willing to do the hard work—then this might not be something you should pursue as a career.

AUDITIONING FOR SHAKESPEARE

▶ By Joe Falocco

The scene unfolds at the Midwest Theatre Auditions, an annual St. Louis "cattle call" where actors seek summer employment. Hundreds of representatives from theaters around the United States wait as a young woman takes the stage. "I will," she announces, "be performing a piece from Shakespeare's *Henry VII*."

There's just one problem. Shakespeare never wrote a play called "*Henry VII*." The speech in question was actually Lady Percy from *Henry IV, part ii*. Apparently, Roman numerals confused this performer.

This unfortunate incident, which I witnessed some years ago, is an extreme example of a common phenomenon. Actors are often woefully unprepared when they audition for Shakespeare. A useful analogy exists with musical theater, where your choice of material should reflect an understanding of the canon—and where, whatever interpretive choices you make, you need to sing the right lyrics on the right notes in a tempo shared with the accompanist. Similarly, with Shakespeare, you need to correctly speak the text in a way that makes literal and emotional sense and does justice to a piece's poetic qualities. In both genres, if you don't meet these basic technical requirements, nothing else you do will matter.

Here I offer guidelines that will enable you to audition for Shakespeare in a competent and professional manner. This approach doesn't guarantee that you'll get work, of course—no one can do that. But it will prevent you from unwittingly disqualifying yourself like the unfortunate actress in St. Louis. We'll look at guidelines for selecting material for monologues, preparing your monologue material, and performing your monologues.

Selecting Material for Monologues

Early in your career, you'll probably have to audition for every acting job you get. With Shakespeare, a typical first step in the audition process will require you to present one or more monologues. If directors like you, they may then ask you to read from the play being cast, but they probably won't do this unless you've done a good job with your monologues.

Ideally, you should have half a dozen Shakespearean pieces ready to perform at any time. That way, you can tailor your choice of monologue to the plays you audition for. At a minimum, you need two contrasting pieces. Each of your audition monologues should be between forty-five seconds and one minute in length. Even if the audition notice specifies a two-minute maximum, there's rarely any need to go longer than a minute. A monologue can even be as short as thirty seconds—especially if it's your second piece. While there are exceptions to this (and every other guideline you'll read here or elsewhere), auditors generally know after thirty seconds whether they're interested in you. As one weary director told me, "I've never seen an audition monologue that was too short, but I've seen many that were too long."

Your audition monologues should be appropriate for your physical type. We must all accept the reality that physical type matters as much as talent and technique in determining what roles we get. For instance, I am a bald, middle-aged, Italian-American who stands 5'8" tall (after yoga class) and weighs 140 pounds. It would be foolish for me to audition with speeches of Falstaff, Othello, or Romeo. It's particularly painful to accept that I'm no longer right for roles I played when I was younger, like Mercutio or Horatio. If I were to audition with material from those roles today, directors would assume I was delusional (a pathology not uncommon among performers).

Joe Falocco (left) as the Portuguese Ambassador in the 2013 Baron's Men production of Thomas Kyd's *The Spanish Tragedy*, performed at Austin's Curtain Playhouse

Photo by Allen Childress

How then should you go about finding audition pieces of appropriate length that make sense for your physical type? First of all you need to . . . wait for it . . .

Read the plays.

Ideally, you should have read all of Shakespeare's plays before embarking on a career as an actor. At the very least, you need to read (more than once) the most produced plays in each Shakespearean genre (tragedy, comedy, history, and romance). As you read these works, be on the lookout for roles you think you can play. If you're not sure if a part is right for you, ask an acting teacher or a professional performer.

Once you find a role, look for long speeches that you can edit down to one minute, or shorter speeches that can be spliced together to achieve the forty-five-second minimum. For instance, Cleopatra is the greatest female role in Shakespeare, but her long speeches (spoken while cradling the dead Antony in her arms or committing suicide by snakebite) are not audition friendly. Yet Cleopatra's description of her dream about Antony, delivered with interjections from Dolabella, is easily something you can cobble into an audition piece. If you're not sure how to edit the material, ask for help. (There might be one or two English professors at your university who are frustrated actors and would welcome the opportunity to contribute.)

The task of finding appropriate material is, alas, much harder for female performers than for men. This leads too many actresses to choose the same four or five pieces. This list of "overdone" monologues includes Juliet's "Gallop apace" speech, along with the Jailer's Daughter from *The Two Noble Kinsmen*, and the aforementioned speech of Lady Percy from *Henry IV, part ii*.

On the one hand, directors know there is only so much material to choose from, so they won't necessarily penalize you for doing something they've heard before. But on the other hand, it's hard for anyone to stay objective when they've seen the same piece five times in an afternoon.

One solution is for female performers to look for "gender-neutral" characters. These include choral figures like Time in *The Winter's Tale* or Rumor in *Henry IV, part ii*, as well as the better known Choruses of *Romeo and Juliet* and *Henry V*. Some directors discourage the use of choral material in auditions because they feel it isn't sufficiently "active." This view, however, denies the relationship of these speakers with the audience, which is just as "active" as that between characters on stage. Choral material is an especially good choice if you are auditioning for a theater that values an actor's ability to speak directly to the audience. The American Shakespeare Center is a good example of such a company. By the same logic, though, you should avoid choral material if you know a director doesn't like it. Finally, many companies regularly cast female performers cross-gender. If you're auditioning for a company that does this, feel free to use speeches written for male characters. But you should know that not everyone welcomes this approach.

Generally speaking, audition with verse rather than prose. You can tell the difference, because in verse, the first word in each line begins with a capital letter regardless of punctuation. Directors want to know if you can handle verse, so you're cheating them if you don't try. An obvious exception would be if you audition specifically for characters who speak prose, like Falstaff or Toby Belch. (And if you possess the physique for these roles, you should have some of their speeches in your repertoire.)

In my opinion . . .

Most of the best comic material in Shakespeare is prose, so if you want to be cast as a clown, you might choose a prose monologue. But I encourage you to avoid Shakespearean comedy in the audition process if you can. Let's face it, the jokes are 400 years old, and many of them have not stood the test of time. Most of the comic material that still works in Shakespeare depends on the interplay of characters within the dramatic situation of the play. This is most evident in the hilarious speeches from the "Pyramus and Thisbe" section of *Midsummer*, which usually fall flat when performed outside the context of that comedy. Some comic pieces work as standalone audition material, but most of these (like Lance and his dog from *The Two Gentlemen of Verona*) are done to death. One possible exception might be Dromio of Syracuse's "fat jokes" from *The Comedy of Errors*, which (although politically incorrect) are quite funny and are material that can easily be edited into a monologue.

One final note about selecting audition material: Most directors appreciate it when you audition with material from the play they are trying to cast. A few, however, don't want this. Whenever possible, accommodate directors' preferences in choosing material.

Preparing Monologue Material

Once you've identified an appropriate audition monologue, there are three steps you should undertake before performing the piece. Let's look at these one at a time.

Step 1: Paraphrase the Text

This is the first step: paraphrasing. It isn't a quest for subtext, but rather an attempt to express the literal meaning of the early modern language through postmodern vocabulary. There's nothing more important than getting your paraphrase right, and you need to do this work yourself. You can find ready-made paraphrases on the internet, but these are not always reliable. And even when someone else's paraphrase is accurate, you aren't necessarily going to understand it better than Shakespeare's original.

The only sure way to know what a speech means is to put it into your own words. Once you think you've got an accurate paraphrase, ask a teacher or professional actor to review your work. This isn't just for beginners. The American Shakespeare Center in Staunton, Virginia, casts its company from among the best trained classical actors in the United States. Yet the ASC's directors require these performers to paraphrase every line they speak on stage—and these expert Shakespeareans each make an average of three mistakes during the course of any play. If not corrected, this would lead a fifteen-person company to forty-five moments during the course of a performance when the audience doesn't know what's going on because the actors don't understand what they're saying.

Step 2: Complete a Textual Analysis

Once the paraphrase is complete, you should do a textual analysis where you scan the speech (if it's verse) and identify key rhetorical figures and other poetic devices. Considerations of space prevent me from describing this important step in adequate detail, so the example of a single verse line must suffice.

At the end of Egeon's long exposition in the first scene of *The Comedy of Errors*, he describes himself as "Roaming clean through the bounds of Asia." Shakespeare's verse is almost always iambic pentameter. This means that a regular line contains five feet, and each foot is an *iamb* (an unstressed syllable followed by a stressed syllable). In the early plays, such as *Comedy*, the verse tends to be quite regular.

For the line in question to yield ten syllables, the word *Asia*, normally pronounced as two syllables, must be expanded to three (*A - zeee – ah*). Such a choice may sound affected to American ears, and an actor might choose to compromise the syllabic count to sound more conversational. However, given its place in the peroration of Egeon's ostentatious outpouring of grief, the extra syllable makes dramatic sense.

Similarly, the first foot of this line, "Roaming," is a *trochee* (a stressed syllable followed by an unstressed syllable), since we never stress the *-ing* of a two-syllable present participle. This trochee has the effect of unsettling the otherwise perfectly regular verse of the speech it resides in, a break in rhythm that signals Egeon is nearing his rhetorical climax. My scansion for this line (with an *x* indicating each stressed syllable) thus reads:

```
  x    -    -    x    -    x    - x    -    x
Roam – ing clean through the bounds of A – si – a
```

Finally, this line employs several monosyllabic words ("clean through the bounds") and long vowel sounds ("Roam . . . clean through . . . bounds . . . Asia"), which cue the actor to slow down and savor the important information and emotion (as when the Ghost of Hamlet's father tells him: "The serpent that did sting thy father's life/Now wears his crown").

This is the type of analysis you need to do (and more, including an examination of rhetorical figures) for every line in your monologue. You can purchase study guides that further explain the concepts of paraphrase, scansion, rhetorical analysis, and audience contact at the American Shakespeare Center (www.americanshakespearecenter.com). Again, if you're confused, ask a teacher or a professional actor for help.

It's a lot of work, yes—but it's part of the business of being an actor. (Cheer up. If you're ever cast as Hamlet, you'll need to analyze all 1,000 lines that character speaks!)

Step 3: Define Your Acting Choices

The third step—once you've made literal and poetic sense out of your monologue—is to make emotional sense by defining clear and distinct acting choices for each moment. There are many ways to do this, but my favorite is to break the text into "beats" and then attach a transitive verb to each beat. A new beat in this system begins with each mark of final punctuation and corresponds with the completion of a character's thought. The transitive verb describes what you're attempting to do to your scene partner during the course of that beat. (In the case of a soliloquy, your scene partner is the audience.)

This focus on active performance choices, when combined with paraphrase and textual analysis, will allow you to bring Shakespeare's text alive in both audition and performance.

Now, onto the next phase . . .

Performing Monologue Material

First and foremost, as you enter the audition room, remember to behave like a functional human being. Look the auditors in the eye and say, "Hello," or "Good afternoon," or "Good morning," in a loud, clear voice. Besides affirming your humanity, this provides an opportunity to test the acoustics in the room before you begin your piece. Clearly and slowly introduce yourself. Your name is the most important thing you will say during the entire audition. Don't mumble it.

Once you've finished introducing yourself, make sure they know that your monologue is about to begin. I always turn my back to the auditors—briefly. That way when I turn around and start talking, they know I'm acting. You don't have to use this specific pattern of behavior, but you need to somehow clearly delineate the start of your piece.

Similarly, when you're finished, remain completely still for half a second, and then say, "Thank you," so they know you are done. If, God forbid, you forget your monologue halfway through, just stop where you are, take a deep breath, and say, "Thank you," as if that was where you planned to finish all along. Do not, at any point during your audition, apologize or explain anything. Do not tell them that you have a cold, or that you have not slept, or that your bus was late, or that you just learned your monologue that morning.

Your audition—for better or worse—will speak for itself.

By the way . . .

Sometimes after you present a monologue, the production team may ask you to make an adjustment and do the piece again. This is a good sign! It means they are interested in you. The director may think this change would be an aesthetic improvement. It is just as likely, however, that they merely want to see if you can take direction. The requested adjustment may be clear and specific ("Do the piece with a Texas accent;" "Make more eye contact with the people in the audition hall"). Often, however, it will be maddeningly vague ("See if you can embrace a different Jungian archetype").

Whatever change the production team asks for, the worst thing you can do is be defensive, take offense, or question whether the adjustment is a good idea. Remember, this is their audition, not yours. (They say, "Jump!" You ask, "How High?") Listen carefully to the feedback and try to incorporate the change into your second pass at the monologue. Whether you achieve the specific adjustment they request or not, make sure that the second time you do the monologue is different from the first.

One of the most difficult issues to address is where you should place your focus while you're auditioning. Shakespeare wrote many of his speeches for the actor to speak to the audience. For instance, Hamlet doesn't spend a lot of time talking to himself. He spends a lot of time talking to the audience. If you go to see *Hamlet* and the lead actor starts talking to himself, run screaming for the exit.

Even speeches delivered to other characters offer you opportunities to "open up" to the audience. Many companies, like the American Shakespeare Center, value an actor's ability to deliver this kind of direct address. Other directors, however, hate it when actors make eye contact during auditions. Even those like myself, who appreciate direct address, don't feel comfortable when performers hold us in an icy stare for their entire monologue. Any solution to this dilemma must involve a compromise approach. The more people in the audition room, the easier it is to look at the audience. If you're at a "cattle call" with hundreds of people out front, then you can look at the audience for your whole monologue—if the piece is written for direct address. Otherwise you can focus sixty percent of your time on an imaginary scene partner and "open up" to the audience during the remaining forty percent. (Make sure to place this scene partner at an angle so you're not just showing profile.)

If, as is often the case, there are only two or three people in the audition room, then don't make eye contact with anyone more than once during your piece. If the monologue is designed for direct address, spend the rest of the time looking at the "invisible" people sitting to the right and left of the actual auditors. Otherwise, focus on your imaginary scene partner.

Again, these are only guidelines and directors vary in their preferences. The more you know about the people you're auditioning for, the better you can tailor your audition to meet their expectations.

If your initial audition goes well, you may be asked to read scenes from the play(s) under consideration. If you're lucky, they'll give you these scenes (or email them to you) and ask you to prepare them for callbacks at a later date. If this happens, you can prepare this material as you do your monologues. Learn the lines as well as you can, but even if you memorize them word for word, always carry the script during the audition to remind them that your performance is a work in progress.

If you're less fortunate, they may ask you to read scenes on the spot the day of your first audition. This is why it's a good idea to read any play that you plan to audition for. As you read, pay special attention to those scenes that feature characters you hope to play. Ask yourself what scenes you'd want actors to read if you were directing, and give those scenes extra attention. You should own a Shakespearean pronunciation guide, the best of which is *All the Words on Stage*, by Louis Scheeder and Shane Ann Younts. Use this to look up unfamiliar words when preparing your monologues, and bring it to auditions in case you're asked to read something on the spot. (Don't ask the other actors how to pronounce a word. They don't know any more than you do!) Carefully reading the play in advance and looking up unfamiliar words will aid you in the difficult task of "cold reading" Shakespeare.

Guidelines aside, remember that the only way to learn how to audition is to do it. Like boxing and standup comedy, no amount of private study can prepare you for the real thing. Although auditioning is initially nerve wracking, with time (believe it or not) you can actually learn to enjoy the process.

Just remember, your goal is *not* to get the job. That's beyond your control. Your goal is to give a good audition. If you do that consistently, you'll eventually get the opportunities warranted by your technique, talent, and physical type.

JOE FALOCCO is a member of Actors' Equity and has per- formed with the Kentucky, North Carolina, Oklahoma, Texas, and Wisconsin Shakespeare Festivals. He has also worked for the Atlanta Shakespeare Tavern and spent a year on tour with the Shenandoah Shakespeare Express. Joe has directed professional and university productions of *Hamlet*, *The Merry Wives of Windsor*, *Macbeth*, *The Comedy of Errors*, and *Romeo and Juliet*. Most recently, Joe directed *Antony and Cleopatra* at Austin's Curtain Playhouse (a reconstructed early modern amphitheater) and performed in *The Spanish Tragedy* at this same venue. Dr. Falocco holds a PhD in English from the University of North Carolina at Greensboro and an MFA in Performance from Roosevelt University in Chicago. He is the author of *Reimagining Shakespeare's Playhouse* (Boydell & Brewer 2010), as well as several journal articles, including "Tommaso Salvini's Othello and Racial Identity in Nineteenth-Century America" (*New England Theatre Journal*, 2012), which won the American Theatre and Drama Society's 2013 Vera Mowbry Jones Outstanding Essay Award. Joe is currently an Assistant Professor of English at Texas State University and has previously taught in theater departments at Arkansas State University and Catawba College.

Joe Falocco

Photo by KennethGall.com

IS A RESIDENT THEATER COMPANY FOR YOU?

An Interview With Richard Rose

▶ By Amanda Nelson

While many dream of performing on Broadway, there are real opportunities off the Great White Way. Seventy-two member companies in twenty-nine states (and Washington, DC) make up the League of Resident Theatres (LORT). According to LORT, these theater companies "issue more Equity contracts to actors than Broadway and commercial theaters combined."[2]

That means a lot of opportunities for work.

Richard Rose
Photo by Ivan Scott

There are LORT companies in the West (including the American Conservatory Theater, the Old Globe, and Portland Center Stage), in the east (for example, Roundabout Theatre Company, Ford's Theatre, and American Repertory Theater), in the Midwest (such as Northlight Theatre, Repertory Theatre of St. Louis, and Goodman Theatre), and in the South (like Playmakers Repertory Company, Asolo Repertory, and Arkansas Repertory Theatre). The companies range in size and scope—some focus on the classics, and others produce new works. Some, like Barter Theatre, Actors Theatre of Louisville, and American Conservatory Theater, offer apprenticeship and training programs that can lead to work in the resident companies.

LORT companies have at minimum a twelve-week season. But many member companies have much longer seasons, including the Barter Theatre in Abingdon, Virginia, which operates year-round, providing fifty weeks of work for their resident company members. Many resident companies provide actor housing, particularly for shorter term contracts. Importantly, LORT Equity contracts establish salary minimums, which are based on the LORT category of theater. Today, the minimum salary range is between $600 and $900 per week.[3]

What a resident company offers the actor, though, goes well beyond a paycheck. It's an opportunity in which to collaborate with a group of professionals on an ongoing basis. It's a place in which to expand and enhance your performance skills. And it's often a place that allows you to interact with the community beyond your work onstage, taking part in local issues.

For twenty-three years, Richard Rose has served as Producing Artistic Director of Barter Theatre, a LORT member company in southwest Virginia.

He is the third artistic director in the historic theater's eighty-two years. He has led Barter to unprecedented growth in attendance and in expansion of programs serving the region. He has served on state and regional nonprofit boards and currently serves on the board of Virginians for the Arts. He was recently honored by his alma mater, St. Norbert College, with the Distinguished Achievement Award in Humanities.

One rainy summer morning, we sat down in his office for a chat about the business of theater and what the resident theater company can offer an actor.

How did the Barter Theatre get its start?

Barter started with a simple notion. Its name really did come from bartering goods for services. It came out of the Depression and out of Bob Porterfield, an out-of-work actor in New York who realized there were a lot of out-of-work actors in New York. So Porterfield brought a group of actors down and started a theater that basically paid the actors by housing and feeding them.

Opening Night at Barter Theatre, early 1960s

Photo courtesy of Barter Theatre

And the company retained its barter model—exchanging "ham for Hamlet"—until after World War II, when it changed to a cash enterprise. I love that the theater still offers special barter performances when audience members are welcomed in exchange for canned goods donated to the local food bank. I notice, too, that Barter is still tightly connected to its community. It's not just the local theater—you and your actors are really part of the fabric of this community.

We want our actors to be engaged politically. We want them to be engaged in other organizations through community service. We want them to help *form* the community, so we've encouraged them to get involved in every aspect of the community. If you're going to expect the community to give to you, they also have an expectation that you'll give back to them—not just your product but your involvement in the community in every way. And I think that's really important. What we do well is connect with the audience, and connecting with the audience means you have to know them. It's about really engaging, and our style of theater tries hard to do that, to connect.

Can you speak a bit more about "connecting" with the audience?
We collectively examine in detail what the *story* of the play is, how best to tell it, what its purpose is from the audience perspective, and how best to utilize what the playwright has given us to make that story come to life. This comes from a belief that people, at their core, are compelled by stories—of their lives and the lives of others. We believe that the need for stories is an essential part of being human.

So tell the story—and don't go down the rabbithole in doing so. Do it with a wink and a nod—remember, the audience is your acting partner, too—and find the true emotion. Avoid sentiment at all costs. It's never really fulfilling for audience or actor. These are what bring a fulfilling connection between actor and audience.

What qualities do you look for in an actor?
We have an adage: *Art equals growth.* Meaning, if you can't continue to grow, and you don't continue to grow, you can't be an artist. An artist has to want to continue to improve his or her skills. That, for me, is the number one criterion for choosing talent. The one thing we guarantee every resident company member is that we're going to find what you can't do and make you do it. And we're going to explore that, and we're going to push you, and we're going to make you do things that are totally outside your comfort zone, and you're going find out if

The cast of Barter's production of *Cabaret* performing "Money"

Photo courtesy of Barter Theatre

you can do them. And if you fail, that's okay—we're not going to penalize you for failing. We want you to be able to grow and get better and stronger. If you're only doing what you're comfortable with, then you're not going to grow.

During my visits to Barter, I've noticed that some actors also direct, or choreograph, or work on the administrative side or in education.
That's very definitely true, and we've done that across the board. We want people to be holistically involved. First of all, it's much more fulfilling. And second, it gives you skills that you bring not only to your acting but also to your life in ways that enrich your work. It also helps you see the world in a bigger scope.

One of the benefits of being part of a resident company is the collaborative working relationship that develops. Can you speak about collaboration in a resident company?
I'll tell you this story. We had an actor—not a regular member of the company—coming in for *Othello*. We were in the second day of rehearsal, and when we got to a moment, he asked me a question, and I said, "Well, I don't know the answer to that." He looked at me and said, "I've been in the theater for thirty years. It's so refreshing to hear a director say, 'I don't know. We'll figure it out.'" With a resident company you really don't have to have all the answers, because we'll figure it out together. It may be best not to answer a question, because sometimes I really don't know what's going to be best there. Try different things and let's find out. You're unlikely to do that in a commercial enterprise where you don't have a

group of people you know how to work with or who trust you in ways that only a group of resident artists do.

The contracts for a resident actor with the Barter Theatre are for fifty weeks a year—fifty-two weeks if you include paid vacations. You've said before that Barter isn't for all actors. What do you mean by that?

If you're looking for stardom, go to New York or Los Angeles. If you want to work, stay here. We're the working-class theater. You're doing a minimum of acting in two shows and rehearsing two shows at any given time. That's not for everybody.

Barter Alumni

You're likely familiar with many actors who were residents at Barter Theatre at one time or another. Ernest Borgnine is a Barter alumnus, as well as Gregory Peck, Hume Cronyn, Ned Beatty, Frances Fisher, and Wayne Knight (you will recognize Knight from *Seinfeld*, *3rd Rock From the Sun*, and *Jurassic Park*). Alumnus James Burrows went on to create and write the television show *Cheers* (NBC), write for *Friends* (NBC), and write and produce *Will & Grace* (NBC) and *Frasier* (NBC).

What do you want or expect from actors who audition for you?

I want them to prepare. I don't want them to come in, do a cold reading, not know anything about the play they're reading for, and not know anything about the company they're preparing for, because it's just not useful. It's a waste of their time. It's a waste of my time. We're usually going to take a few minutes to talk to them. If we're interested, we're going to take a lot of time to talk to them, because we want to know they share at least a philosophical basis.

I want to work with actors who really want to act and who really want to explore a wide variety of aspects of themselves. I want somebody who's going to come in and make choices, and then if I don't like that choice, I'll say, "Hey, I get it. I get why you went there. It was great. But can you try this?" And then you have to be flexible, because if you're not, if you're locked into that choice, I'm never going to be able to direct you and you're never going to be able to grow because you're locked in.

Never audition for anything you're not interested in, because there's nothing worse than getting the person excited or interested in you and then you say, "I'm really not interested in doing this. I'm auditioning because I've got to audition." I don't want that. You may not get hired for this project, but it doesn't mean we've forgotten about you. I've hired people I saw four years ago.

Joining Barter's resident company is a commitment—a commitment for the actor and a commitment on the part of the company.

All of our contracts are automatically renewable, unless we speak with you at least four to six weeks in advance of the contract renewal date, or unless you're not interested, at which point we need to know four to six weeks in advance if you're not going to renew.

So the renewable contract is a show of commitment and trust.

For both actor and Barter. When we commit to somebody, we commit to them for the long term. I think that kind of relationship is really important in a business that doesn't have much of that.

There's another way to become part of the company—through the Barter Players. Could you tell me about that?

The purpose of the Barter Players is to introduce young actors into the professional world of theater. While they do some crew work, ninety percent of their time is spent acting, and so it really is an intensive acting program. And they're going to tour as well as perform here. Generally, the Players are here for eighteen

Esco Jouley and Stephen Wormley in Barter's production of *A Streetcar Named Desire*

Photo courtesy of Barter Theatre

months. They come in May and they stay through August of the following year. They'll also understudy, and they'll frequently get to go on because it's a resident company. We're here year round—people get sick or have family emergencies. Understudies are pretty important for us.

So typically, a Barter Player would be someone who's completed a program, whether it's conservatory or college?
Generally, they have an undergraduate degree, or some have their MFAs already. Many of them become a player and then want to go on for an MFA.

Could you talk about the "rite of passage" for Barter Players that occurs at the end of their contracts?
One of the last things they do as a member of the Players is take whatever they've identified as their greatest fear and do it for the company. The entire company gathers in the theater, and all the players come out and do what they call the Player Projects. We believe that if you can conquer your fears, you can conquer anything—because fear is the greatest thing that keeps you back.

How many of your current resident company members came up through the Barter Players?
We have eight currently.

So, let's take a moment to talk about challenges.
Let's talk about diversity, a tough issue for us. The challenge has been keeping minority actors, because there's no significant minority population here. I'm not a type caster. In fact, I'm the opposite of that, and we want a variety of people in our company. But it's unfortunate. We have always posted notices and casting calls encouraging minorities to audition. We've hired a lot of minorities for non-traditionally minority parts. We have a reputation for casting minority actors, but it's still difficult.

You've also remarked that Barter actors have been called on to play characters of the opposite gender as well as characters either much older or younger than themselves.
You're going to play a wide variety of roles here, and you're going to play everything you think you're never going to be able to do.

The advice I heard over and over again in theater classes and workshops was "if there's anything else you can do with your life, do it."

Oh yeah, that was the whole thing in theater—if you don't *have* to do theater, don't do it, which I don't believe at all. First of all, there are lots of jobs in the entertainment industry. It's a hard life being an actor, but there's lots of work out there. There are a lot of regional theaters. And there are lots of entertainment options. There's a ton of cable channels, there are boats to be part of the companies on, and there are theme parks. So there's lots of work in the entertainment industry. I grew up with that same advice, and they still say that.

So what advice would you offer to the aspiring actor?

My advice is to be well rounded, and by that I mean be well rounded in terms of the way you look at life and skills. And be flexible. Don't be rigid and say, "I'm only going to do this." You may find that your skills lie elsewhere as well. I don't care where you went to school. I don't care what degree you have. Don't be afraid to take jobs that aren't exactly what you thought you were going to do.

How do you define success?

Oh, *define success*. For us, success is really about how many people we can employ, how large a resident acting company we can have, how well we can support the other artists, all of our craftspeople.

What do you hope an actor, having worked here, will take away and share with the rest of the field?

The holistic approach. It's not just about a role you play—it's about the bigger part you play in the company and in the community.

> Rose was one of the first-ever recipients of the Town of Abingdon's Arthur Campbell Award for extraordinary contributions to the community.

AMANDA NELSON directs the MFA in Arts Leadership for the School of Performing Arts at Virginia Tech. She joined the faculty in 2013 after working eleven years for the world-renowned Alvin Ailey American Dance Theater in New York, where she oversaw membership programs, government relations, corporate sponsorships, and foundation support. She holds a PhD in Drama from Tufts University, an MA in Drama from San Francisco State University, and a BA in Drama from the University of California at Irvine. Amanda teaches arts management and acting and is a freelance theater reviewer for the *Roanoke Times*.

Amanda Nelson

Photo by Logan Wallace, courtesy of Virginia Tech

Notes

1   "Occupational Outlook Handbook: Actors," United States Department of Labor, Bureau of Labor Statistics, accessed May 1, 2016, http://www.bls.gov/ooh/entertainment-and-sports/actors.htm.

2   "About LORT," LORT League of Resident Theatres, accessed April 28, 2016, http://www.lort.org/About_LORT.html.

3   "2013-17 LORT-AEA Agreement," LORT League of Resident Theatres, accessed April 28, 2016, http://www.lort.org/Agreements.html.

CHAPTER 2

STICKING IT OUT

"The best way to guarantee a loss is to quit."
Morgan Freeman

You've taken the first step and have begun your career, and now it's time to move into the next phase: "Sticking It Out."

How long is this stage? you might be wondering. The short answer is, longer than you think. You won't just stick it out until you achieve the success you're looking for. If you're in this for the long haul, you'll stick it out until you're ready to retire. That is, if you do retire. Because artists, as you know, have the luxury of continuing their work long after the age of 65.

Sticking it out means making a decision to stay in the game even when all signs seem to point you in a direction off the board. Sticking it out means weathering the low-lows. It means finding a way to be happy for your friend who just landed a lead when your agent just dumped you. It means practicing the accent for your new role for ten or twelve hours instead of only the two hours you were required. It means showing up for the audition even when you've lost all confidence.

In this chapter, we'll delve into the work involved with *choosing* to participate in an acting career. It's all about choice—hard work, tenacity, creating your own opportunities. There will be lean months. There will be entire years when the only acting jobs you get are the ones you create for yourself. There will be eighteen-hour days with two jobs and acting class at night. There will be roles you get but have to give up for one reason or another.

Who Knew?

The overnight success stories you've heard of in the business are actually stories of dogged determination—people working quietly, tirelessly for years before that overnight success occurred. Morgan Freeman made his Off-Broadway debut in 1967, debuted on Broadway in 1968, and continued his theater work for years before receiving the Obie Award in 1980. He didn't find success in film until 1987, in a supporting role in *Street Smart*, and he landed the films *Glory* and *Driving Miss Daisy* in 1988, at the age of 51.

If you want to reach the next stage of your acting career, you must first commit to this stage. In this chapter, we'll discuss:

- How vocal training prepares you for a career in acting
- What vocal training looks like for the highest paid actors in the business
- Getting headshots, where to meet friends, and where to take acting classes
- How to get an audition, what to wear, and how not to panic when you get there
- The importance of managing your mental health
- How much appearance matters for actors
- How acting for the stage in Germany compares to acting in the United States
- What it looks like to overcome significant personal obstacles and stick it out against all odds
- How the art of acting compares to the art of working as a visual artist
- How to create a life as an actor and find a healthy balance between work and play
- Why it's often a good idea to take a break from acting if you need to

But you're not ready to take a break just yet. Let's start with vocal training and see what that looks like for the actor in Los Angeles.

TRAINING YOUR VOICE FOR THE JOB

▶ An Interview With Bob Corff

Bob Corff has been working as a voice coach in Los Angeles for more than three decades. His film, television, and stage clients over the years have included Hank Azaria, Angela Bassett, Jason Bateman, Don Cheadle, Toni Collette, Jesse Eisenberg, Sally Field, Maggie Gyllenhaal, Samuel L. Jackson, Anna Kendrick, Jennifer Lawrence, Andie Macdowell, Ewan McGregor, Julianne Moore, Olivia Munn, Gwyneth Paltrow, Vanessa Redgrave, John C. Reilly, J.K. Simmons, Emma Stone, and Channing Tatum, to name a few. (For a complete list, visit Corff's website at http://www.corffvoice.com.)

Bob Corff

I'm worried you're evaluating my voice.
I know. I'm off duty, though—just here to serve.

So you work more with screen actors than theater actors, but you have a background in theater yourself, right?
Right. I'm old enough that I trained and then starred in three Broadway shows before I got into coaching, so I got my beginning on Broadway—I learned how to fill a house.

Could you tell me a little about your path to this career, your background?
Basically, I graduated from high school and decided that being in a rock band would be a good idea, so I put together a couple of musician friends, and we had one rehearsal and opened at a gas station. And as fate would have it, somebody from MGM records came in to get gas and found us. So I started as a lead singer in a rock group called "The Purple Gang." That was the first taste of show business for me. I'd started taking voice lessons as soon as I thought about being an actor or a singer, because in those days, that's what everybody did. I didn't know anybody who didn't do acting class, dance class, and voice class.

When was that?
Oh, this is back in the late '60s. So I've seen how things have changed. Then, after I was in the rock band, I auditioned and got the lead in *Hair*. I took over for Jimmy Rado, who was the original star of it, and I did that for 11 months.

And this is important in terms of what we're discussing here. Tom O'Horgan was the director, and after the first night of my doing a show, Tom said to me, "You know, in the second act, your voice needs to be much bigger. You need to fill the theater." And I remember thinking to myself, this is a lot of intimate stuff going on with this character, and it felt really wrong to be talking so loud. But what I love about myself looking back was that I was smart enough to know that I didn't want to lose that job. So I just talked really loud during the second act.

And I'll tell you, it really didn't feel good to me. And every night, Tom would come back and go, "Great!" And about the third night, it stopped feeling so weird. And then I just realized that to do a good job in the second act, it took that much vocal energy, and then it stopped feeling uncomfortable.

So it was just the newness of using your voice in that way.
It was. So what happens to a lot of people is that when you learn voice or some new technique, it's uncomfortable in the beginning because it's not natural. But the people who are successful are the ones who are willing to go through this discomfort to get to the place where it finally relaxes and they can say, oh, *this* is now my instrument.

Were you concerned that you looked like a bad actor in that second act? I imagine to some degree it's a matter of trusting the director.
Well, I trusted him because I didn't want to lose the job, and he was a famous director. And really, as smart as I thought I was at that age, I thought maybe he was

smarter. But what I do with my clients now is, I tape the lessons—or now we're using smartphones. So I say, "Now, you know that part where it felt really uncomfortable—too big, too loud, too exaggerated? Let's listen to it." And they're always shocked and surprised, because it's not. It's just that if you have a very soft voice and then you start to talk a bit louder, it feels like you're yelling, but you're not.

And the more you talk at that volume, the more natural it feels?

Yes, but it can take many, many hours of that before it feels natural. I've had a chance to work with a lot of stars, and one of the things I admire and enjoy about working with those kinds of people is how hard they're willing to work—how willing they are to do whatever it takes to get the result. I've had people who have said, "You know, I worked eleven hours on this yesterday," and I would think, wow, I wouldn't have the courage to tell them to practice eleven hours. But they did whatever it took so they could break through.

I think people sometimes attribute an artist's success to luck or connections or something outside of his or her control.

No. People who are very successful work very, very hard—harder than you think. It's not like, oh, I *kind of* would *maybe* like this to happen in my career. No. It's, in two weeks I'll be making a film that people can see for 100 years. Or in two weeks I'm going to be on stage in London. I'd better get my voice handled. So it's real for them. They have to get it done, and they're willing to do whatever it takes. So it's rewarding for me, obviously, to work with people whose commitment is that complete.

What about talent? Are there some people who are just more talented, more capable of getting the accent, or getting rid of the accent? How do you tackle that?

The answer to the question is, yes, some people are more gifted. Being a singer, I think that's why I was able to do accents—because I heard the melody, the stresses, the placement—so it was just a little song to me, that accent, so that was my way in. There are some people who have very good ears, and they're quick to pick things up. But I've worked with really big stars who didn't have that natural talent for accents. And for them, it was hard. It was just bone-crunching hard work, but they got it anyway because they did the work.

But yes, clearly some people get it more easily. That's the first thing that everybody wants to know—how many lessons will it take? And I say, well, I would love to tell you, but if anybody tells you that they're just making it up. I can give you an idea. It could be a couple lessons, or it could take you a couple of months. It depends how quickly you pick it up, how hard you work, and your commitment to consistency, doing it day after day.

Daily—and what about during the day in the actor's real life? Do you recommend that actors practice the accent, incorporating it into their routine?
I do. It's very hard for a lot of people to do it 100 percent of the time. I've had people who went in, auditioned with that accent, did the movie for three months, and when they finished the picture, they talked to that producer with their original accent and blew their minds. That's an extreme case, but I would say that you should go to restaurants where you don't know the waiter, in the taxi, or in the market where it doesn't matter. Always do it there first, because you want to do it in a safe place before you start doing it in auditions or when you're shooting or in rehearsal.

Is it always a matter of hard work then? Have you never come across an actor who simply wasn't able to get a certain accent or get comfortable speaking loudly?
I have a sign next to my piano in my studio that says, "Change is possible." A lot of people just think, hey, this is my voice. My shoe size is nine, and that's not going to change. But your voice is a matter of muscle and coordination, so you *can* change your voice. But you have to believe it, because if you're sure it *can't* change, then you'll be right.

What would you say are the most intimidating vocal problems for an actor to tackle?
I think it's just confronting the sound of your own voice. People feel very uncomfortable when they listen back to their voice for the first time. The reason you're uncomfortable is that when you talk, not only are you hearing your voice with your ears, but you're hearing it bouncing around inside your own head, so it seems much more resonant and big inside your head. And then when you hear it played back, you're just hearing it with your ears, which is how everybody else hears it. It can be uncomfortable at first, but you need to hear it.

You can't fix something unless you can confront what's really there. So that's why I tell them, you've got to listen for these things. You *will* get better. But you've got to be willing to not be good for a while—that's what it takes to become good.

I like that, "you've got to be willing to not be good for a while."
I'm jumping off track a bit maybe, but as a personal side note—I have a friend who is a very successful screenwriter and then became a director, and we were having lunch years ago, and I said to him, "Don't you think we've been lucky that we've done so well in our careers?" And he said, "Lucky? I wrote bad scripts for ten years before somebody finally hired me. I did my homework, and so did you."

That's how people become good. Every once in a while somebody gets something on no work. It's like going to Vegas and putting in a quarter and winning $1 million, and then 20 million people come and lose. So it can make you think, maybe if somebody did it with no work, I can, too—but that very seldom ever happens.

Sure, and then where do you go from there? At some point—soon—you're confronted with work!
Exactly. It's a myth, that.

I'd love to talk more about the most common vocal problems and how to tackle them. So learning to deal with the sound of your own voice. What else?
I would say the thing I see most often now is that people don't breathe properly. The voice is all about how you handle and organize and send your air out of you. So when people don't breathe properly, the voice is weak—you can't get it to go where you want it to go. And because there's so much pressure today, more than ever, our stomachs are all locked up—beyond the fact that we want to look good and hold our stomach in! I find that's pretty universal nowadays.

But when people start to breathe properly, it's better for their health, too— because all of a sudden they feel better, they have oxygen and blood flowing in their system the way it's supposed to, as opposed to being tight and living in a position of "I'm ready for the hit" all the time. That's what happens, the stomach locks up like it's ready for an attack, which isn't a good position for art or life.

Do you think there's any correlation between emotional stressors—or even personality temperaments—and the way actors speak or are able to speak?
Absolutely, and yet, there are people in show business who are very successful who are tense and crazy as a loon, but they have an instrument that works for them, so their voice can be good even when they're not good. That's what technique is for. It's not for the days that you're inspired, because those days you don't

need anybody. Those days, it's all, "I'm flowing today—my choices are good, my voice is open." But that doesn't happen every day no matter who you are. So if you have an instrument that knows how to do its job, then when you open your mouth, out comes this big sound, and you go, "Oh, I'm here." It grounds you, and then you can do your job.

If you were working with an actor who's just about to showcase for agents, perhaps at the end of an MFA program, what kind of advice would you have for that actor?

Well, you only have two things to work with on a physical level—you have your body and your voice. People work on their bodies all the time—they go to the gym and dermatologists, they get their hair done. They do all kinds of things to get themselves looking as good as possible. But so often, they don't do the work on the voice. And as a director friend of mine said a few years ago, your voice is your other face. It's your instrument, and you need to train it to be capable of doing what your impulse wants to do as an actor. In the same way that your body can make someone take notice, can get you in the door, your vocal instrument can make the difference between getting the job and not getting the job. And when it's working for you, that can make you feel strong and powerful—you know that you've done your work, and it showed up for you.

Do you have clients who are screen actors and then they transition because they have a theater gig?

I have that all the time. I have big stars who go to Broadway, London, or somewhere for a show. They have three months, and they panic and go, "I've never done theater!" So they have to come and really do some quick work to get that instrument working. Because if your body isn't used to talking loud for two hours, your voice will go out. You'll lose it.

You've been doing this a long time. Have you found over the years any analogies between being successful in your career and how you're able to use and manipulate your voice?

Absolutely. Today more than ever—it's always been true, but today especially—young people don't want to be uncool. Really at any age. And one way to prove that you're cool—as opposed to uncool—is to speak with everything on one level. *[mimics]* "See, I'm just not going to get too excited about anything, because that really shows weakness, I think. So I won't show too much nuance. Just keep it flat and cool."

But you've got to give of yourself. I say to my clients, your job is to wake people up, to excite them about whatever it is you're talking about. Otherwise, they'll give the part to somebody who *is* interesting to be around. You may think you sound cool, but you sound like you're putting it on. You have to believe that. We see right through it. The best storytellers make you feel like you're there. The best actors take you on a journey from their experience. They're using their instrument to take you on that ride.

By the way . . .

Bob says there are two keys for actors who want to make their voice work for them: articulation and resonance.

Articulation

"You have to be clean and clear so people can understand you. You don't want to be over-articulate, because we don't speak that way anymore. But if I don't understand you, I tune you out—and, before that, I get frustrated. So you have to think, as an actor, is that something you want to do? Frustrate your audience? Force them to tune you out?"

Resonance

"When your voice is anchored into your body, then your body resonates and you vibrate. What happens is, you're using your body, it resonates you, and then it resonates the room, and people in the room become resonated. They go, you know what? I like him. They don't know why. But they're tuning in to you because they see you, hear you, and feel you—and those are the things you get when you tune up your instrument, your voice."

What about casting directors? Do you think they're tuned in to why they like a particular actor—that the actor's voice might have something to do with it?
There are some casting directors who have no sense of that, and there are others who, if your voice isn't good, they say, go to Bob, go to him right away. Some people are very voice aware and some aren't—but either way, if your instrument is good, they'll be getting a better you.

What I do is really kind of a secret. There aren't very many actors who are that aware about voice anymore, but there are enough of them to keep me and my wife very busy. Most people don't have the benefit of an instrument that works for them—and the ones who do, they do much better and feel better about themselves.

Bob's wife Claire began as an apprentice to Bob and has since become a renowned dialect coach herself. She teaches private lessons at Corff Voice Studios and accent reduction classes at the Strasberg Institute, and she continues to develop audio accent courses with Bob.

Claire and Bob Corff Voice Studio, Los Angeles

I wonder if there's a correlation between that human instinct to fight against change or the willingness to embrace change as a means to success. Yes? No?

Yes, absolutely. I have such great respect for schoolteachers, because people come to me, they pay me good money, and they say they want me to help them, and then they resist anyway—because that's what humans do. So when teachers are working with people who don't even want to be there, that must be horrifying.

But I'm lucky. People at least—even though they're resisting—they're still trying. They're showing up and doing the work. We're in a process. We come, we work, we fight a little against change, because nature isn't happy when things change. But the people who are brave and strong and successful are the ones who are willing to move through that discomfort.

**When I think of stage acting and voice, I think of that "actor's voice"—
do you know what I mean? Seems like that might be different from what
you're teaching, though.**

Look, you can go too far with just about anything. You might sometimes meet
a stage actor who says, *[mimics voice]* "Hello, it's so nice to meet you"—and you
know instantly that you're in the presence of an "actor." But nobody talks like
that anymore, unless you're playing a character like that. So I'm not teaching that,
but it was definitely the vocal style at one time.

Do some voice instructors still teach this, though? The actor's voice?

Well, there's a wonderful woman, Edith Skinner—she's got a very famous book,
Speak With Distinction. And she was a great, great teacher, but she was a great
teacher in the 1930s and '40s and '50s. And listen, I have great respect for her.
The material is great. It's just that nobody talks like that anymore—that was the
way they spoke in the studio days. It's called the mid-Atlantic accent. It's in the
middle of the ocean—not American. We have achieved a standard American
accent now. In my programs, we have a lot of the same kind of exercises, but just
with the pronunciation that people use today.

The thing is, you want to bring your voice up to the level of excellence, not
excess. In this town, I've been doing it for thirty-five years now, and just about
everybody knows who I am because I'm teaching what gets people jobs. A lot of
voice teachers will teach you their "gift." They have this big bass baritone body,
and they always had that voice. I'm a tenor, so any bottom I have in my voice I
had to put there. But no, if you sound phony and exaggerated, that's not going
to get you the job. That's not what we're striving for.

Next steps for the young actor?

Having a good voice will be a benefit to you whether you do stage or film. I've
worked with a lot of really good actors who talk very soft when they're doing
a film, but their instrument is choosing *exactly* what they want it to do. And if
there's a high emotional scene, the instrument will take care of it. And if they do
a show on Broadway or in London, their instrument is prepared for that. Your
voice will follow you—wherever you go.

ESSENTIAL KNOWLEDGE AND HABITS

For the Working Actor

▸ An Interview With Jordan Lund

Jordan Lund has been act-ing professionally since the 1980s. He has made more than eighty film and tele-vision appearances and performed in more than 150 plays. He has worked on Broadway, Off-Broadway, in regional theater, and with some of the best Los Angeles theaters, including the Ahmanson, Pacific Resident Theater, the Blank Theatre, and the Odyssey Theatre.

Jordan Lund

Photo by Alex Monti Fox

Lund received classical training at Carnegie-Mellon University and began his career on Broadway at the Belasco Theatre for the New York Shakespeare Festival, in *Romeo and Juliet*, *As You Like It*, and *Macbeth*, all directed by Estelle Parsons. His Off-Broadway credits include *All's Well That Ends Well*, *Measure For Measure*, *The Golem*, *Twelfth Night*, and *King John*, all at the Delacorte Theatre in Central Park for the New York Shakespeare Festival. Also in New York, Lund was in Eric Bogosian's *I Saw the Seven Angels at the Kitchen*.

Lund is an Associate Artist with the New American Theatre in Los Angeles, where he has appeared in or directed twenty-two plays since 1997. He has had roles in films such as *The Bucket List*, *Doc Hollywood*, *Speed*, *American President*, and *The Rookie*, and in television shows such as *NYPD Blue*, *Cheers*, *Frasier*, *Firefly*, *LA Law*, *Law & Order*, *Star Trek DS9 & TNG*, *Enterprise*, *ER*, *Chicago Hope*, and *The Practice*. He has been teaching acting in Los Angeles since 1999.

You've been doing this a long time. What advice do you have for the aspiring actor?

The biggest advice I would give young actors is to get more than just actor training. Get a real training in the world. Learn about things that are going to bring you depth as an actor and as an artist. If you're just learning voice and speech and movement and dance and acting technique, you're not going to have any opinions or attitudes about politics, or religion, or education, or family—the things that you develop as a human being when you're out in the world.

Any thoughts on paying the bills while you're trying to get work acting?

Yes, you've got to earn a living. I've had long stretches of my career where I would work, and then stretches where I wouldn't have an acting job. So it's a good idea to figure out how to bring in income when you're not working on the stage. You should have skills that you develop outside of acting.

What about acting skills? What do you think is the most important skill for actors to acquire?

I've learned over the years that the most important thing an actor can master is relaxation. It's what stands in the way of an actor having authentic human behavior on stage. The stories, the plays, the movies, the TV shows—everything we do is pretend. The only authentic part is what we bring in our emotional life to the role. The very best actors can access their own personal life in those parameters, and that's when we see an authentic, emotional performance.

Emotional availability and emotional expression is a really important part to the early development of an actor. I've worked with people in their 40s and 50s who have had conservatory training, and they've been working professionally, and the assumption is that they have emotional availability and also the ability to express it freely. But they don't always, and when they don't, it's because of tension and self-consciousness. It's impossible to be completely vulnerable and intimate in a public place if you're self-conscious and tension visits you. So the actor has to continue to work on the ability to relax and let the expression come through.

Is some of the tension that you're referring to in auditions? How can actors master the art of relaxation during the auditioning process—especially when it's a coveted or potentially career-changing role?

Part of mastering the audition is understanding that it's not about being rejected. We all have this feeling that if we don't get the part, they're rejecting us. But that's not what it's about. If I'm going into an audition and there are three other people auditioning for the same role and none of them looks or seems exactly like me, we're not really in competition with each other. If they cast the other person, is it a rejection of me or is it an acceptance of the other person?

I've never walked into an audition where the people doing the auditioning were repelled by me, where I walked in and they said, you're just too ugly, or I hate your voice, or my God, this guy stinks. Nobody's ever done that in an audition. What they've done is treat me mostly with respect. They usually show you respect because you have a craft and they want you to do the best work so that you might be the one they cast.

And the reason they do or don't cast you can be arbitrary. Maybe it's because I'm three inches taller than all the other leads, and they don't want me to stick out in terms of height, so they need somebody shorter. There are so many reasons why they pick somebody, and I've never imagined that any of those reasons has been because they rejected me. Actors need to cut that word out of their vocabulary. They can't think about rejection.

> "I've learned over the years that the most important thing an actor can master is relaxation. It's what stands in the way of an actor having authentic human behavior on stage."

Do you have any examples of getting cast for an arbitrary reason?
I know for a fact that one job I got was completely arbitrary, a guest star on a show on ABC for one season. When I was in the audition, one of the executive producers was wearing a golf shirt with the name of a golf course that I had played in New Jersey, and I mentioned it. We had a five-minute conversation about our experiences on that particular golf course. I got offered the role, and my first day of work, I walked onto the set and the producer came over to me immediately to ask if I'd played any rounds recently.

What about trying to land a leading role? Does that have more to do with talent? Is that a less arbitrary decision in the casting?

When it comes to talent, so often what you'll see with young people coming into the business is that they censor themselves, so they don't have full control over their craft—and that's when the people casting can't see their talent. They think they have to be perfect, that they have to make themselves look perfect. And unfortunately, that's always going to work against them. So what happens is, they edit themselves in their work, and they try to behave in a way that they think people want to see.

I always tell my students to think of it this way—it's okay for the audience to see me at my worst. If I'm going to bring a real human life to light in my performance, it has to be someone who you can sit in the audience and recognize. But that only happens when you watch fallible human beings. So we have to be willing to show the sides of ourselves as actors that we're not proud of. It's something that actors should try to start to get in the habit of from the very beginning of the journey, a willingness to show the side of themselves that they're not proud of. It's that willingness that allows an actor's talent to emerge.

Do you think we confuse the idea that the lead role in a play—or film or TV show—is a hero? So actors have a sense that they should portray the character in a heroic way?

Look, if all I wanted to do was show you the heroic side of a character, then I wouldn't be doing my job. I'm not illuminating a life. So I have to be willing to reveal weakness. And I have to be willing to seek the dark side in myself, in

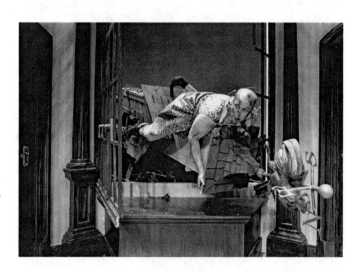

Jordan Lund as Sgt. Match in Joe Orton's *What the Butler Saw*, Great Lakes Theater Festival, 1997

Photo by Roger Mastroianni

my own personality. How else do you play Jack the Ripper, or any of the other sociopaths that we get to play? They're the most fun characters, but if you're just play acting, it's never going to be as moving to the audience as if you find the ugliness in yourself to bring to that light.

But being emotionally available is very different from being emotionally unstable. There used to be this idea that actors had to be unstable emotionally to be great artists. But actors *shouldn't* be unstable emotionally. Actors should have psychological health so they're able to go deep into themselves and utilize their emotional life without damaging themselves.

What about the aspiring actor who knows that he or she is emotionally unstable? Can a person with fragile mental health hope to succeed in this career?

Sure, some actors just need another outlet to learn how to express themselves honestly, and maybe that means a twelve-step program. Maybe it means a group therapy. Maybe it means talking to a clergy. Maybe it means talking to therapist. Any of those things are good. The key is to take care of yourself emotionally.

The Actors Fund

For information about counseling services for actors, visit the Actors Fund at http://www.actorsfund.org. Administered from offices in New York City, Los Angeles, and Chicago, the Actors Fund is a national, nonprofit organization serving all entertainment professionals through comprehensive services and programs. In addition to providing counseling, substance abuse, and mental health services, the fund provides emergency grants for essentials such as food, rent, and medical care. The Actors Fund was founded in 1882, serving performing arts and entertainment professionals in film, theater, television, music, opera, and dance.

How important are looks in this business? Does a serious actor pay attention to appearance?

If you want to spend time working out, getting healthy, doing your hair right, picking the right clothes, there's nothing wrong with that. Beauty is prized in our business, so the better you look, the more opportunities you're probably going to have. But you can't do it at the expense of your emotional strength and life. And you can't do it at the expense of your craft, doing the hard work of being an actor.

For so many people, fame has become an end result, a goal. I have plenty of contemporaries who have expressed that they would like to be successful as actors. But for most of them, the important thing was always to be an actor, to get the work. My contemporaries who I respect, if they could work all the time, that would be the greatest thing of all. It was never about being famous or looking perfect.

Every actor wants to get an agent. How do you advise your students about this?

Nobody gets an agent until they're hip deep in it. But in the meantime, you send out emails to agencies with your picture and resume. Or you send out snail mail of flyers and postcards of shows you're doing—try to get them to see shows. Also, there's a new tool for marketing actors that hasn't been around too long: casting director workshops. The only kind of workshop a casting director can conduct is one where there's no promise of work, and very often they can't even advertise where they work. But that can be a great way to introduce yourself and your work to people who are in the business of casting actors. And casting directors work with all the agents, so instead of contacting one agent at a time, this way you can talk to a casting director who has your back, and maybe he or she will introduce you to some people. The key is you have to be constantly proactive, either networking, seeking out representation or people to see you, self-generating work, doing scenes and monologues for classes, doing plays. If you're in Los Angeles and New York, you should be auditioning constantly for plays and doing as many as you can, no matter what they pay you—and they probably mostly won't pay you much.

> "Beauty is prized in our business, so the better you look, the more opportunities you're probably going to have. But you can't do it at the expense of your emotional strength and life. And you can't do it at the expense of your craft, doing the hard work of being an actor."

Can anybody audition? If you move to New York or Los Angeles and you don't have an agent yet, you can just audition for plays?

I'm not talking about Broadway plays. They're little theaters. Some of them are under union supervision, some of them aren't—but even the ones that are under union supervision are allowed to cast nonunion actors. Backstage also has auditions for plays at some of the little theaters around town, so on a weekly basis there are auditions available.

Also, in Los Angeles, there are about 200 membership theater companies. They all have websites with links to audition information. You join the company, and then they have to let you audition for plays. You pay your monthly dues. Some of them have meetings. Some of them you have to do other kind of work, like box office, or clean the bathrooms, or build the sets to donate hours for the company—and some of them don't.

But that's how actors without agents get considered for acting roles, and there are people who get them regularly through those vehicles. And sometimes you get lucky—you do a play, somebody else who's in the play brought her agent that night, the agent sees you, and bingo, you meet an agent. There is no one way to do it.

Have you ever known that to happen?
Where someone's agent first saw them on stage? Oh, yeah. I've known several people that's happened to. That's actually the best way. The agent was there for a client, but you knocked it out of the park that night.

Are there agents who only represent theater actors?
Agents don't really do that anymore. But the opposite is true—there are agents who won't represent actors for theater. Out here in LA, there are a lot of agents who will only represent actors for commercials, or on camera, or for voiceovers. They discourage their clients from auditioning for theater.

Because it doesn't pay?
Right, and because LA theater is kind of the redheaded stepchild. At the Ahmanson Theatre and Mark Taper Forum, the contract has an eight-week out. Meaning, if I want to get out of the play, I have to give eight weeks' notice. That's pretty unrealistic, but its purpose is to discourage actors from looking for other work. Although it doesn't stop people, and there are still plenty of people who work all the time in film and television during the day during performances of their shows. So no, if someone wants to just do theater, LA is the wrong place.

What are the options if you choose not to live in Los Angeles or New York?

Go to some of the smaller markets if you want to start a theater career. Markets like San Francisco, Seattle, Minneapolis, or Chicago—those markets have very vibrant theater scenes, and most of it is nonunion theater. A smaller market, or regional theater. That's another real option for young actors coming out of school, to seek the regional theater life.

Should actors just starting out get headshots for theater work and different headshots for film and television work?

It's all the same now. Everybody uses the same thing, a color headshot. And all you've got to do is go online. Every headshot photographer has a website. And everything is done digitally. Very few pictures are printed.

There's so much rejection for actors. How can an actor know whether he or she has enough talent to pursue the career?

It's an intangible. There is no way to know for sure. But you have to know that you're enough. That's another thing I try to impart to students all the time. You're enough. No one is like you. Everybody is completely unique. So if you just simply exist honestly and authentically up there on that stage, then you will be perfectly you. When you try to start being somebody else, that's when it gets cliché and no one wants to watch it.

Any final words of advice?

Don't become complacent. It's a real seduction to have an evening job, working at a restaurant or bar where you're making some decent money and you have your friends. You're going out drinking and partying, and all that fun stuff that actors do. And that's important for actors to have fun. But if you're doing that, don't sleep until 3:00 pm and do nothing all day. You have to be proactive on a daily basis. Do something every day for your acting career, every single day. No matter what it is, do something. Maybe it's a learning thing or a marketing thing, or maybe you're working on a scene or monologue for a class.

You're working in a solitary way so much of the time as an actor, so it's a good idea to have a coach, or a friend to work with, or an acting class to go to. You want to make sure you have somebody to work off of when you're practicing a monologue or preparing for an audition, so it's not just a vacuum and you're not relying only on your instincts. But you should always be learning. It takes a lot of work to be an actor, and it should be work. Any job that you succeed at, you put work into it. It doesn't just happen.

THIS IS NOT MY BEAUTIFUL HOUSE!

A Semi-Imaginary Interview With Berliner Ensemble Actor Laura Tratnik

▶ By John Crutchfield

Setting: *A two-bedroom flat in Berlin-Kreuzberg. Tastefully but minimally furnished w/beige couch, a few mismatched chairs, a bookshelf crammed with titles in English and German, plus an assortment of DVDs in no particular order. At one end of the couch LAURA, a svelte European woman in her early thirties, sits with her legs folded under her. At the other, JOHN, a somewhat scrawny American man in his mid-forties, sits with a laptop on his knees. For some reason, he wears an obviously fake black mustache. From OFF we hear the sound of a CHILD singing to herself— a bilingual mash-up of the* Frozen *soundtrack.*

JOHN: *[calling OFF]* Polly? Could you sing a little more quietly, please? Mama and Daddy are working in here. *[The singing continues unabated.]* Okay. I guess we'll have to deal.

LAURA: Um, can I ask you a question?

JOHN: Sure.

LAURA: What's with the 'stache?

JOHN: I thought it would make things more objective.

LAURA: It's weird.

JOHN: Exactly. A little Brechtian *Verfremdungseffekt*. In fact, for purposes of this interview, I'd like you to call me *Klaus*.

LAURA: Uh huh.

JOHN: But before we begin, I should say that this is for a chapter called "Sticking It Out."

LAURA: Which means . . .?

JOHN: You know, keeping the dream alive, not giving up just because you haven't had instant success right out of drama school. Which now that I think of it, doesn't really apply to you.

LAURA: No.

JOHN: Okay, well, so you're a counterexample. We can work with that. You graduated contract in hand. The Berliner Ensemble, no less. So: to what do you attribute your success, Ms. Tratnik?

LAURA: Right. Well, I would say that my success is due in large part to the reputation of my school.

JOHN: Ah! The Ernst Busch Academy of Dramatic Arts!

LAURA: That's the one. It's seen here as sort of the West Point of drama schools, where artistic directors from major houses all over Germany, Austria, and Switzerland scout new talent. I had several offers before I completed my studies.

JOHN: Amazing. But how did you end up there to begin with?

LAURA: Luck had a lot to do with it. In this profession, there's always an element of luck and the magic of the moment. If you're in good form on the day of an audition, then maybe, during those few brief minutes, you manage to concentrate and at the same time let go. Of course, I get nervous during auditions, but usually I'm pretty focused. My basic attitude is always, Now I'm gonna show you people! Probably because I found my way to theater by accident.

[From OFF, the CHILD sings, "Here I stand . . ."]

JOHN: *[calling OFF]* Uh, Polly? Maybe you want to go back into Mama and Daddy's room to sing?

CHILD: *[OFF]* No!

JOHN: *[to LAURA]* Wait. You found theater by accident?

LAURA: I had an arts-based education in the Waldorf School, but I never thought about theater as a career. In fact, I came to Berlin to study Japanology at Humboldt University. And even that was really just an excuse to move to Berlin.

JOHN: Japanology?

LAURA: Yeah. "Japan" plus "ology." "Japanology." Maybe it's a German thing. Anyway, one night I went down to Vienna for this art opening, and out of nowhere the gallerist tells me I have something special and I ought to apply to acting school. No one had ever said anything like that to me before, but somehow it resonated. So without telling anyone, I started preparing for an audition at Ernst Busch.

JOHN: Knowing that something like 2,000 people apply there every year? And they accept 15?

LAURA: Well, I figured I might as well go for the best. I had nothing to lose.

JOHN: And you think that attitude helped you?

LAURA: Absolutely. It made me more open and emotionally available. I mean, I'd worked really hard on my monologues, but my feeling walking in was like, Hey, let's just go for it and see what happens.

JOHN: And . . .? What happened?

LAURA: Um, honey?

JOHN: Klaus!

LAURA: Your 'stache is coming off on that side.

JOHN: *[investigates face]* Oh. *[Reattaches mustache.]* Thanks.

LAURA: And I wonder if it's really necessary? I mean, it makes you look like Kaiser Wilhelm II. After chemotherapy. Or maybe an institutional delousing.

JOHN: I think it's working just fine. You were saying, Ms. Tratnik?

[A moment of indecipherable nonverbal communication between spouses.]

LAURA: *[sighs]* So I made the first cut and then the second cut—and with that I was an acting student.

JOHN: I see. And meanwhile, the other 1,985 people who'd been dreaming of this their whole lives and preparing for months and going without the refined pleasures of Japanology . . . What did they get? A set of steak knives?

LAURA: But that's what I'm saying, "Klaus." I think it actually helped me that I hadn't been dreaming of it my whole life. I had other experiences. Even Japanology helped me somehow.

JOHN: So, what's the upshot here? The way to become a successful actor is to not want to become a successful actor?

LAURA: Kind of.

JOHN: That's totally Zen.

LAURA: Or is it fate? I mean, I'm here now, and certain factors led me here, a particular combination of talent, choice, luck, hard work, timing, circumstance. Take away one small thing, and the outcome would be totally different. Or would it?

JOHN: This is getting mystical. I don't do mystical. No one named Klaus does mystical. Ever. Let's get back to the facts. *[Reads from computer screen.]* "You've worked in both Europe and North America. How would you characterize the difference?"

LAURA: Well, certain things are the same everywhere—how people function together, the power structures and hierarchies. But there are differences that change the way you experience the work. What I love about working in the US is the concentration on the actor. Often, what the actor offers in rehearsal becomes the basis for the whole staging of the play.

JOHN: Are you suggesting, Ms. Tratnik, that actors are creative artists? Good God!

LAURA: They can be. And it has to do with curiosity. Not only curiosity about the world—history, politics, the arts, the natural sciences—although that is extremely important too. But also curiosity about oneself. A desire to find out things you don't know, to break open your idea of who you are and look deeper. Your curiosity has to be stronger than your ego and your need for security. That's why courage is so important for an actor.

JOHN: And you think American actors are strong in this way?

LAURA: Well, I think American culture encourages people to see themselves as creative, but it only goes so deep. When I watch American TV series or films, or go to see plays in the US, the actors often have this wonderful naturalness about them. But over time, you notice that this becomes a sort of habit. In a way, American actors mostly play themselves—which explains why they're so good at it. Like even you, right now, you're still just John.

JOHN: I beg your pardon. I am most certainly not "John." Need I remind you that I have a mustache? And please consider my nervous tick. *[does something with eyebrows]* It's a character choice.

LAURA: Except it's the same character choice you make for every character I've ever seen you perform—and frankly, you do it at breakfast too.

JOHN: Have you never heard of the Method?

LAURA: Is this interview over yet?

JOHN: Far from it. You have yet to tell us anything about how the actor is viewed here in Europe.

LAURA: Well, the dominant principle here and in much of Europe is *Regietheater*, or director-centered theater. So the director is more the star than the actor. The stage actor's purpose is really to bring about the director's vision.

JOHN: Is there an actors' union in Germany?

LAURA: No, so that's another big difference. But really, the professional circumstances are difficult to compare. We have a lot of state-supported ensemble theaters, even in smaller cities, so working actors in Germany are more likely to be salaried than freelance. Which is nice, because it means you get to live and work in one place.

JOHN: Think of these American actors, where if you want a career you have to be completely flexible, traveling to jobs and living out of your suitcase for months on end. You come back home to your partner, and they're like, "You talkin' to me?" And then the mohawk. It gets ugly.

LAURA: True. Which is one reason so many artists end up together. It takes one to know one. The only problem then is that your partner is equally overworked and underpaid and torn between the limitless demands of art and life, and so who's going to pay the utilities this month and who's going to pick the kid up from daycare? "Oh shit, we have a kid?" And so on. Actually, artists should marry dentists.

JOHN: How long have you felt this way?

LAURA: But the whole cultural paradigm is different here. Being an artist in Germany actually confers a certain social status, even if you're living hand to mouth. Artists are seen as doing something important in the culture. In the US, it's more of an all-or-nothing view. Unless you make lots of money or get a zillion views on YouTube, no one seems particularly interested in whatever it is you're doing with this so-called art thing. People look at you funny and assume it's a cover for laziness or something illegal—which is pretty discouraging for the artists themselves. On the other hand, it can lead to a kind of solidarity and love of the work for its own sake. I mean, look at you guys at the Magnetic Theatre. You have this tiny space, and everybody has to have a day job, but you've got total artistic freedom. Sure, your annual budget wouldn't pay Bob Wilson's laundry bill, but at least it's your own thing you're doing, and you know the people you're doing it for. And who knows where it might lead?

JOHN: You make poverty and despair sound so nice.

LAURA: And by the way: 'Stache Alert.

JOHN: Oh. Thanks. *[investigates face, reattaches mustache]* Can you tell us about your work at the Berliner Ensemble, Ms. Tratnik?

LAURA: Yeah, you know? This whole *[air quotes]* "interview" thing? What are you doing? This isn't even me. These words aren't even mine. If they were, they'd be in German. And worst of all—it's not funny!

JOHN: Who said that was my artistic intention? Believe me, after living in Berlin for three years, I am so far beyond that, Ms. Tratnik. Oh, so very far. You have no idea. So maybe you could just get with the program here? Your work at the Berliner Ensemble?

[Another moment of indecipherable nonverbal etc.]

LAURA: The Berliner Ensemble is a repertory theater. Dozens of plays rotate through the schedule every season. Meanwhile, new productions are premiered, while older ones—or ones that aren't doing well at the box—get retired. Certain productions are considered classics, though, and will play till doomsday: Tabori's *Waiting for Godot*, Wilson's *The Three Penny Opera*. This season, I'm in fifteen different plays, some supporting roles, some leads, and during the day I'm usually in rehearsal. But my schedule is extremely unpredictable, and it changes on short notice. The total hours per week range between thirty and ninety, depending—and is out of all proportion to the salary. The contract is officially year to year, but generally, if you do a good job, your contract gets renewed. So even though we don't have a union, there's some degree of security.

JOHN: *[reading]* "What would you say is the greatest professional challenge you've faced, and how did you . . ."

LAURA: Shhhhh!

JOHN: What?

> *[A faint sound from the next room. Matches being struck?*
> *Tissue paper being torn into interesting shapes?]*

LAURA: *[calling OFF]* Polly?

CHILD: *[OFF]* Yes?

LAURA: *[calling OFF]* What are you doing?

CHILD: *[OFF]* I'm making myself beautiful!

Theater makeup? That's easy!

LAURA: Uh oh. *[calling OFF]* Like what exactly? I hope you're not getting into my makeup . . .

[silence]

JOHN: *[calling OFF]* Polly, are you playing with Mama's makeup?

CHILD: *[OFF]* No.

[beat]

LAURA: Is she lying?

JOHN: Does she even know you can do that?

[beat]

LAURA: My greatest challenge—staying true to myself. Going my own way, however difficult that is. Not becoming dependent on external circumstances or the demands or moods of directors and colleagues. In this profession, you have to preserve your inner equilibrium. You have to let yourself be challenged without losing your bearings on who you are. Only then are you able to do your best. Very rarely does everything just click from the start. Usually, you have to fight to be recognized in your full depth and complexity as a human being and an artist. This is extremely important early in your career, because it sets the tone for the kind of collaborator you're going to be.

JOHN: *[reading]* "At one point, you took a break from your career, moved to the US, got married, and had a child. How did this experience change you?"

LAURA: It changed everything. I'm no longer constantly at war with myself. I have a healthy counterbalance to my professional life that puts a lot of things in perspective. At the same time, I'm less driven than I was before, and my need for peace and quiet is greater.

JOHN: So how do you manage career and family?

LAURA: Good question. During a big production last year, for instance, I realized at one point that for three weeks I hadn't put my daughter to bed a single time. That made it clear to me that something had to change.

JOHN: I suspect you weren't the only one who felt that way . . .

LAURA: No, "Klaus," I don't believe I was. And would you mind if I stuffed that mustache up your nostrils using my thumbs?

JOHN: *[reading]* "What advice would you give actors just starting out in their careers, especially those struggling to 'make it'"?

LAURA: I'd remind them that life outside the theater is also important. In fact, it's what we create out of, and it's what we present on stage. Acting is the most beautiful job in the world, but it also eats its own young. The only way to survive is to be obstinate, and to do it for your own joy and satisfaction. Not to get famous. That's mostly out of your control anyway. Better to love the work itself. Then if the big break happens and you get "discovered," super—and if not, who cares? You still have this thing you love that you can keep doing. All you need is your own creativity and the respect of your collaborators. As long as you keep your spirits up and your love of the work alive, it will continue to give your life meaning. That's what it means to have integrity as an artist.

JOHN: *[reading]* "Where do you see yourself in ten years?"

LAURA: Somewhere else. Earning more money, so that I can travel and have my own house and a garden. Doing artistic projects only if they make me happy and stimulate me and involve people I like.

JOHN: You'd walk away from your acting career?

LAURA: From the career, yes. From acting, from the art itself, no.

JOHN: *[reading]* "If you could go back to the day you graduated from acting school, what would you do differently?"

LAURA: Nothing.

JOHN: Nothing?

LAURA: Nope.

JOHN: Not even crash a few parties at the School of Dentistry?

[A side door bangs open: a small CHILD wobbles in on a pair of women's high-heeled shoes, wearing a pink tutu turned inside-out and a small plastic crown. Dark red lipstick covers much of her face and arms.]

CHILD: Ta-da!

[Curtain]

Husband-and-wife team **JOHN CRUTCHFIELD** and **LAURA TRATNIK** currently make their home in Berlin, Germany, where Tratnik is a member of the Berliner Ensemble and Crutchfield teaches courses in creative writing and theater at the Freie Universität Berlin. He is also a Founding Member of the Magnetic Theatre in Asheville, North Carolina, where he continues to direct and perform original work, including, most recently, *The Jacob Higginbotham Show*. In addition to her acting work at the Berliner Ensemble, Tratnik has appeared in two of John's plays, *The Strange and Tragical Adventures of Pinocchio* (Magnetic Theatre) and *Come Thick Night: A Shakespearean Gruselkabinett* (FringeNYC 2014), both of which Crutchfield also directed. More is sure to come.

John Crutchfield   Laura Tratnik

Photo by Lauren Abe (press
photo for *The Songs of Robert*,
2007)

WHEN IT FEELS IMPOSSIBLE
An Interview With Regan Linton
▶ By Jason Dorwart

Regan Linton is a professional stage and film actor. She uses a wheelchair due to a spinal cord injury from a car accident in college. In 2013, she graduated from the MFA Acting Program at University of California San Diego (UCSD) as the first wheelchair user to do so. Prior to graduate school, she worked for six years with Denver-based community theater companies and was honored with numerous awards for her performances, including the Colorado Theatre Guild Henry Award and Denver Post Ovation Award.

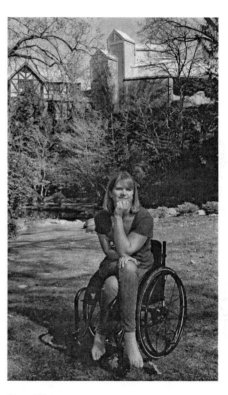

Regan Linton

Photo by Kathy Hollis Cooper

Can you tell me about yourself and your spinal cord injury?
Sure. I grew up playing sports and was very active. In undergrad, at University of Southern California (USC) in Los Angeles, I was in a car accident and came away with a T-4 complete spinal cord injury where I was paralyzed from my chest down. Basically, I have no sensation or movement below that, and I use a manual wheelchair. It definitely wasn't something I ever planned, and it has changed my life in many ways—mostly for the better.

Did you have dreams of getting into acting before your spinal cord injury?
I did. I started performing when I was a kid. I took theater classes, acting classes.
I was a shy, introverted, do-gooder child, and theater was the place I could act
out and let that other side of me—the darker, angry side—come out. Theater
was where I processed a lot of emotions as a kid. In high school, I had dreams
of going to a major conservatory, but I didn't get in. I went to film school and
started doing other things.

What prompted you to start acting again?
Immediately after my injury, I was like, "There's no possible way I'm ever going
to perform again. How can I even do that?" All of a sudden having a two-thirds
paralyzed body—in my mind, I couldn't act without legs. I couldn't act without
full abdominal breath support. But I still had a passion for it. But afterward, I
completely changed the way I thought about my body—and about my body
on stage—and it reinvigorated my confidence that I could get on stage and do
some acting.

At what point did you think to yourself, "I can make a living at this"?
I'm still trying to convince myself, but not because I'm an actor on wheels. It's
because that's the way the actor life is. When I auditioned for the UCSD MFA
program, the head of the program, Kyle Donnelly, asked me point blank in the
audition, "Do you think you can work as a professional actor?" There was something inside me in that moment that thought, "Absolutely, yes. Of course I can."
The confidence I had gained competing city wide with other theater companies
and being honored with a couple of local acting awards made me think, "Oh, I
can do this! The only thing I'm lacking is professional training, technical training,
and the experience of getting myself out there."

**Sometimes people attribute an artist's success to connections or
something outside of the artist's own control. What is your take on that?**
What is out of my control is how people are going to respond to me as an actor
on wheels. Sometimes they think I'm very inspirational, and sometimes they're
amazed and don't know how I do it. Sometimes they think I'm doing it as a
character choice, and they don't know I actually use a wheelchair full time. There
are not a lot of professional actors out there with different physicalities and my
level of training. I was looking into the possibility of grad school and found
only a handful—five people—who use wheelchairs and had gone to school and
trained.

"Oh, I can do this! The only thing I'm lacking is professional training, technical training, and the experience of getting myself out there."

What *would* you say an actor can control?

The biggest thing actors can control is how they respond to feedback. The way you respond to the world is within your control. You have the choice in life to be like, "Okay, people have said no, and that means no, and therefore I'm not going to continue." Or when you get rejected, you can say, "Well, screw that. I'm going to continue to improve and go forward." It's my inner competitive spirit to go against the lack of expectations people might have for me.

In your mind, what is the difference between talent and skill for an actor?

Oh, my! A skill is your toolbox. In grad school, that's what I was gaining—tools to build skills. Repetition and experience are needed to build skill. It's a trade. To do it well, you have to do something over and over again so it becomes part of you. But talent is sometimes an arbitrary concept. The greatest talent in acting is the willingness to be vulnerable. One of the things I had the ability to do partly because of my injury—which was also enhanced by my training—was just *be*. Just be on stage and be in the world.

Regan Linton as Don John and Barret O'Brien as Borachio in *Much Ado About Nothing*, Oregon Shakespeare Festival, 2015, directed by Lileana Blain-Cruz

Photo by Jenny Graham, courtesy of Oregon Shakespeare Festival

At the end of its MFA program, UCSD has an actors' showcase. What was your experience with that as an actor in a wheelchair?

It's one of the most beneficial and absurd things all at the same time—to spend so much time preparing for the tiny amount of stage time you're going to spend in front agents and managers. Part of me thought, "This is the most ridiculous thing." It seems like such a silly blip on the radar, and yet I got a good agent out of it who has really been beneficial to me and has helped me grow in my professionalism.

For me, a lot of my time was spent educating the agents and managers: "Oh, this is my experience. Yes, I use a wheelchair. Yes, I can do things. I can get out of my wheelchair. I'm not glued to it." Educating about larger disability things but also giving them an idea of what kind of an actor I was. There aren't a lot of actors on wheels. Often, I go into an audition, and it's like I'm not only proving my talents and worth and capability as an actor but also my worth as a human being—and even sometimes trying to prove that I should be alive.

How many meetings did you get compared to your classmates?

My response from showcase was much lower than most of my classmates. Maybe three agents total wanted to meet with me. Managers, I got one meeting. I have classmates who got responses from twenty managers in Los Angeles. I got a much a lower response. But that said, the response I did get was very genuine. Often, when they encounter actors, it's like, "We don't really know who this person is." Maybe my authenticity was more on the surface, and the people who did meet with me were genuinely interested in me as an actor and not something superficial about my wheels and my physical persona.

I know you moved to Los Angeles and had auditions but weren't getting a lot of work at first. What did you do to keep yourself in shape and mentally sharp before landing your first role?

I moved to Los Angeles in June. That timing was weird because of the casting cycle. Summertime is dead. I had a few hard months, even as we started moving into the fall when things start picking up again. They say in Los Angeles or New York, it takes at least three years to have people even be aware of you. That's with having a really great agent or manager. Most people take a job—becoming a waiter or valet or something. Those jobs are very labor based and weren't workable for me, so I struggled a lot with, "How do I keep myself engaged?"

I ended up doing small projects I got through grad school contacts. Then I did land a part on one show, but the show was cancelled three days later, so I never ended up filming that. So I stayed pretty regular with physical activities. I would swim and work out with a trainer, and I would try to do whatever I could to pick up side jobs. Eventually, I decided to write my own material. That ended up taking a good amount of my time when I was in Los Angeles. I wrote my own show for the Hollywood fringe and also worked on some web series ideas with friends. That was a lot of my daily work.

When you go to an audition, do casting directors know you're in a wheelchair beforehand?

Yes, typically they do. My agent would make an extra phone call to say, "Hey, this is my client. She's really a great actor, and by the way, she uses a wheelchair . . ." Most of the breakdowns that come out don't mention a wheelchair, so the casting directors aren't thinking of the possibility that a person on wheels could be in the role. When I'm presented to them, a lot of reactionary things go through their heads, "Would she survive on set? Can she work an eight-hour or ten-hour day? Does she need an accessible dressing room? Do we have that?"

It's always helpful having an agent who has been in the business for a long time and has personal connections with the casting directors, because they respect her opinion. Often she's the one who gets me in the door to a lot of auditions, because she'll make a call. I put that I'm a wheelchair user on my resumé because I feel like, ultimately, they're going to hire me or not hire me, and they're going to have to know I use a wheelchair. I don't really like the idea of surprising somebody by just rolling into the room. I realize my privilege of having an agent who'll submit me and make that extra phone call to give a heads up.

Are there roles that you might resist taking because of how they portray disability?

Luckily, my agent has been pretty careful and approached me as an actor and not as a disability charity case. She knew I'm a diverse entity. I'm not a common entity, but she wasn't ready to exploit that.

There was one breakdown in particular that read, "People with disabilities needed to sit around Jesus and accept his love," or something like that. I used it as material in my Hollywood fringe show I wrote. I can often tell from the breakdown wording that it's something I wouldn't do. It's a hard decision—many disabled characters portray the same storyline, but at the same time, it's giving you stage time and visibility. There was a play I was offered about a young woman who had become paralyzed and how her family was dealing with it. It was the worst play I've read about disability. The playwright had taken every cliché about becoming paralyzed and everything sensational and shoved it together. That was a major playhouse, and I ended up turning it down because I felt, "This is not a story I want to be telling." A lot of the people writing these roles aren't writing from a disability perspective, and often they don't feel complete to me. I would rather go for roles without disability written in and re-envision the role instead of playing these poorly crafted characters with a disability.

> "I put that I'm a wheelchair user on my resumé because I feel like, ultimately, they're going to hire me or not hire me, and they're going to have to know I use a wheelchair. I don't really like the idea of surprising somebody by just rolling into the room. I realize my privilege of having an agent who'll submit me and make that extra phone call to give a heads up."

Life is more expensive for disabled people. Is this accounted for in your contracts?
Life costs more because of my disability, no question, but I don't get paid any more than other actors, so I end up absorbing the extra expense. I have to buy wheelchairs and pay for maintenance—casters, wheels, tubes, cushions. I'm using my own chairs during shows, so I have to buy supplies more frequently. And it's a murky area as to who's responsible for these expenses during the show. My chair could easily be considered a prop or costume, like someone's shoes. But there are no guidelines I've found to help theaters clarify whether they should help with the expense. So yes, it definitely costs more to be an actor on wheels, but this isn't accounted for in my salary.

When I was hired for an NBC show, they were trying to figure out whether I was going to need an accessible trailer. My agent intervened and advocated for me and said, "This is something you have to provide under the ADA regardless of whether it is an extra expense for you." I also know for Oregon Shakespeare Festival (OSF), it was definitely a consideration. As a union actor on a ten-month contract, they're required to provide housing. At the time I was hired, they had no wheelchair-accessible housing, so they ended up renovating a unit. From their perspective, because they're a great theater company, they thought it was something they needed to do in general. If they renovated, it would be available for all of their actors, including a wheelchair-using actor.

When I don't get a project, I don't know whether it's them thinking through the logistics of if I'm actually going to be able to get on stage, or is the dressing room accessible, or do they have an accessible actor apartment? I don't know how much that factors in to their ultimate decision.

Have you had any issues with Actors' Equity health insurance because of your pre-existing condition?
No. That's one of the greatest benefits. In Los Angeles, I was without insurance. I'd gone off of my co-insurance, and Obamacare hadn't started yet. I ended up using some free clinics. When I finally started at OSF, one of the best perks of being a union actor is the health insurance. It's been wonderful. It's really good health insurance. It's difficult to keep, because you have to keep working—but for the time I've been on it, it's been great.

Is there anything backstage that you need accommodation for, such as for quick changes or pants or specially constructed costumes?
It depends on the show, but in general, I'm able to do lot of my backstage work on my own. I do my own makeup. For one of the shows I was in at OSF, I did all my own costume changes. If I have a quick change, stuff is built with Velcro, or it would

be laid over the top. For *Much Ado About Nothing* at OSF, there was a part where I put a dress on for a party. It was put over my fatigues, which was part of the design concept. But the dress only zipped from my torso up, so it didn't actually go underneath my butt—but it looked like it did, so you couldn't tell. That's one adaptive accommodation. But I'm probably one of the least high-maintenance actors up there this year.

Regan Linton as the Mysterious Woman in *Secret Love in Peach Blossom Land*, Oregon Shakespeare Festival, 2015, written and directed by Stan Lai

Photo by Jenny Graham, courtesy of Oregon Shakespeare Festival

One major accommodation at OSF—it's a repertory theater, so they're changing the set and putting different sets in and out. They built ramps for all of the entrances instead of stairs. But they're beneficial! The entire crew uses those ramps for taking sets on and off stage. Really, it ends up being a universally accessible design for everybody. There are still definitely inaccessible things, but OSF is good about making accommodations whenever needed.

Advanced age and disability are often conflated. Have you found yourself reading for characters who are older than you because of your wheelchair?

Funny you should ask, because I was just asked to read for a project that I didn't get—but I was asked to read for *As You Like It*, and it was an all-female production. The breakdown even said, "Somebody who should be able to read older." I once played Ouiser Boudreaux in *Steel Magnolias*, who's supposed to be like 50-plus years old. I don't necessarily mind that. I love those roles. As a female, those are the roles I gravitate toward anyway—they're the wiser, more experienced, more messy roles. I like that I fit into those maybe more than I would without my wheelchair.

But you're right—there's a lack of awareness of the fact that somebody can be young and vibrant and capable and productive and also have a different ability. Even with *Much Ado* this year, the particular take on my character, Don John—she's the villain, and the take on her was that she had been injured in battle and is a veteran coming back. There are certain storylines that tend to pop up, because it's what the public is aware of when it comes to disability—and often that's an injured veteran or somebody who is indigent. We rarely see the storyline of somebody young and living their life and working and raising a family or those types of progressive storyline.

Now that you're actually working, what's your daily routine? Do you have time for training or skill maintenance while rehearsing and performing?

The rep acting lifestyle is pretty intense. It doesn't sound like it's going to be when you hear that you'll have six shows a week. Initially it didn't sound to me like it would be that taxing, and I thought, "Oh, I'll have plenty of time for doing side gigs."

The most difficult part is that your schedule is so irregular. You can't say, "Okay, every night I'm going to have a show at 8:00 pm, and therefore I can set up my day. It's like one night you'll have a show at 8:00 pm, and then the next day you have a double. Then the next day you're off, and the next day you have a matinee. The irregularity makes it really difficult to establish a routine, whether it's exercise or physical therapy.

My daily routine often involves one show a day, maybe teaching a workshop or doing a discussion, training, or doing physical therapy. Then also, because I'm this unique actor entity, I'm frequently contacted by people from all over for articles or school papers, so often I'm doing that kind of advocacy or education work as well.

Any advice for the actor who's really struggling to break in?
Oh, my word. You mean any general actor, not an actor with a different physicality? Really, it's all the same. I've discovered—and you often hear it—"If you're doing good work, people are going to hear about it. If you're focused on what really, truly matters to you, then the rest will come. The success will come." I know that can seem like a load of jargon, but I truly believe it. I think I've been a more effective actor post-injury. Not because I'm a unique entity, but because I have a better sense of self and of the stories I'm really passionate about telling, the places I'm passionate about working, the places I feel like I fit.

How do you get away from going through the motions and being this kind of empty vessel?
It's weird, because that's what we are. We're an instrument—a vessel for other characters to flow through. Experience is great, but at some point, pull back and ask, "Okay, what really matters to me?" If you want to be a Shakespeare actor, don't waste your time doing stuff that doesn't apply. If you want to be part of Cirque du Soleil, go up to Canada and bang on the door until they let you in. Don't stop learning and dreaming and believing you still have something more to learn or gain from people from all different experience levels or ages. I feel like the most beneficial thing I've held onto is probably that thirst for still being curious at all points of the game.

JASON DORWART is a PhD candidate at the University of California, San Diego where he is researching performances by and about people with disabilities. He is also a standup comedian and was a recurring company member of the Nebraska Shakespeare Festival. His work has previously appeared in *TheatreForum*. With his wife, Laura, Dorwart is editing a forthcoming anthology entitled *mad/crip/sex*. Dorwart's assistant directing credits include *A Play on Two Chairs* (University of Colorado), *Narnia* (CenterStage), and *As You Like It* (Nebraska Shakespeare Festival). He holds a BFA in Theatre from Creighton University, an MA in Theatre from the University of Colorado, and a JD from the University of Denver.

Jason Dorwart

Photo by Chris Dorwart

A DIALOGUE ABOUT THE ART OF WORKING AS AN ACTOR

▶ By Kate Kramer and Elizabeth Stevens

Elizabeth and I met in the spring of 2012 when we became neighbors in West Philadelphia. Our friendship quickly developed when we discovered that we shared common ground in the arts and in higher education. We're both educators and scholars, and both artists—I'm in fine arts and Elizabeth is on the stage.

As we've been at this game of working and living and teaching in the arts for a combined forty years now, we're intimately familiar with the struggle and exhilaration of what it takes to "make it" in the arts. We welcome this opportunity to share our insights and concerns about the complexities of the artistic journey.

Kate: In the arts, I encourage artists to pursue work at whatever pace they can manage. In the juried situation, artists have a lot of work to do once they're selected. They have to make the art for the exhibition, to get physical work ready for the show itself, and sometimes to build crates for shipping. A calendar of submissions and activities can help them keep track of submissions and the work required to fulfill their commitments or upcoming opportunities. Are there similar cycles in theater and auditions, or similar seasons?

Elizabeth: Hmmm . . . not exactly. Casting for plays can happen months, or even sometimes years, before the play, depending on the project and the kind of theater. And those things happen all the time. The good thing is that most actors and artists already know that they need to work their butts off. We're told over and over that if you're not working or trying to work all the time, if you're not making drastic sacrifices, you'll never make it. So actors and artists don't really need to hear that they need to work hard, because they already know it. All of the auditioning can be exhausting.

Kate: Right! I think every successful artist I know is a work-a-holic. And by "successful" I mean someone who is doing the craft, involved in *making*.

Elizabeth: I think actors and artists might need to hear the flipside of this: You need to take care of yourself and have a life. Actors tend to audition for everything without discernment. And it's hard to go to auditions and have a day job. Careers require making priorities, so the things you really care about auditioning for, the people you really want to work with, these are the things you should make sacrifices for—like asking for time off of work, or not hanging out with your friends, or missing that trip you've been planning for a while. But I think going to every single audition, which some people recommend—while it does give you practice in auditioning and in getting used to the constant "no"s—it isn't sustainable forever. And it's probably not how you're going to get work.

Kate: Will actors find their people, their peers, at these auditions? Will they make connections with actors as well as casting agents, casting directors, or directors?

Elizabeth: Not really. The audition situation necessarily puts the actors in an unequal status relationship with the rest of the team. A big casting call is typically a table of people who are watching and judging you for about two minutes and then dismissing you. And while it might possibly be a chance to get your foot in the door, it's downright demoralizing if it's the only thing you're doing to get work.

Kate: It sounds completely alienating.

Elizabeth: Yes, I think it often is. If you can enter an audition with a positive mindset—that we'll all be lucky if we find I'm good match for this project, that I know I have a lot to offer, that I'll work really hard—it can be a good counterbalance to the typical dynamic. You're not just a beggar saying, "Please, please sir! Might you spare a role for me? I'm just a lowly actor." Artists get so little power in the whole enterprise, so you have to claim some power for yourself. And remember that auditions aren't the only way to get work.

Kate: Let's talk about that. You've alluded to the work of an actor, the work that occurs without the audition, but also to the work people need to do to survive—the job that is flexible enough to let an employee take off a day for auditions, for instance. How many of the working actors you know also have other means of support?

Elizabeth: All of them.

Kate: Really? *All* of them?

Elizabeth: Well, the vast majority. There are plenty live theater artists who are fortunate enough to have other means of support so they don't need to find supplemental income, but most actors do need day jobs.

Kate: Wow.

Elizabeth: And let me say, there's nothing wrong with having other means of support. There aren't many better things to do with money than to use it to enable you to be an artist if that's your calling. Do it! It's too bad every actor doesn't have financial support. I should say that there are a few actors I know who make a living working onstage because they're willing to be on the road, *a lot*, or don't mind doing the same role over and over in a successful production. There aren't many actors who imagined working this way when embarking on theater careers. We usually dreamed about playing a number of different roles and somehow making a living. But it's a rare actor who's lucky enough to have that kind of career. Don't count on it happening. Actors probably need to find another means of support for at least some portion of a working life.

Kate: Besides focusing on a positive mindset, how else might an actor seek more empowering support, more sustenance in the chosen craft?

Elizabeth: Take a class in a theater you respect. There are a lot of great classes. Most of the actors I know and respect, even after thirty-five-year careers, keep working on their craft by going to classes. The other actors you may meet can support and inspire you as an artist. Classes are an important way to make community in a noncompetitive way. Perhaps the most useful advice I can offer is to find other actors and directors.

> "The vast preponderance of jobs are developed through people you already have a relationship with. It's just like any other enterprise. Or maybe even more so in the arts because we tend to make these tight little networks and work with the same people over and over."

Kate: The "it's not what you know but who you know"?

Elizabeth: Yes! The vast preponderance of jobs are developed through people you already have a relationship with. It's just like any other enterprise. Or maybe even more so in the arts because we tend to make these tight little networks and work with the same people over and over. We come to trust each other's judgement. It's almost always the case that you'll be recommended for a part, or pursue a director you know and ask to be seen for the part. Or you'll initiate making work with a group of people who don't have other artistic work at the moment.

Kate: And if you're a loner?

Elizabeth: If you feel like you really don't have anyone—nobody you went to school with, nobody you worked with in a different venue and you want to start making connections now—go see as much theater as possible. Find the artists you want to work with, especially the directors and the theater. See the plays, go to as many events as you can, ask to meet with people.

Kate: Right. I often recommend artists reach out to people they admire and talk about their work, their careers.

Elizabeth: It can't hurt to try reaching out to an actor who's not a big-deal star or maybe someone who's starting out but whose work you really like. Ask if you can take them out to coffee, if you can talk a little bit about their work. Most people, unless they are flooded with these invitations, are very flattered and like to talk about themselves and their work.

Kate: The worst thing that can happen is that someone can say "no."

Elizabeth: You definitely get to take some control by engaging in these activities. Looking for connections is the most effective way to get work. If you wait to be discovered at a big "cattle call" audition and you think you won't ever have to worry about finding work after that, you're kidding yourself. The way to free yourself from that myth is by working—making work, seeing work, getting work, plugging in, asking people to see your work. The more people you come into contact with, the more possibilities there are for you. And then you're not just playing the industry lottery anymore.

Kate: I like this metaphor of the lottery. This ability to take control by being selective about auditions, taking classes, getting to know people you admire, working harder, making work, seeing work, being seen . . . all of these are appealing ways for an actor to feel strong. I'm wondering about other ways an actor can feel in control . . .

Elizabeth: Maybe the most important thing you can do is remember the reasons why you started doing theater in the first place. Go see the work that inspired you. A lot of actors fall into the trap of not seeing and appreciating theater anymore because they are so focused on just finding an acting job. Finding the reasons why you care about this work involves seeing stuff, a whole bunch of theater. Remember your mission. Theater is a joyful, complex, intimate art form. Enjoy it as much as possible. You can find cheap tickets. You should try to go to as many different things as possible. Go to the weird avant-garde thing in the basement, because maybe you'll love it. Go to the rep theater and the big musicals. Look for your contemporaries who are making things that intrigue you. Often directors and actors who are starting out are also on the lookout for people to work with.

Kate: I would imagine that such people are more open to innovations.

Elizabeth: Yeah. Often young companies are more interested in collaborative models. And if that's interesting to you, that's about as empowering as you can get in the theater.

Kate: We talked earlier, privately, about this notion of a mission, of an actor having a driving force to keep her grounded. I wonder if you could talk about that a little bit more.

Elizabeth: We all get demoralized. Of course we do. It's not easy when people say no, that they don't want to work with you. No, you don't look the way they need you to look. No, you don't sound like what we need . . . It's hard not to take that personally. But these people may have bad taste, or there may be a million reasons why they're looking for someone who isn't you. Casting has nothing to do with your value as an artist or a person.

> "You have to believe in your intrinsic value. The only thing that can actually pull you through is remembering your purpose. Remember why you like doing it, the first play you loved, who really inspires you, what you believe is special about theater beyond 'I just want a job.'"

Kate: And you have to believe that.

Elizabeth: You have to believe in your intrinsic value. The only thing that can actually pull you through is remembering your purpose. Remember why you like doing it, the first play you loved, who really inspires you, what you believe is special about theater beyond "I just want a job." Remember what you're passionate about as opposed to focusing on that pain-in-the-ass schlepp to auditions.

Kate: That's such an important part of the work, right? Remembering the joy.

Elizabeth: Yes. And being clear about what success means to you.

Kate: It's such an individual thing, determining an acceptable level of success. How many roles a year? What kinds of role? How much money they do or don't make? What kind of work they might need to do to support their living expenses?

Elizabeth: Right. And how does work fit into your life on a larger level . . .

Kate: . . . and your success as a person.

Elizabeth: This life does demand a lot from people. But it doesn't demand your soul. It's important to preserve your soul, your health, your sanity, and the other elements of life that are important. For example, ask yourself if you want to be away from home and travel? Or if you want a garden and a cat? All of these things have to be factored into the equation. Looking for work shouldn't be the only focus of your life. Because if you let that happen, it will be very hard to stick it out.

Kate: One of the things I keep coming back to is how much actors are physically putting themselves out there in real time, in real spaces. Dedication at some point has to pay off at some level.

Elizabeth: Remember that you, the actor, are the one making the choices here. That doesn't mean that you get to control whether people will want to hire you, but it does mean that you get to control whether you stay in the game, how you choose to stay in the game, and how flexible you are about it. It means that it's your choice to keep working at it, not the world forcing you into it.

Kate: That brings us to flexibility, being able to shift gears when necessary, depending on circumstances as well as roles. One of the things we talked about when we first discussed the possibility of doing this interview was how individuals have so many opportunities to make choices (roles, theaters, genres) and that those opportunities all fall to the individual.

Elizabeth: There are so many different kinds of theater that you can do.

Kate: What about those instances where you're not involved in a particular project and you find yourself out of work at the moment. Can you volunteer or somehow be otherwise involved in theater work? Or is that a career killer?

Elizabeth: You can always try asking to audition if you don't get invited. But I would beware of taking a job in the "area" of theater where you aren't working creatively. Julia Cameron wrote a wonderful book about maintaining your faith in being an artist, *The Artist's Way*. She talks about the danger of becoming a "shadow artist" as opposed to an artist. It's easy to fall into this trap. For example, you think, "I want to be a writer, but I'm scared to be a writer, and nobody's going to like my writing, so I'm going to work as an editor's assistant so I can still be in the field."

Kate: And then you get to be in the field but not the work you want to do in the field.

Elizabeth: Right. And in theater you might think, "I'm going to work in marketing, or in the box office, or in ushering, and that'll help me get my foot in the door." That isn't actually a great way to get said foot in door. Once you're working in the box office, especially if you're good at it, everyone will identify you as such. "Janet from the box office wants to audition? Sure, we'll see her." But Janet is already in those people's minds as "Janet from the box office," not "Janet the aspiring actor."

Kate: That's excellent advice. You're a faculty member now, but could you share the types of job you've had over the years?

Elizabeth: I've always had other jobs. I worked in cafes and restaurants—prep cooking, dishwashing, serving, making espresso. I worked as a temp in a number of weird offices—logging videotape and working in law offices. I worked in publishing as an assistant to a literary agent. I worked a million different jobs. Teaching is a career that works for me, keeps me working with actors, but there are other sustainable creative careers, and the goal should be finding one that can keep you in the game.

Kate: Keeping actively involved.

Elizabeth: Maybe it's that you don't think of yourself only as the noun "actor," because that really reduces who you are as a human being. Maybe you think of yourself as a person who acts, of "act" as a verb.

Kate: But you aren't only an "actor." Your life is broader. I wonder if acting is something that you can move in and out of. Can performers take a break and go back into it? Does it go away?

Elizabeth: People do burn out, of course. And that's really okay. It's hard to sustain. If you need to step away for a while, it's not the end of the world. And you can come back to it. The theater has plenty of breathtakingly good roles for older actors.

Kate: You are a person who acts. Who wants to act. Your core isn't the rejected actor. You're a person . . .

Elizabeth: . . . a person capable of continuing to make decisions about your life.

An Assistant Professor at Swarthmore College since 2006, **ELIZABETH STEVENS** has directed plays in New York, Philadelphia, Dallas, and Atlanta since 1994. Venues range from experimental, Off-Off-Broadway (like world-renowned avante-garde La MaMa Theater in New York) to large regional theaters (like the acclaimed Dallas Theater Center). She's taught at Southern Methodist University, Bryn Mawr College, and the Yale School of Drama summer program. She is currently at work directing *A Bright Room Called Day* with her students at Swarthmore. She can be found at kelizabethstevens.com.

Elizabeth Stevens

KATE KRAMER has been a Senior Fellow in the Critical Writing Program at the University of Pennsylvania since 2011. Her essays in contemporary art, design, and writing for artists have been published in scholarly, shelter, and regional publications as well as in exhibition catalogues. She is currently working on *Write to Work: A Practical Primer*, a book based on a business of art-writing seminars she's been developing since 2000.

Kate Kramer

Photo by Alan Magayne-Roshak, copyright UW-Milwaukee Photo Services

CHAPTER 3

FINDING SUCCESS

"Success? I don't know what that word means. I'm happy. But success, that goes back to what in somebody's eyes success means. For me, success is inner peace. That's a good day for me."
Denzel Washington

How many actors does it take to screw in a light bulb?

A quick web search reveals that there are many possible answers to that question. But history tells us that it took one man a significant number of tries before he got it right. Thomas Edison failed a staggering 10,000 times before finally succeeding. Or as he's quoted to have said, "I have not failed. I've just found 10,000 ways that do not work."

Nobody succeeds after one or twenty or fifty tries. Not light-bulb level success.

Ten thousand is a good number. It's also the number of hours psychologist Malcolm Gladwell suggests it takes to become a master at any given skill.

Scientists have argued the validity of the number—but nevertheless, it's something to strive for. What would make anyone think they can master a challenging task in a just a year or two?

People often think getting an agent is the ticket to success. But that 10,000 hours isn't only about practice and mastery—it's also about building a body of work. If you work on your craft six hours a day for four and half years (do the math!), think of the work you can create. Think of your reel, your fan base, your resumé, your portfolio. It's when you have a salable body of work that you become desirable to agents. You don't need to claw your way onto an agent's roster. Your job is to produce the work.

Who Knew?

Speaking of producing work, a lot of actors write, direct, and star in their own material, effectively casting themselves. There's a long history of women who have created their own opportunities, writing complex roles that wouldn't have existed otherwise. This is especially true of women who don't fit the typical leading role type. Think of Whoopi Goldberg's one-woman Broadway show, *The Spook Show* (1985), or Nia Vardolas's one-woman show, *My Big Fat Greek Wedding* (1997), which led to her film with the same title.

We're going to spend some time exploring definitions of *success* in this chapter. It's an important exercise to engage in this discussion, because not only do our definitions differ from one other, but our definitions are also fluid. They change over time. They might even change within a week or day.

In fact, here's an experiment: Take a moment and jot down your own personal definition of *success*, and then tuck it away until you've finished reading this chapter. After reading, be sure to come back to it with your fresh perspective and see how you would revise it.

Here's what you'll read about in this chapter:

- Ellen Burstyn's thoughts on why vulnerability is key to success and the work you do at home as compared to in rehearsal
- The many "people" you have living inside of you and how you can access them
- Strategies for networking, money management, touring internationally, creating your own opportunities, and social media branding

- An agent's perspective on maintaining success and developing healthy relationships in the industry
- Why you should commit to your training, even when you've been training for years
- Expanding your view and definition of *success*
- Choosing to work in community theater and developing a professional attitude about amateur work

We'll begin with Ellen Burstyn. Let's get an up-close view of grand success and see if we can unravel why success happens when it does and how you can take control of where your success leads you.

THE TRIPLE CROWN OF ACTING

The Road to Winning an Oscar, Emmy, and Tony

▶ An Interview With Ellen Burstyn

Ellen Burstyn is widely regarded as one of the great actresses of stage and screen in the past five decades. She is one of only twenty-one actors to achieve the Triple Crown of Acting, winning an Oscar, a Tony, and an Emmy. In 1975, she was awarded both the Oscar and the Tony—the Oscar for her performance in *Alice Doesn't Live Here Anymore*, and the Tony for her work in *Same Time, Next Year* on Broadway. She won her first Emmy in 2009 for her guest appearance on *Law & Order*, and she was awarded a second Emmy in 2013 for her performance in the miniseries *Political Animals*. In 2013, she was inducted into the American Theatre Hall of Fame.

Ellen Burstyn

Kelly Sullivan/Getty Images Entertainment/Getty Images

Burstyn began her career in the theater in New York in the 1950s and worked in theater and television throughout the 1960s. Her first film role was in Paul Mazursky's *Alex in Wonderland* in 1970, starring opposite Donald Sutherland. Two years later, she received an Oscar nomination and Golden Globe nomination for Best Supporting Actress for her performance in *The Last Picture Show*, directed by Peter Bogdanovich. The following year, she starred in William Friedkin's *The Exorcist*, receiving an Oscar nomination and Golden Globe nomination for Best Actress.

Burstyn took the reins on her career after these successes, shepherding *Alice Doesn't Live Here Anymore* from script to screen. The film is often credited as one of the most important movies released during second-wave feminism in the 1970s. Burstyn was offered the opportunity to direct the film, but instead she selected Martin Scorsese after seeing his debut film, *Mean Streets*, at Francis Ford Coppola's recommendation. Although Scorsese didn't have experience telling stories about women, when Burstyn questioned him, his response sold her: He didn't know a lot about women, he said, but he wanted to learn. (Scorsese famously accepted the Oscar on Burstyn's behalf for the film, as she chose to honor her commitment to being on stage in *Same Time, Next Year*.)

In 1982, Burstyn became the first female president of Actors' Equity Association in its sixty-three-year history, and in 2000, she was named co-president of the Actors Studio with Harvey Keitel and Al Pacino. She is currently the Artistic Director of the Actors Studio in New York.

In 2007, Burstyn became a national bestselling author with her memoir, *Lessons in Becoming Myself* (Riverhead Books). In the memoir, she shares her personal, professional, and spiritual journey, exploring her memories growing up in a turbulent household in Detroit, her early days in New York, her work in theater and film in the decades that followed, and her personal evolution.

I loved your book. How long did you work on it?
Thank you. I worked on it for about seven years, because I was acting in the meantime. I would go away on location and then come back and have to light the fire again.

You talk in your book about working with Lee Strasberg to get to the heart of who you are, to remove your mask. Could you tell me a little about that process and how you think that ultimately helped you in your career?
As I recall, I didn't know my mask was a mask. I didn't know that the personality I developed—which was serving me in getting through the world all right— I didn't know that it wasn't me. It was something I put on because I thought I was supposed to, to be charming and cute and flirtatious and an adorable girl. I didn't recognize that it was a false face, though, until I worked for Lee and he saw through it. He said, "You're very natural, darling, but you're not real." It was like a sword going through my armor when he said that, and I could feel where it landed. I could feel that he got to a level of me that I didn't know was there.

So that was painful, that realization?

I just remember crying for several weeks, because I thought, if that's not who I am, then who am I? I had no idea.

How old were you at that time?

I was in my 30s, mid-30s. I had a career. I was working, but not at the level that I later was able to work.

So that process of figuring out who you were, and being brave enough to expose yourself, to be vulnerable, do you think that was key to your success?

Oh, absolutely. I think a masked personality is not of interest to anyone really. It's only when we're able to peek out from behind the mask and really say, hello, here I am—it's only then that people can see you. And even though it's through a character, and the character's circumstances might be totally different from yours, if you can be alive in that character, not be protecting yourself behind the character's personality, then you can speak your truth.

And what about the vulnerability involved with risking making mistakes, or possibly failing?

Lee said something to me about this early on. It was the first time I did an exercise for him creating my morning liquid, my morning cup of coffee, and I was feeling the weight of the coffee cup in my hand as though it was real—and after a while Lee said to me, "Do you ride horses?" And I said, "Well, I used to." And he said, "When you rode, did you ride well?" And I said, "Yes, pretty well." And he said, "Well, you don't have to ride that cup." And I looked up at him shocked, and he said, "What if you made a mistake? Go on, make a mistake."

You see, you have to be willing to make a mistake to be vulnerable. You can't be concerned about the effect you're having on people. Instead, you have to just be with what's really happening.

And that was the turning point for me, when I realized that I was terrified to make a mistake. Because my experience growing up was that if you make a mistake you get a pretty violent reaction. So being willing to make a mistake, which simply means that you're concentrated on the task at hand and not thinking about the result in somebody else's opinion—that's being vulnerable. That was a really big lesson to learn.

That lesson, allowing yourself to be vulnerable and potentially make a mistake, do you think you applied that to the business side of acting? To business decisions?

I didn't really think in terms of business. I thought in terms of getting work that I wanted to do. If I'd thought about business, I don't know, maybe I would have ruined the whole thing. I just thought, how do I get to play this part? How do I get to tell the story I want to tell? The show business part never appealed to me. I never thought in terms of building a career.

> "It's one of the advantages of having a difficult childhood—that you don't sink. You do recover. You become a survivor. It's like when they make steel stronger by pounding on it. So I've never been one to give up. It just doesn't interest me I guess. If one thing doesn't work, I try another."

I wanted to ask you about your ability to bounce back after rejection. For instance, you describe in your book this moment when you didn't get cast in a part you really wanted before *The Last Picture Show* . . .

Five Easy Pieces.

You didn't get cast in that film, but this was just a year before *The Last Picture Show* and getting the Oscar nomination and all of the other awards and nominations. Another actor might have been so disappointed that she would have given up, or never fully recovered, after *Five Easy Pieces*. But you were able to put it behind you and move forward.

It's one of the advantages of having a difficult childhood—that you don't sink. You do recover. You become a survivor. It's like when they make steel stronger by pounding on it. So I've never been one to give up. It just doesn't interest me I guess. If one thing doesn't work, I try another.

You describe in your book how you became depressed when you found out that you couldn't get pregnant. Did you ever get that low because of something work related?

No. I mean, a couple of jobs I didn't get, I cried. I really wanted them, and I was disappointed. But I didn't linger there. That just doesn't do any good. The hard part of the business is the amount of rejections you have to suffer, and if you can't handle rejection, you get into another business. This business is about going in to sell yourself—doing an audition and coming out feeling that you either did or didn't do a good job. It can go either way. And if you don't get it, you have to just get over it and be willing to try again. That's the job.

Was auditioning a strength for you?

Yes, I have to say, I was one of the people who could audition. There are some really fine actors who just can't audition. But I had a fortunate thing happen when I was married to my second husband. He was an executive in a television studio, and he came home one day just exhausted and kind of depressed, and I said, what's the matter? And he said, "Oh, we just are having the hardest time casting this part. I don't know what we're going to do, because so many actors read but none of them are all right." He was really anguishing about casting this part, and suddenly I saw the other point of view—that they're not just sitting there with all the power and we're begging for a job. They're worried whether they'll be able to find somebody who will solve their problem. So after that, I took the point of view that I walked into an office and was there to solve their problems.

Oh, that's fascinating.

It really helped. It shifted the power so that I had it going in. "I'm the answer to your prayers. Here I am!"

Which takes confidence.

The big enemy is a lack of confidence. If you don't have enough confidence, you just can't do it. So it's all about finding the answer for you—for each person, the thing that will make them have the confidence they need to go through this horrendous process of auditioning.

When you say you've known some great actors who couldn't audition, are you specifically talking about nerves?

Nerves and lack of confidence. Once you have the part, you're into the work. But before you have the part, you're into *getting* the work. And getting the work has a plea in it. You're selling yourself. It's a horrible feeling. You're trying to make people like you. You go in with an empty purse begging for coins, and it's very hard to do the work under those circumstances. You feel it in your stomach, and the more you want it, the worse it is. The more you love the part, the worse it is.

But once you've got the part, then all of that relaxes and you can address the work. And there are some actors, by the way, who are wonderful at auditioning, and then that's it. You've seen everything they're going to do. And that's a nightmare for directors. But they are different processes—doing the work and auditioning.

Once you have the part and you're ready to do the work, what does that look like for you? The prework, the work you do on your own before you get to rehearsals or the set?

It varies with each part. Sometimes I get a part and it just reveals itself to me right away. I can feel the character. I read the script out loud, and I'm full of the character's emotion, and then all I have to do is memorize the lines and let her rip through me. But other times, I read a part after I get it and I go to work on it, and then I start to think, "Why does she do that? That's a funny thing to do." And once I start asking those questions, those questions will lead me deeper and deeper into the character. And I find there are always surprises. Everything that I didn't know, that I didn't understand about the character—that becomes my creative process. The answers to those questions become the character that I'm building.

So, *Same Time, Next Year*, you do that kind of work on your own before you meet for the first time with Charles Grodin, and then in your work together you begin to learn more about your own character?

Yes, exactly.

Is there preplanning? Do you try to make things happen, or do you let things happen?

Oh no, I let them happen, definitely. I love to be surprised. If I know who the character is, that's my preparation. I know who she is, and I know where she's coming from, and I know what makes her tick, what her intentions are, what her drives are, what her soft spots are. But then, once I go into rehearsal, I have no idea what's going to come out, because that's what happens between the actors—and that you can't know ahead of time, because the other actor evokes it from you. What you say lands on him in a certain way, and his response isn't anything you could have predicted, and that affects you in a way that you had no idea you would feel. It's alive then. It's all about the space between the two characters. What happens there is the play.

And what you're describing is all in the rehearsal, but once the play is up and running, how do you keep that aliveness?
Well, that's the big question, and it's a combination of things. There's remembering that first reaction you had the first time you did it—wanting that to happen again but not necessarily forcing it to. It's really about being alive in the moment, especially in a long run. You can do the lines inside out or up and down and around and change them or not, keep everything exactly the same—but alive. It's such an inner process, it's hard to describe. It's just being in the moment.

In terms of being in the moment, you mention in your book that you've gone into a dissociative state several times in your life, stepping outside of your body and looking at yourself in that moment in order to survive it. Do you think there's any connection between having the ability to be alive in a moment on stage and the ability to step outside your body and witness yourself?
It's complicated, because it's so delicate, the states you're talking about. I've experienced moments on stage where I was completely inside the moment. It's 100 percent what I was playing and doing and feeling and experiencing and expressing. It was 100 percent from the inside out. But very often, there's also a witness, and the witness can be impartial and just noting for later—saying, oh, that was good, you should try to go for that tomorrow. It's like an overseer that doesn't interfere with what you're doing. It's only witnessing.

But then other times, there's the witness that's the judge, and that's a negative thing. You don't ever want to have the judge onstage with you, because the judge inhibits you. I don't know how that relates to dissociating. I'm not sure. It might be the same. The judge might be a split off part that's observing in an uninvolved way, not feeling the inner experience. It's stepping outside and judging—but that's not a good state for acting.

The state you were describing when it's 100 percent from the inside out, when there's no witness—how common is that?
Not very common. There are certain times when you're doing a play and it takes off—where you're not doing it, it's being done through you. And those times are

blessings. They don't happen often. In the run of a play, it might happen once or twice or three times. When you feel that, it's like ecstasy—and everybody who has experienced that wants it again. There's something slightly addictive about it, because you know that's the height, that's the art of acting at the most sublime.

> "We're all such multilayered beings, and I've never liked playing a character who is just one thing. First of all, I don't ever believe it. Even the toughest characters are going to have their tender sides, and I think everybody's trying to do the best they can."

So, you were just talking about stage acting. It's different with acting for the camera, I know—but for instance, would you say you achieved that with your _Requiem for a Dream_ monologue?

Yes, because when I read one of the crucial scenes out loud for the first time, I felt an emotion on a certain word—and it surprised me. And I knew once I said it, everything after that would be acting. It was only going to smile at me once with that same immediacy, and I knew that if we did other takes, it would just be reproducing that. So I asked Darren [Aronofsky] to shoot it so that I only had to do it once. And that's what's in the film.

One take.

I was right about that, my instinct. But that's just knowing your instrument. Strasberg used to refer to our _instruments_, which people have made fun of since then. But it's true, because we're both the piano and the pianist, and the violin and the violinist. We're playing with this instrument. There's no other way to say it. And tuning into that is the artistry.

So with your monologue for _Requiem_, does that mean that you didn't practice it at home?

No, no. You don't practice it in terms of practicing emotions. You learn the lines. You say the lines, but you're not playing it. There's a difference. I never practice the emotion. I practice the meaning, but the emotion is what I call on in the moment, and that's what makes it alive. Telling the story for the actor is not with the words. The writer tells the story with the words, but the actor tells the story with the feeling.

> Burstyn was nominated for an Oscar, a Golden Globe, and a Screen Actor's Guild Award for her work in *Requiem for a Dream* (2001). The film received a total of 61 nominations and was awarded 32 wins, including an Independent Spirit Award for Best Female Lead.

After reading about your childhood, I'm curious how much you draw on your mother for some of your characters.

Well, my mother has worked her way into a lot of different roles. She was such an impactful character. As you know from my book, she was a very forceful woman, and consequently I was introverted. So I find very often that there are different characters I play who aren't really much like me, but I can call on my memory of my mother. But I've also used her in lighthearted characters, because she had that aspect to her personality, too.

Your mother character in *Another Happy Day*—she's complex. She's tough, but there's a kindness to your portrayal of her as well.

We're all such multilayered beings, and I've never liked playing a character who is just one thing. First of all, I don't ever believe it. Even the toughest characters are going to have their tender sides, and I think everybody's trying to do the best they can. Some people can just do some things better than others. As I recall, that character was not a warm character, but she was conscientious. She was trying to be a good wife and mother, but she wasn't very capable. And she couldn't stand to be vulnerable.

I wanted to ask you, what are some drawbacks to success? Anything particularly difficult about achieving your level of success?

I don't know. I can tell you that it's hard on a relationship when a woman is successful and a man isn't. That's hard. I don't know if it's hard the other way around, if the man is successful and the woman isn't. I think society has certain attitudes about this that make it difficult.

But I was talking to a friend of mine the other day who's in her 60s, and I'm in my 80s now—and we were talking about being disappointed with your life. She said, "Everybody's disappointed when we get to this age. We all feel like we're failures as mothers, failures in our careers." And I said, "It's true! It's absolutely true." Other people would consider me successful, but there are so many things I wish I had done, or wish I had done differently, or shouldn't have done.

So I don't know if being a success changes that. It hasn't for me. I know I have a career and I'm successful because other people tell me that, but I don't feel like a success. I tend to dwell on the things that I didn't do right. I don't know what that's about. It's some bad habit of mine. But I don't think being a success really changes who you are. You can be a success and not feel like a success, like me—or you can be not so successful but feel perfectly happy with what you've achieved.

I wonder if it's true for everyone—if there are moments when we all feel good about ourselves, like we can call ourselves successful, and other times when we just feel like failures.

I was reading something the other day by [the philosopher] Alan Watts, who said that whenever anybody would compliment him and say what a kind, wise man he was, he used to always feel like a fraud, because he felt somewhere deep down there was its opposite, too. And then over the years, he came to realize that not only is there the opposite, but there's everything in between. We're just experiencing what's on the surface right now, but all that other stuff is there, too. If we're aware of the many people we've got living inside of us—that we're not just one perfect person—then we can relax into it.

Do you make a conscious effort to keep moving forward? To keep working on yourself?

Yes, in every way I can. I work on myself all the time. I've done a lot of therapy and a lot of studies in healing, and also I'm very interested in the brain and all the things we're learning about the brain now. It's so helpful to understand.

What about work-work, moving forward in your career?

I like the doing of the work, like we were talking about before. But I don't like the getting of the work. Right now, I've been trying to raise money for two different shows—one that I'm directing and one that I'm producing, and acting in both. And dealing with the financiers, this is the least fun you can imagine. But I love to work. Even now, that's why at 83 I'm still working.

I just read a great book. Did you ever read *Gilead* by Marilynne Robinson?

It's been on my list, but I haven't read it yet.

Well, I'll tell you, I'm so in love with this book. It won the Pulitzer, and then I found out that Obama says it's his favorite book. You should read it. I think you'd really like it.

It's just gone to the top of my list. How would you describe what it's about?

It's about humanness, about what it means to be a human being.

Ellen Burstyn's memoir, *Lessons in Becoming Myself* (also available as an audiobook, which she reads out loud herself), is a lesson in acting and sustaining a career on stage and screen, but it's also a lesson in what it means to be human—the lifelong journey of self-discovery.

CAREER STRATEGIES FOR PERFORMING ARTISTS

▶ By Amy Guerin

As you begin to find success as an actor, you'll see positive changes emerging in your career. Perhaps you'll be able to afford to live without roommates. Perhaps you can reduce, or eliminate completely, the need for a day job. Or perhaps you'll have developed a strong enough relationship with your agent, casting directors, and directors that you get phone calls about available parts rather than having to audition.

Success as an actor takes many forms. In the pages that follow, you'll hear from a handful of theater professionals living across the United States and abroad about strategies for achieving success as a professional actor: the ins and outs of networking, managing finances, working internationally and touring, creating opportunities, and social media branding. We'll discuss practices you can start doing now to help set yourself up for success—and if you're finding success, what you can do to make that success sustainable.

First, defining *success* . . .

As a regional theater actor, Justin R.G. Holcomb has worked in New York City and around the States. When did Holcomb decide he'd achieved success as an actor?

Justin R.G. Holcomb, NYC

Photo by Kent Meister

In this business, success comes in teaspoons. You strive to work with more renowned companies and increase your asking price, but sometimes you take a gig for health insurance, for a specific role, or just to work with people you enjoy. I've worked with incredibly well-known LORT houses and Tony award-winning creative teams, then turned around and done a show in an NYC basement for less than $300 a week. Playing the Old Man in *A Christmas Story* at Actors Theatre of Louisville, playing the lead in the Off-Broadway production of *Channeling*

Kevin Spacey, and finally signing with an agent after thirteen years of mailings, these were all game changers. They changed how people perceived me on paper and in the audition room.

Annie Donley, an actor specializing in improv comedy, has worked in both Chicago and New York. Donley's own realization of her success happened this way:

Annie Donley, Chicago and NYC

Photo by John H. Abbott

> Success is subjective, but for me it happened over a period of time. I found myself writing and performing pieces that came from my point of view, and it was extremely fulfilling. At some point, I realized that I had an audience who enjoyed watching and reading those as much as I enjoyed producing them. I'd say the meeting of the two was the moment of success for me.

Networking

One can argue that there's no success without an expanding professional network. As you continue to work as an actor, you'll meet other theater professionals that you want to work with again—and in return, they'll want to work with you.

Guy Roberts, Artistic Director of the Prague Shakespeare Company, notes that successful networking makes continued acting work possible.

Guy Roberts, Prague

Photo by Ashe Kazanjian and Kaja Curtis, courtesy of Prague Shakespeare Company

> Almost all theater work is seasonal, so your only hope of a sustainable theater income, if you're not a member of a company, is to be very good at what you do and be very pleasant so people want to keep working with you from job to job.

Over time, that professional network grows from outside the boundaries of your home base to include contacts across the country and perhaps even across the globe. It becomes a source of information about available work, emotional support, and long-term collaborations that provide you with an artistic home.

Regional theater actor and Juilliard graduate Tracie Thomason has this to say about the notion of an artistic home:

> Ideally, my creative home base, no matter how large or small, would support a thriving artistic community wherein every individual had a great sense of belonging. I want to be challenged and supported but also enjoy an environment beyond its theatrical endeavors, because I believe in the idea that growth as a person ultimately equals growth as an actor.

Tracie Thomason, NYC

Photo by Kerry Beyer, KerryBeyer.com

However, this network can't survive on passivity. Even successful actors can't rest on their laurels and wait for the work to come to them. You must make a lifelong effort to connect with your network and communicate with them regularly—letting them know when you have a current gig or that you're looking for the next one.

Theater director and producer Philip Olson describes the importance of a professional network this way:

> Investing in relationships with decision makers in the theater and film scene will pay huge dividends. And no, this doesn't mean partying with your fellow actors. Good old-fashioned networking goes far. Industry mixers, events, and ceremonies are great. As a theater director myself, I'm much more likely to cast an actor I know and like over one I don't know (assuming similar talent and style fit). Use that to your advantage! Casting directors, directors,

Philip Olson, Austin, TX

Photo by Diana M. Lott

> and producers are fantastic opportunities. Follow them on social media. Research their work. Maybe even reach out, asking for an internship. You may not make any money, but it'll be of huge value.

Leaning Into Your Network

If you're not sold yet on the importance of building and maintaining your network, consider how you can lean into your network to support you in expanding your range of roles, playing higher prestige venues, and making tough career decisions.

To the first point, "expanding your range of roles" means getting cast in roles that positively impact your resumé, rather than just take up space. Expanding roles suit your type and increase in line load and plot importance. Your network helps you find those roles, connect with people personally about the roles, and supports you regardless of whether you book the gig.

To the second and third points, higher prestige venues can move you into larger cities, nationally known companies, better spaces, and better pay—except when you choose not to take the gigs. When you're in the lucky spot of having two contrasting offers for the same time period, one offer for a less prestigious venue but a lead, and the other for a more prestigious venue but a smaller role—what do you do? How do you make the best decision for your career? You take the question back to your network. Use their expertise to help guide you toward the decision that's best for you.

Jacklyn Collier, a regional theater actor, points out that these kinds of decision aren't always easy.

> Sometimes I want to do a low-paying show and I know I'll have to give up other opportunities to do it, but I need it to feed my artistic soul. When I leave town to do a play, I know it means giving up commercial, TV, and film auditions, so I have to weigh those opportunities carefully.

Jacklyn Collier, NYC
Photo by dirty sugar

Managing Money

The moment in your career when you're finding success also means that you must get smart about how you manage your money. While performance is art, being a performer is business —and the better you understand and manage the economics and business of *you*, the more freedom you'll have to pursue opportunities that may take you away from your home base or day job.

But how do you get there? What are the economics lessons to put into play at the start of your acting career that help lead you to and sustain your success?

Philip Olson, who has the distinction of being an accountant as well as a theater professional, says that first you need some commercially valuable skills in the real world:

> I recommend developing a technical skill that is valuable in all markets such as coding, mechanics, or writing copy. For ninety-nine percent of performing artists, finding commercial success is an endeavor that's years and years in the making. You'll need stamina, longevity, and a frugal lifestyle. And you'll need to enjoy these years or you'll eventually be more likely to quit. The most successful artists and creators I know have developed viable commercial skills that they use when the money from theater/film isn't flowing in.

The idea of developing a marketable skillset might fly in the face of the romantic notion of the impoverished artist fighting the valiant fight in the name of art, but one could easily view the actor with both a successful business career and a successful theatrical career as an even more committed and driven artist than the "artiste" who is only committed to waiting tables.

So when is it time to call on an accountant? What is the benefit of having an accountant review and manage your finances? To these questions, Olson answers:

> If you earn over $5,000 as an independent contractor, you need an accountant, plain and simple. That's any pay from theater, commercial acting, television, or film. An accountant knows the tax code the way you know the Bard or Beckett. Your accountant can see the missteps you'll make before you make them. She'll make you realize that, for instance, you *can* deduct that gym membership! Have a pro help you out, and you'll save yourself tons of money.

Saving for a Dry Spell

Olson also suggests that you "avoid debt like the plague." As he says, it'll come between you and your dreams every time. If you're in debt, he recommends keeping only a month's worth of expenses in savings. All extra income is money you should throw toward your debt. For the actor who is out of debt, he recommends building up a healthy emergency fund—around three months' worth of regular expenses. This should be somewhere in the range of $10,000–$15,000. This will insulate you against surprises, emergencies, and bad luck. And it can also serve as your "amazing opportunity fund"—freedom to take that bus to New York for open casting sessions or to fly to LA for pilot season. Olson says to think of this fund as your "passport to good, protection from bad" fund. Keep it safe, stable, and unsexy.

Working Internationally and Touring

Successful actors can be found everywhere—in New York City, in other major theater cities across the States, on a cruise ship, on a tour bus, or even in a foreign country. There are different paths to success that don't go through New York City or Los Angeles.

Guy Roberts has lived in the Czech Republic since 2008, producing, directing, and acting with his company. The Prague Shakespeare Company's international work has grown to include tours in Europe and America.

> We have toured select productions internationally for the last six years to the United States and Hungary. We had an educational five-actor *Romeo and Juliet* that toured France, Slovakia, Austria, and Poland as well. This season we'll take *Twelfth Night* and *Venus In Fur* on tour to the US in January of 2016.

As an artistic entrepreneur, Roberts recognizes both the advantages and disadvantages of creating your own work:

> I always wanted to be personally responsible for my successes and failures, and so for me, running a company where I was directly in charge of my future was the only way. Is it a sustainable life? I am not sure—that depends on the success of your company in some ways. It's so difficult waiting on someone else to give you a part or an opportunity. I really feel that for some people, creating their own work is the only way to have agency in the profession.

Touring actors have challenges and opportunities to embrace. True, as a touring actor, you're working, getting paid to travel, and playing to audiences hungry for your work, but you're also missing auditions for other work, separated from your family, and playing the same part in the same show night after night.

Roberts has experience with this aspect of an actor's career as well:

> I toured for a year with the first Broadway tour of *Big! The Musical* and shared the road with many people who had done it for years . . . I think early in an actor's career when they can work cheaply, it's a good idea to get experience this way and also perhaps play roles that they normally wouldn't get in a big market such as New York or London.

Creating Your Own Opportunities

Besides touring or moving to another country, other options do exist for entrepreneurial artists to create and fund their work. For seven years (2008–2015), Jenni Rebecca Stephenson served as Executive Director of Fresh Arts, an artist support organization in Houston, Texas, that provides career services, educational workshops, gallery space, and exhibitions to artists of all kinds.

As she says, "Most of the funding opportunities for theater makers of which I'm aware involve the creation of new work (not interpretive work) or the presentation of theater for children or underserved communities."

After years of work helping artists find ways to succeed in the marketplace, while also keeping a finger on the pulse of the marketplace itself, Stephenson's view on sustainability as an artist sounds a familiar refrain:

Jenni Rebecca Stephenson, Houston, TX

> I know all too many performers that started ensemble companies to create their own opportunities to act or dance who end up spending more time marketing, fundraising, and playing janitor than on their art. But I hope that warning doesn't deter anyone—creating your own work allows you to carve out a career on your own terms. The sad reality is that so few performers are making their entire living from their art, so if you're going to have to juggle a day job, too, you might as well make sure you're in love with the majority of your projects. In a way, that allows for the freedom and investment that keeps the dream alive over time.

Social Media Branding

Beyond proactively managing your economic reality as successful actor, whatever your geography, you must also be as equally proactive with your social media branding. The care and feeding of your social media brand is an entrepreneurial skill that working artists of any kind—and at any age—must learn. Branding can directly and positively impact your career.

Travis Bedard is a Minneapolis-St. Paul-based producer, actor, and blogger. A frequent contributor to the theater blog 2 AM Theatre, Bedard also maintains an active Twitter presence. Bedard defines social media by saying:

Travis Bedard, Minneapolis-St. Paul

Photo by Will Hollis Snider

> When you decide to use social media in a professional capacity, you're effectively deciding that all of the content you're creating on a platform is a reflection of your values. The best brand messaging for individuals serves as the beginning of a conversation between you and a new customer, an old customer, or colleagues in your field.

New York City-based actor and playwright Bernardo Cubria is the moderator of the popular theater podcast "Off and On" and is also on Twitter regularly. He says that social media branding is something he thinks of in terms of honesty as an artist. "I want my brand to represent the things I stand for and the things I believe in—the kind of actor or writer I am. I hope my social media brand represents that."

Bernardo Cubria, NYC

Photo by Bixby Elliot

But what if you're shy about social media? Or if you think it seems self-serving or self-promoting?

It is! And it should be. As Cubria says:

> I think the mistake many theater people make is being shy about their work. I want as many people as possible to be exposed to my work, to see the things I create. I want a full house at every show. So why not take advantage of all of the social media tools available? If the main problem in modern theater is that our audience is getting older and older, then why not use a tool to help us reach a new audience?

Distinct, but connected to Cubria's idea of using social media branding as an audience-building tool, is Bedard's pragmatic answer to the question of why having a social media brand is so necessary:

> Because sometimes people do come looking for you. When people attempt to meet you online, they're doing the same thing you are—they're looking at your webpage, your publicly available Facebook content, or your Twitter feed. You want to control that. You want to know what they see, because you created it.

The most effective social media platform for both Bedard and Cubria is Twitter. Bedard makes the case, saying:

> Material pushed to Twitter can achieve a very broad reach very quickly if it hits the right eddies and currents of opinion and attention. The open nature of the medium means it can reach anywhere frictionlessly, but mostly it needs to be well aimed at affinity groups (hashtags and thought leaders) and

repeated for different times of day to appease the ever-flowing river nature of the platform.

Cubria seconds this notion: "If it wasn't for Twitter, my podcast would have never developed a larger audience than my friends and relatives."

Okay, message received. Have a website featuring your work. Have an active social media presence, preferably on Twitter. But what do you tweet about? Blog about? The theater universe is vast with more than enough actors out there. How do you set yourself apart?

Bedard says:

> The goal of social media branding is to contextualize yourself. In a crowded field, you want to differentiate yourself. Define yourself with two or three words or phrases, and use those to guide your content. Are you in love with edgy new plays? Musicals? Puppets? Share articles about it, images from productions of it, and your thoughts on it. In the negative space, we begin to see you. You'll draw others involved in those communities to you as you broadcast whatever your Venn diagram of interests are.

Cubria points out two major pitfalls in social media branding:

> Don't try and be someone you're not. So be true to yourself, and that will make an audience come to you. Also, while negativity can be helpful in building certain kinds of brands, I believe that artists should avoid posting negative thoughts on other people's work.

Adding all this up, we see that for you as a successful actor to grow and sustain your hard-won success, you must be proactive in managing your finances, positive in your social media branding, and on the lookout for networking opportunities and unexpected ways to work in the theater. With this kind of daily practice—and it is daily!—theater acting becomes your lifelong vocation.

Careers have their ups and downs, and there might not always be obvious signs of success, but with a vocation, the joy of purpose in what you do can remain constant.

AMY GUERIN is an Assistant Professor in Theatre at the University of Alabama in Huntsville. She previously taught at Texas A&M University in the Department of Performance Studies for nine years. In 2009, Guerin's production of *A Midsummer Night's Dream*, a collaboration with A&M's Department of Computer Science and Engineering showcasing flying fairy robots alongside human actors, was featured in *Wired Magazine*, on NBCNews.com, and on the NPR program Science Friday. She also directed the plays *Lend Me a Tenor*, *Les Liaisons Dangereuses*, *The Conduct of Life*, *Bus Stop*, *Measure for Measure*, *An Ideal Husband*, *Tartuffe*, and *Machinal* at A&M. She blogs about theater at discoballtartuffe.wordpress. com. Guerin received her BFA in Theatre from the University of Oklahoma, and her MFA in Directing from the University of Houston. She co-founded Nova Arts Project, a Houston-based theater company, which received the Houston Press MasterMind Award for Outstanding Creative Contribution in 2009.

Amy Guerin

Photo by David A. Brown

YOU'RE SUCCESSFUL! NOW WHAT?

An Agent's Perspective

▶ By Richard Lucas

"I was 25 years old when I was nominated for a Tony Award for Jerome Robbins' Broadway. I did not work on Broadway for pretty much five years after that."

Charlotte d'Amboise[1]

You've achieved some success in establishing yourself in this very challenging and competitive profession. You're a union member, have solid professional credits at the top of your resumé, some good reviews, and even a few bucks in the bank.

Now it's time to take a careful personal and career inventory to ensure you maintain or raise your place on our industry's precarious theatrical ladder.

We all know more than just a few talented actors who aren't having the success they deserve. Conversely, we see other actors who we consider less talented artists enjoying great success. The difference is probably that the former doesn't understand the business of acting. As Andy Warhol once said, "No matter how good you are, if you are not promoted right you won't be remembered."[2]

The cruel reality is that the actor who books the job often isn't the artist who gave the best audition. I've been an agent in this industry for more than three decades, and I've had the great pleasure of working with some of the most talented and successful actors in Canada. I'd like to share with you what I've learned about how actors can train their business minds to make smart, intentional decisions that will propel their career in the right direction.

Healthy Relationships

Agents

As your career grows, it's important to reevaluate your relationship with your agent to be sure the fit remains just right. Like a teenager getting your first set of wheels, sometimes you start with an older, less expensive car instead of the top-of-the-line brand name that you really want. Do you require a more powerful engine or maybe a newer model? It's admirable to be loyal, but this is your career and you must take the reins and be your own best advocate. And sometimes, recognizing that you deserve an agent who can help get you to the next level is the smartest decision you can make. Here are a few things to reflect on as you think about your agent and your current needs:

- **Experience:** Is your agent knowledgeable with proven theatrical contacts?
- **Theater vs. film:** Some actors represent themselves for theater, and their agent services their film and television work. If this is the case, consider if you should upgrade to an agent who will also represent you for theater.
- **Support:** If your agent is taking commission for your theater work, then an agency representative should be obliged to see all of your in-town work and make the occasional effort to see your out-of-town work. If your agency doesn't take commission for your theatrical work, then their attendance is optional. That said, it's a great sign if they do show their support by coming to some of your plays and becoming more familiar with your work.
- **Regular check-ins:** Does your agent still seem enthused to represent you? Does she or he promptly return your phone calls? Have you had calls for auditions lately, or perhaps just a "check-in" call or email? Has your agency seen some of your recent work? If you don't have positive responses to these questions, it may be time to consider finding some fresh energy.

Accountants

The most dreaded word to many actors is *taxes*. Make sure you have an accountant who's experienced in doing taxes for self-employed individuals and arts and entertainment professionals. These are the type of things your accountant should advise on:

- **Incorporating:** Should you or shouldn't you incorporate? And when is the right time in your career to incorporate? My rule of thumb is that when you've booked a high-paying job or a long engagement that will result in having more cash coming in than you need, it's time to look at incorporation. You don't want to pay the government more tax dollars than you have to.

• **Investing:** When you get that fat contract and know you'll have extra cash coming in, ask for recommendations of reputable investment advisors to interview. Find the right person to help you set up investment accounts and to advise on the management of the union and employer contributions to your retirement funds.

• **Tax deductions:** Which expenses are tax deductible, and which aren't? If you're unsure about what's allowable, it's always better to keep the receipt and let your accountant decide.

Tip . . .

If you're bad at keeping records, keep a shoebox handy. Take a few seconds to write on your receipt what the expense was for, and then just toss it in your shoebox. When you go to do your taxes, all of your materials will be in one place. And if you aren't good with money, simply deduct 15 percent from any check you get, and throw those funds in a separate savings account. This can take the stress out of tax time if you find that you owe a bundle to the government.

Directors, Artistic Directors, and Casting Directors

These are all important people. Keep in touch with past and potential engagers. Phone calls, emails, and letters are all nice, but I find that cards are the most effective method. Because we consider these a thoughtful gesture, we don't throw them away as we might an email. Even a postcard from your present gig reminds a past engager that you want to work with them again in the future. It helps them to keep you in mind while also letting them know what you're up to and when your present contract is over.

Also, a small holiday gift and card to your agent, accountant, or someone who has cast you or directed you in a show that year is always appreciated. Keep it simple like a nice bottle of wine, flowers, or a box of treats. If you go over the top with an extravagant gesture, they may feel uncomfortable.

Tools of the Trade

Raise your odds by keeping your tools sharp. If your promotional materials aren't current, it can appear that you don't care about your career. And if you don't care, then why should the people who hire you?

- **Resumé:** Keep your resumé up to date and to one page. When you were just out of school, your credits were slim at the top with your theater school, professors, and classes having prominence. Now that you're more established, make sure you've dedicated more room for your professional credits. Remove some of the older information at the bottom to make room for new credits at the top. Watch the spelling. Double-check that you've correctly spelled the name of each project and director. And don't shy away from asking a few friends to proofread.
- **Headshots:** Keep your photos up to date. If you're a character actor, maybe you only need to update every three or four years, but if your look changes, be sure to change your photo. If a beard or a mustache has come or gone, if you've gained or lost weight, or if you have a new and different hair color or style, then you need to update your headshot.
- **IMDb:** Keep IMDb and industry casting profiles up to date. Social media platforms including Facebook, Twitter, Instagram, and a personal website can be helpful to build your career, but if you create these platforms, you must keep them updated.
- **New opportunities:** Your career should be like a well-balanced stock portfolio. Examine your strengths, and see if there are additional areas of the entertainment industry that you could or should focus on. In addition to stage work, many actors enjoy the variety and income from voice acting, commercials, teaching, and film and television work.

Tip . . .

Staple your resumé and photo together, but don't put them in a plastic cover. Directors and casting directors often like to write notes about you or your audition on your materials for future reference. And if you also audition for film and TV, have two resumés—one with theater credits at the top of the page, and one with your media gigs getting top billing. Make the theater folks feel they are most important when auditioning for them, and vice versa with film and TV.

Monologues

Veteran actors often feel that once they've achieved success they should never have to do "generals" or monologues again. And they're right. They shouldn't *have* to . . . but this business isn't always fair, so you should always be ready to cheerily perform party pieces when required. Know that producers and directors are impressed with veteran actors who demonstrate pleasant aggressiveness to get a job:

- **Read the play.** A professional theater actor will never randomly pick a monologue from a book, the web, or from a film or television script. Choose from a professionally produced or published play. And read the whole play.
- **Choose the right character.** Find a character and a monologue that you love. Make sure this character is suited for you and that it's a role you could be cast in today.
- **Keep it fresh.** If you've been doing Juliet since you graduated fifteen years and thirty pounds ago, it might be time to switch it up and learn the Nurse.
- **Keep it short.** The perfect length for a monologue is two minutes, and no longer than two and a half minutes.
- **Keep the preamble short.** And always take a moment to focus (as in five seconds max). This lets the audition panel take a breath before you begin your piece with a clean attack.
- **Avoid profanity.** It's best to stay away from monologues that have a lot of swearing. Also, most auditioners don't enjoy being yelled at.
- **Don't perform directly to the audition panel.** This is especially true if it's dramatic material. Playing to the panel can make them uncomfortable and tends to demand their attention (as opposed to *command* their attention). I recommend choosing a specific focus above their heads to make sure they see everything. That said, if you're performing a comedy piece that they're enjoying with gusto, it could be very successful to adjust your focus and play to the auditioners.
- **Don't get thrown off your game.** Even when you catch your audition panel writing, texting, or eating lunch during your audition. It happens, and it can merely mean that you've already nailed the callback or the job.
- **Never surprise the audition panel by pulling out a weapon in the middle of a monologue.** If such a prop is required, show them the replica or prop knife, gun, or object before you start. Never use a real weapon!
- **Play the room.** If you're auditioning on the stage of a 500-seat theater, you want to vocally play to the auditioners in the house. In a small rehearsal room, though, dial it down appropriately.

- **Don't do "the face" after completing your monologue.** Far too many actors finish with that stretched out *how-did-I-do-might-not-have-been-my-best* look. Instead, on your final line, take a moment, give a confident yet gentle "I'm done" nod, and then look at the auditioners and wait for them to begin the after-monologue conversation.
- **Don't apologize.** *Blank* in the middle of your monologue? It even happens to veterans, but you can save your audition by simply not saying a word, composing yourself, and then bravely carrying on. Your auditioners will be relieved that you didn't ask to start again or say the dreaded words, "I'm sorry."

> Emmy-nominated casting director and former Chair of Capalano University's School of Performing Arts Stuart Aikins says:
>
> Never apologize. "I'm sorry" may be music to the ears of your significant other, but in an audition, it is a negative by which you draw attention to something only you may see as wrong. If you make a mistake, just go back and redo it. Avoid drawing even more attention to it with an apology.[3]

Auditions

Auditions are a tricky thing. Most actors fresh out of theater school are ready and eager for them, while many veteran actors become jaded and can even be unprepared. Remember that every audition you go to is an opportunity to advance your professional life—getting the role is just a bonus. Even if directors have worked with you in the past, they may wish to see your take on a very different role or style of play, or it may be a chemistry read to see if you have a connection with another leading character. There may also be other producers or artistic directors who have cast approval and haven't previously worked with you.

Auditioners are always impressed when veterans arrive looking like they're happy to be there, full of positive energy, and armed with an updated picture and resumé and prepared with any specific audition requirements.

- **Do your homework.** Know the show. Know the director. Look like you're informed and want the job. I like to say, "If there's Google, there's no excuse."
- **Be on time.** In fact, be early. Don't be late. Ever.

- **Cover your tattoos.** Unless you're auditioning for Puck in a punk version of *Midsummer's Night's Dream*, it is best to cover them up.
- **Clean up nice.** And ladies, don't wear hooker heels unless you're auditioning for the role of a hooker. Gents, there's a new invention called an *iron*. Use it!
- **Leave your water bottle in the waiting room.** You can survive the audition without it, and the audition panel isn't there to watch you nervously suck on it every two minutes.
- **Always have pictures and resumés with you.** The only correct response to someone on the audition panel asking for them is "of course," followed by a flourish of said materials.
- **Read the room.** If the panel seems to want to chat, then chat. If they seem to want to get down to business, then hop to it.
- **Take the direction.** If you're given bad direction and asked to apply it to your scene or monologue, take a deep breath and go for it. They may know it's bad direction and simply want to explore if you can do anything else, or perhaps it may be an "attitude check" to see what you're like to work with.
- **Ask for time.** If they give you a new scene and ask you to do it on the spot, feel free to ask for time. Again, you're your own best advocate. You know a cold read isn't going to show you at your best, so simply ask if you can come back later in the audition day. Say something like, "Would you mind if I take some time to prepare this piece? I'd like to present you with my best work."
- **Save the kiss.** If you have a love scene in your audition, just *indicate* the physical contact. Unless you've rehearsed and have agreed how to play with your scene partner, you want to blow her a kiss rather than frenching her. Save the heavy stuff for after you get the role.
- **Turn off your damn phone!**

It's never about just this audition. It's also always about the next job. The director in today's room may be the artistic director of a company tomorrow. Whenever you feel snarky about having to go to an audition, remember Sally Field. Even winning three Emmy Awards and two Academy Awards was still not enough to be offered the role of Mary Todd Lincoln. Even she had to audition . . . twice. (She subsequently received a third Academy Award for her work in *Lincoln*.)

Cautionary Tales

As you move forward in your career, the cruel realities of the profession can arise to take their toll on the human psyche. Many in our business are sadly prone to depression, eating disorders, or addiction. If you're someone who faces such demons, know that you're not alone. In my career as an agent, I have watched three beautiful and talented clients take their own lives. There's a lot of help out there if you need it. If your career hits any such roadblocks, be brave, get honest with yourself, and reach out for assistance.

I do have stories about the "casting couch," and, at this point in your career, maybe you do too. Firmly and professionally deal with inappropriate sexual attention or acts from anyone in your workplace. Most theaters, studios, networks, and your unions have very explicit policies on the subject. Your agent will always be your first line of defense and should help you decide how to handle a situation. If you don't have an agent, talk to your stage manager, Equity deputy, or union staff.

When you're not working, work out. Try to make healthy choices for your body and mind. From meditation to step cardio to taking a workshop or scene study class, keep your chops in shape. If you're short on funds, you can meet informally with friends to exercise and read new plays. Staying connected with colleagues and friends is an important part of staying positive when you're in between engagements.

As Michael Shurtleff famously says in his book *Audition*, "To stay there once you've made it requires unceasing hard work and discipline. Luck aside, the reason a lot of talented actors don't make it is because they don't work hard."[4]

Throughout your career you will experience highs and lows. I hope my thoughts here will help you to avoid some of those lows.

Since 1986, **RICHARD LUCAS** and his team at Lucas Talent Inc. have proudly represented many of Canada's leading actors, directors, and writers. Lucas holds a BFA in Acting from the University of Alberta, an MFA in Directing from the University of British Columbia, and he's currently enrolled at the University of Victoria working toward a PhD in Theatre History. He has shared his workshop *The Business of Acting* in post-secondary and acting schools from coast to coast and was Department Head of Acting and Actors' Voice for three years at the Canadian College of Performing Arts (CCPA). Lucas has worked across Canada as a theater producer, director, and an actor.

Richard Lucas

Photo by Kevin Clark Studios

EXPANDING YOUR VIEW OF SUCCESS

Notes from the Acting Coach

▶ ## An Interview With Scott Fielding

Scott Fielding is the founding director and master teacher at Michael Chekhov Actors Studio Boston. He is on the international faculty of the Michael Chekhov Association (MICHA), has taught on the faculties of the Graduate Opera Studies Program at New England Conservatory, Emerson College, and Tufts University, and has given master classes and workshops at schools such as Yale, NYU, and Carnegie Mellon. During several years abroad, Fielding taught and directed extensively throughout the Balkans, as well as in England, Switzerland, Germany, and Brazil. In Croatia, he held a full-term appointment at the Academy of Dramatic Art, Zagreb, and a guest professorship at the Academy of Arts, Osijek.

Scott Fielding
Photo by Kippy Goldfarb/Carolle Photography

Fielding has received international awards for his stage directing. Notable productions include *John Cage: A House Full of Music*, *(His) Three Sisters*, *Night Just Before the Forests*, *Mud*, and *4.48 Psychosis*. He collaborated with Slovenian director Tomi Janežić for *King Lear* and *The Blind*, and at the invitation of renowned Buddhist monk Thich Nhat Hahn, Fielding directed the US premiere of Nhat Hahn's *The Path of Return Continues the Journey*.

As an actor, his stage credits include Off-Broadway productions as well as productions in Chicago and Los Angeles.

I'd love to begin by discussing your definition of *success* for an actor. As a teacher, how do you—or do you—discuss this concept with your students?

I think everybody has to come to their own definition of success. I define it for myself simply as artistic or creative achievement and creative fulfillment. Doing the kind of work I want to do with the people I want to work with—this has much more to do with success, for me, than money or fame. What I would say to young people is that if fame and big money are your benchmarks for success in acting, then you may never be able to call yourself a success. So take care. Money and fame in acting are hard won. People do attain them, but at the end of the day, it's not the outer results that truly satisfy you, it's your own personal sense of achievement that brings lasting fulfillment.

When actors do have success, by their own definition, what kind of work would you say is necessary to maintain that success? Can you describe what that level of hard work looks like to you and your students?

I think it was Hemingway who said something like, I sit down at nine o'clock in the morning and I don't get up until one o'clock. I put in my X number of hours a day, every day. I start with that blank sheet of paper, and I work. I have days when I'm inspired, and I have days when I'm not. But I sit down and I do my work.

For the actor, one of the challenges is that most of us don't have access to an empty studio, and few actors go into the living room at nine in the morning and say, I'm going to work on my acting for X number of hours. But that's the hard work—the practice. Yeah, you have to do the business part, but from my point of view, persistent training is the essential work.

For actors, the work of training and conditioning yourself on a regular basis is hard. I know a lot of professional musicians in the classical world. They get up, and they practice their music every day for hours—it isn't even a question. And this is the same for an athlete. In my training with students, I frequently use those two analogies.

Right, and we don't have the image in our head of the actor standing in front of the mirror practicing for hours a day.

I discourage people from working in front of a mirror. But there's a vital need for the actor to work on a daily, regular basis. The actors who do practice hours and hours a day on their own, those actors have intrinsic motivation, and it's the real key to success. I do everything in my power to help nurture and inspire that, but it's really on the individual. If a person isn't intrinsically motivated to learn and grow in their field, it's not going to happen.

This is a problem for the actor. If you're waiting until you get the audition or until you get the part, how can you possibly expect to do well when that moment appears? You might get lucky now and again, but you certainly can't expect to be consistently achieving under audition or performance conditions when you're not working daily.

Stanislavsky talked about how an actor needs a daily *toilette*, a French word that essentially means the kind of thing we're talking about here. He instilled in his actors the idea that they need to train and condition themselves on an absolutely consistent basis in order to grow and stay sharp.

> "For the actor, one of the challenges is that most of us don't have access to an empty studio, and few actors go into the living room at nine in the morning and say, I'm going to work on my acting for X number of hours. But that's the hard work—the practice."

Do you think it has to do with the collaborative nature of acting? Could that be why the actor might not think there's a lot of solo practice to be done?

Uta Hagen starts off her book, *Respect for Acting*, by saying that she had this question when she was coming up as an actress: What can I do to work on myself, by myself, at my house to develop myself? And from there, she developed her valuable series of exercises.

Before Hagen, there was Michael Chekhov, who—while acknowledging the essential collaborative nature of the actor's art—also offered creative exercises that the actor could do alone anywhere, at any time. Chekhov said that the actor is an actor twenty-four hours a day, and his work offers insight into how we can be exercising at any moment. The question is, will I have the initiative to do it?

Fielding teaching at Michael
Chekhov Actors Studio Boston

Photo by Kippy Goldfarb/Carolle
Photography

**Do you think it's that initiative that makes a difference, if you're willing to
go that extra mile?**

Darryl Hickman, my first teacher, used to tell us about working with Gene
Kelly. Kelly had already been on set for two hours by himself practicing before
anyone else arrived. And at the end of the day, Kelly stayed and practiced again.
That was his work ethic. Whether the performer is an actor or an athlete, ease is
the mark of a master—and it's developed, earned, only with hard work. Actors
like Tom Hardy and Meryl Streep, they make it look easy because they work
like hell.

**Yes, and with them it looks like it takes no work. They seemingly just
have this ability to be believable. It's "naturalism."**

But it's an illusion. With naturalism, you get this idea that acting is just getting
up there and being yourself. Why learn to speak? Why learn to move? Why
learn an inner psychological technique? The truth is, the actor's command of
her instrument and craft, acquired by training and practice, is absolutely key to
believable acting in every genre or style.

**I do think that actors might have a particular advantage in the arts of
faking it till you make it. An actor has the ability to act, to put on an
attitude of success or air of confidence.**

You might be shocked by the number of actors with poor self-esteem and fear.
Just a week ago, I read a piece about Dame Judi Dench, where she talked about
the terror she experiences at the possibility of failing in every new role. Laurence
Olivier basically quit stage acting because he couldn't face a live audience anymore—the terror of that. And that's a remarkably common phenomenon with
actors.

**Let's talk about that. I do feel like once you achieve a certain amount
of success, you might be terrified that you're not worthy or maybe the
success was just a fluke—living with the weight of your success.**

It doesn't necessarily get any easier with success—and it very frequently gets more difficult. And that takes us again to the fact that the best remedy is mastery of your technique. When you know what you're doing, it eases the fear of failing. If you're continually cultivating that mastery, you're in a better position to keep at bay the demons that plague the soul when you're faced with the challenge of a new role.

**Do you address with your students the practical steps for tackling anxiety
in an auditioning scenario, a callback scenario, or a first read-through?
Do you encounter students who develop or struggle with severe anxiety?**

Yes, of course, we all do. There's almost no one who doesn't struggle with this. So besides the importance of consistently working on yourself, the second thing you need is very thorough preparation for whatever specific work lies in front of you. If you're coming to an audition unprepared, you're almost guaranteed to be full of anxiety. On the other hand, if you're coming to an audition having really put in the time it takes to audition properly, you'll have confidence.

Training and preparation go together. I have a great interest in sports psychology. Imagine the pressure of being a major league pitcher, or a NBA player, or a tennis pro. The science of sports psychology offers a lot of very concrete techniques that an athlete can do to facilitate his best performance under pressure. And what I find is that these kinds of technique are valid also for the actor. For example, techniques for relaxation and concentration—the twin pillars of all acting technique—visualization, breath work, self-talk. These are techniques that are extremely useful for an actor under audition or performance conditions.

**So, for the actor, I would imagine that part of moving forward in your
career means taking on different types of role as you age. But there
are challenges to that, particularly for actresses. Can you address the
strategy for tackling that?**

It seems like every week there's another story about Hollywood actresses, in particular, and how when they hit 35 or 40, there's just no work. It's really a problem. The roles become fewer and fewer. And that's when you have to think, what's your mark for success? Those years of having success, youth, and beauty can be short lived for the actor. So if you don't have a passion for the art, craft, and work of acting, then what do you do?

I'm thinking of someone now who was a significant actress in her 20s or 30s who I had the good fortune to work with in the 1980s when I was just starting out. Now she's in her 60s, and she does theater. She's played roles on some big theatrical stages, but she also does work on stages that most people probably wouldn't know about. Her love of acting is what fulfills her. I'm sure some part of her would still love to be the ingénue she used to be, but she loves to act. So she acts, every chance she gets. It's the satisfaction of being a creative artist that's the name of the game in terms of longevity.

> "This country has a tremendous wealth of working actors who sustain very fulfilling and lucrative careers whose names you never know."

So, she reinvented herself as a stage actor. Was this by necessity, or did she start on the stage, went to film, and then came back?

Maybe by necessity. On the other hand, a lot of our really fine, "celebrity" actors sustain parallel careers, both in front of the camera and on the stage. There are more and more celebrity actors on Broadway. But even beyond Broadway, there are an awful lot of really wonderful household-name actors who are working on stages in LA and New York and elsewhere. They'll tell you that the satisfaction of working in front of a live audience is often far more fulfilling than the work they do in front of the camera.

Right, there has to be a reason that the celebrity actors continue to work on the stage.

Absolutely, and it isn't for the money. And it's not just the celebrity actors, by the way, but the working actors. This country has a tremendous wealth of working actors who sustain very fulfilling and lucrative careers whose names you never know. J.K. Simmons comes to mind. This guy had been a relatively unknown working actor for decades when "suddenly" he had the wonderful good fortune to be recognized with an Academy Award for his work in *Whiplash*. But that's icing on the cake when you look at his achievement of a sustained career as a working actor.

So when you say "working actor," can you define what you mean by that?

One definition of a working actor is an actor who has the opportunity to sustain a living through acting. That's one definition, and it's a rarified level. But there are a lot of people who do achieve that. You're also a working actor, though, if you're a bartender who more or less frequently also works as an actor. Maybe you're working for scale, or maybe you're working as a nonunion actor, but you're doing those plays or independent movies. The fact is, there are a lot of actors, believe it or not, booking television jobs or even movie roles, and they still have to make a living doing other work.

Many young actors want to become a union member, and that's perfectly fine as an early goal. But there are an incredible number of union actors who, unfortunately, don't have the opportunity to support themselves with acting work.

When I think of a working actor, I think of somebody whose face we've seen a thousand times but whose name is relatively unknown—the person who continues to get cast repeatedly because he or she has a reputation, but there's nothing about stardom or celebrity here.

That's right—there are those actors whose faces you know but whose names you don't. There are also a tremendous number of actors whose faces you don't know but who work all the time. They appear in small parts. There are tons of actors who are, in a way, invisible to the average viewer. Believe me, Hollywood and Broadway need those actors, because they have technique and they're reliable. They're hired because a producer knows they're going to get the job done. They're professional.

Working actors who are invisible to your average viewer. That strikes me as a challenge, because invisible is the last thing an actor wants to be. Actors want to be memorable, I would imagine, no?

I heard Dustin Hoffman say that when he was coming up, he just wanted to act. It wasn't even a question of being visible or invisible. He just wanted to act, just to have the opportunity to act. I think if the young actor's aim is to be visible, to be known, it's not the right aim. I'd invite young actors to give it a little thought. Think of Van Gogh. He died an unknown painter. But he painted with an incredible passion to create. That was his motivation. That's what drove him. Van Gogh painted because he *had* to paint. I think the road to success as an actor has to do with doing what you *have* to do because it fulfills some fundamental impulse in you.

It's hard work, but an actor has to love every facet of the art of acting—not just performing in front of people, or getting your name in the paper, but living with a script for weeks and months, sometimes years. From the stretching, yoga, and weightlifting to going to that dance class or singing class. You should love learning a new dialect, reading the novels that open your soul, and all the many things that are, in fact, necessary to our profession beyond just learning lines and hitting your marks, as Spencer Tracy said.

> "Think of Van Gogh. He died an unknown painter. But he painted with an incredible passion to create. That was his motivation. That's what drove him. Van Gogh painted because he *had* to paint. I think the road to success as an actor has to do with doing what you *have* to do because it fulfills some fundamental impulse in you."

I try to teach actors—in addition to all that pertains strictly to craft—to cultivate a compassion for all human beings and a curiosity about all things. That's really all part of an actor's work and training. And that's not always in the minds and vision of young people who aspire to have success in the profession. But maybe it should be. I would hope they cultivate a breadth of interest in the world, and in history, and nature. This is what will enrich their lives—inside and outside the profession.

NOT STANDING ON CEREMONY

How To Be an Amateur in the Theater

▶ By Phillip L. Beard

This is about pursuing work in the theater for love, which, as you probably know, is the linguistic meaning of being an *amateur*—one who does something for the love of it. Nonetheless, this won't be a romance of amateurism. If you decide to be an amateur of the theater arts, this will be a short guide for how to nurture its best challenges and reflect your committed love of theater, both in the art and in your broader existence. This means, especially, becoming a good-natured foe of clichés and uncertain ceremony.

The Challenge of Being an Amateur: Make It a Plane

The challenge will be ongoing, and it's worth it. Amateur arts, including sports, are generally not as good as their professional variants. I may be upsetting you already, but that's okay. I'm confident that there is ample evidence that this is a pretty stable truth. The Central University Fighting Chipmunks don't play at the level of the New England Patriots, neither do the little ineptitudes of the Fighting Chipmunks make their moments of grace and efficiency more entertaining than those of professionals. The string section of the volunteer-based Smallville Civic Orchestra will likely not have anyone who plays a musical instrument as well as a member of the Alban Berg Quartet. For similar reasons of training, talent, and experience, amateur theater is seldom as good as professional theater. But the challenges can be exhilarating.

I was once in an undergraduate play, and the word came out that our college's president, a somewhat aloof, intellectual guy who had also been a US Army major in Vietnam and later a critic of the war (we respected him as a Renaissance man) would likely not come to see our play. "I detest amateur theatricals," he had said, chuckling, recusing himself. Many of the cast were surprised or hurt by this—the nerve of that guy, et cetera. But I wasn't upset. I understood him perfectly, and he had my sympathies. I knew already that watching amateur theater can be as tedious as long-distance bus travel.

Curiously, our president *did* come to see the play, and he unaffectedly liked it. We evidently rose to some challenge. Thus, another side to amateurism is this—in some endeavors, like flying an airplane, you have to be nearly as good as a pro, regardless of whether you're getting paid for it. In the theater, this both is and isn't so. You have to *choose* to take up this challenge. The deaths are figurative, but amateurs can (and should!) aspire to avoid theatrical death with the same dexterity of a pilot.

If one chooses to be devoted to amateur art, it can even be a key to a meaningful life, by being a model of committed, freely chosen, thoughtfully determined action. By "commitment," I mean two very simple things that the mechanistic, mannerism-focused training and egocentric goals of actors sometimes obscure: *studying* the script devotedly, in multiple dimensions, and *listening* to your fellow actors.

Acting is not a ceremony (an uncertain repetition of ritualized conventions or manners), and it is not about you. Acting is a reflection of the actor's unique knowledge in a particular place, for the sake of bringing a play to light. If you choose to do this for no money, good for you. Just know that commitment does not mean saying something that you half understand with "intensity." Politicians may pitch their spiels in this spirit, but actors, even amateurs, don't have to. One of the advantages of being an amateur is that you get to pick the scripts you work on, something only the highest level professionals get to do with the same liberty, ironically. With this liberty, you should be better able to devote yourself to the scripts you play. Sometimes, you'll literally pick the script you play. As an amateur, I encourage you to be a cast member who helps the group fly from mere clichés of companionship toward real, artistic collaboration. Despite magnificent parodies that reveal how this ambition can go wrong (think *Waiting for Guffman*, for instance), there need not be anything exotic or pretentious about this. Studying the script and listening to your fellow players may actually be the only satisfying remedies to amateur pretension.

> "If you choose to do this for no money, good for you. Just know that commitment does not mean saying something that you half understand with intensity."

Cost-Benefit Analysis and the Funny Animal Costume

There are a few good (and certainly disputable) reasons not to become a professional performer, and you probably know some of the top ones, such as, it involves risky investments of personal energy with an uncertain payoff. There may be a long, undignified apprenticeship of pecuniary unreward and personal unrecognition. Once you're paid, the performer's life and its requirements to travel, not sleep, and work odd hours alongside or in a funny animal costume may literally make you a shade of crazy, a fate not reserved to struggling theater artists, by the way, but also to the class of famous and often very good actors. Likely you can recall a few celebrity actors who have had publicly bad days off the stage. But frankly, if you have a tolerance for these (in the cosmic scheme of things, quite tolerable) risks, please do take them and learn to relax. And by that, I mean, study the science of relaxing, involving no hypnotic or narcotic substances. I'm serious. Learn it.

Otherwise, it's more likely that you may choose to be an amateur in the performing arts because you feel you have another significant calling, perhaps as an engineer or teacher, and perhaps life makes better sense to you by ordering your priorities in this way. That's fine, and the bulk of my address here will consider a few significant aspects of this way of being.

I should first mention an obvious practical benefit: The theater arts may also end up being a complement or component of your "other" professional life outside any conventional theater. Most actors have good, inventive, and adaptive public speaking skills, and that's important in many jobs, especially to managers and teachers. Many of these same jobs also involve light or sound production in meetings or presentations. Any Skype call in a serious business situation is a small theatrical production. The gods have not ordained that Skype conference calls have awful back lighting, duckface-downward-gazing camera angles, and tinny sound, but most people without a background in theater don't think about light and sound dynamics in ordinary workplace communications. As a theater person, you likely will, and your skills and aesthetic good sense will be valued and can be an educational resource. Many teachers address a room as if they're speaking into a rotary telephone receiver while trying not to disturb visitors sleeping in the next room. If you have a background in the theater, you won't be one of those teachers. In other ways, being a teacher may engage many of the skills and recall many of the rewards of stage performance—if you love the material you teach, you'll have what are, in effect, great scripts, day in and

Phillip Beard and Michael Prickett in *The 39 Steps*, Auburn Area Community Theater (2015)

Photo by Chris Qualls

day out. You'll have good, challenging audiences. Your performance skills will regularly be called into play. There are recurrent ways your theater skills may be useful within a professional life.

The more significant issue here, though, is what you make of your amateur theatrical life. Likely, you'll be glad to be in any theater at all, and if you have significant experience or training, you'll be a real asset to an amateur group in which, at any moment, a certain number of adult volunteers are experimentally working in the theater for the first time. Community theaters can be some of the loopiest and most fun places to work. Nonetheless, there's ultimately a happy, useful place for a kind of unapologetic seriousness within amateur theater, and it's actually identical in many ways to what one would do in a professional theater.

The conclusion of this brief address will be a portable definition of what "love of the theater" means, against what it is not. Hamlet like, I will dare to end abruptly.

> "Community theaters can be some of the loopiest and most fun places to work. Nonetheless, there's ultimately a happy, useful place for a kind of unapologetic seriousness within amateur theater, and it's actually identical in many ways to what one would do in a professional theater."

For the "Love" of Theater

A love of amateur theater is often expressed by those who work in it in dreadful clichés and in sentimentality. This is an awkward reality, because, as the poet Wallace Stevens says, "sentimentality is a failure of feeling," and a theater is supposed to be a chamber of vivid emotional truth. People who work in a theater may often say, "This group is like a family to me." They may mean no harm, of course, but they're usually lying. This statement can mean, "Thank God I'm getting away from my real family several times a week and that I have no really meaningful responsibility here." Theater can provide companionship, and *that* is called loosely, and inaptly, "family." And that is not to be sniffed at. In fact, I endorse it.

But companionship isn't artistic collaboration, and collaborative work, often involving significant, caring self-sacrifice (of time, effort, and other opportunities) is the only way a cast can become in any meaningful sense a "family." I don't recommend that you attempt to achieve this goal too easily. I wouldn't treat the notion as an automatic effect of any theater, and I hereby dissuade you from using the expression "like a family" glibly.

Another sentimental cliché of amateur theater is that people generally "love *it*." They too are usually lying, because if they really loved "it," they (and thus I mean anybody working on a play) would know their scripts the way airplane pilots know the machine they're sitting in, because there are many lives that depend on it. People who say this easily seldom do this work. By "it," they may mean the social and vaguely festive atmosphere of a theater. They are compensating, typically, for *not* knowing their scripts.

Left to their own devices, without good models for what it means to be an amateur, many people within an amateur theater—including its directors, producers, and stage managers—may shift into a mode that treats the theater as a social venue. A consequence of this attitude is that socializing and theatrical work can become confused. A simple test of this is if audible conversations occur in your theater while actors rehearse onstage (you should politely quiet them, please), or if personal conversations (sometimes in the guise of a vaguely therapeutic prelude) routinely delay the start of rehearsals. I'm not referring to the necessary conversations of technical or managerial crew. I'm warning that amateur theaters can be run like social clubs first and theaters second in a misunderstanding of the playful atmosphere of the house.

Some of this evasiveness of acting within amateur theaters comes not from obliviousness but from a shame at not being a professional. That is legitimate, and it should be creatively sublimated into the amateur's craft. But one's shame at not being a professional should not be indulged in wasting people's time during rehearsals by talking about oneself or about anything unrelated to the play.

Again, companionship is not artistic collaboration. There is a time and place for companionship: it is called a *bar*, and I wholeheartedly endorse the sane and judicious use of bars for theater groups, especially community theater groups, to socialize in. (Those that don't do this are, in my experience, impoverished.) At the risk of sounding crabby, I don't endorse the use of theaters for socializing in, and I especially reject the assumption that a kind of loose affability is a necessary foundation for good acting. In fact, its pursuit—or a tolerance for it during rehearsals—may merely distract players from rehearsing meaningfully. In performance, it will be obvious if the director and cast spent (or wasted) rehearsal time in unfocussed preambles to targeted, imaginative work with the script.

Let me make it plain, meanwhile, that I too enjoy the social and festive atmosphere of a theater. It tends to make actors giddy, and it fools many of us into thinking that we're suddenly funny. Beyond its social environment, I love many of the crazy little things about theaters, including the hallucinatory feeling stage lights give me (even if they aren't on), and the way fresh cut wood smells backstage. That's cool stuff. But enthusing about these social or architectural qualities isn't acting. As an actor, you must bring any enthusiasm back to the play itself and your fellow players, or these accessory amusements can lead your performance into becoming a vague ceremony.

Ceremony means doing something that you don't really understand with the stale, unconfirmed hope that somebody, somewhere (often an audience member who doesn't really exist) wants it to be that way. This hope is not only a bad criterion for acting but a near guarantor of bad acting. Please know that you can, in measured ways, bring a professional level of commitment to amateur theater, and it's also fine, as an amateur, to hold that if it isn't good, it isn't fun. This doesn't mean that you'll be a prima donna, control freak, or belligerent know-it-all. You actually will *not* be any of these, because these are all signs of self-loathing and insecurity, and you, as a real amateur, will calmly know what the hell you are doing.

If you become a real amateur in the theater, you can be a model of what it means to act for love. This should be a quiet, jealous, fierce love that doesn't boast easily (if ever) of its real commitments. It will simply blaze forth happily in lived moments on the stage. There are two reasonable ways to do this, which I've addressed briefly in relation to the concept of commitment, and they are two, related forms of surrender. They are stupidly simple and infinitely demanding:

Devote Yourself to the Script

This doesn't mean that you idolize or become uncritical of the script. It means you're a devout, passionate expert on that script. In other words, if you were to meet a scholar of that script's author at a conference, or the playwright herself in the supermarket after a rehearsal, you should be able to stun each of them with the stuff you know about the script. I'm not talking about memorizing lines, which is an oft-fetishized terminal zone of amateur acting, especially among people who haven't acted much. That's certainly important, but acting isn't recitation.

Acting is based on a soulful, multidimensional knowledge of a script—where it came from, the historical moment it represents, its cultural background, the geography of its setting, the meaning of its dialogue, and even (surprise!) the meaning of individual *words* in the script. If you, as an actor, are shaky about any of these aspects of the script, you may be building an incomplete, ceremonial performance. You may be shouting things that you half understand with great enthusiasm, and your director may have lied to you that this is just fine. But it's not. Act like you know better.

Devote Yourself to the Other Players

By this I mean that you're listening and relaxedly responding to the actors on stage as though they are real people living in serene real time. As amateurs, your fellow actors may be merely waiting for you to stop speaking so that they can say their lines on cue. (You should expect this!) By relaxed, I don't mean that you play a character as lax or loose—unless, obviously, that character is so. I mean that within your performance, you are so at ease with your choices that you're relaxed within the character and thus can listen to the other players and respond to them in that moment. Trust that this commitment may be matched, contagious or inspiring. And that is love in the theater. Anything less than that isn't.

PHILLIP L. BEARD teaches English Literature at Auburn University. He has an MA from the University of Virginia and a PhD from the University of Maryland. He has taught American Literature as a Fulbright Scholar at Friedrich Alexander University in Erlangen, Germany. He has worked in amateur theaters, in several states and abroad, his whole life.

Phillip L. Beard

Notes

1   Wienir, David, and Langel, Jodie. 2004. *Making it on Broadway.* New York: Allworth Press, 2004.
2   Pace, Alison. 2005. *If Andy Warhol Had a Girlfriend.* New York: Berkley Books, 2005.
3   Aikins, Stuart. 2014. "5 Keys to a Killer Audition." *Your Daily Cap,* 2014, accessed July 29, 2015, www.yourdailycap.ca/5-keys-to-a-killer-audition.
4   Shurtleff, Michael. 1978. *Audition.* New York: Bantam Books, 1978.

CHAPTER 4

GETTING AHEAD

"As one goes through life, one learns that if you don't paddle your own canoe, you don't move."

Katharine Hepburn

The idea of getting ahead in your acting career can be intimidating, especially when so much of it seems outside your control.

The goal of this chapter is to help you think about acting from a different point of view. Whatever your daily practice and perspective looks like now, you'll be comforted to know that there are actors who approach their careers entirely differently. These approaches may or may not look appealing to you, but just knowing they exist can help to nudge you off the rung where you're currently living.

This is what often happens after a period of time in any career. You fall into habits and convince yourself (often without thought) that these habits are working for you, so it becomes difficult to change them. Sure, they might have worked at some point, and they even might still be working now. The point is, though, to take time to reflect on them—to be conscious of your habits and whether they're helping more than hindering.

"Don't rock the boat." "Don't fix what isn't broken." "Look before you leap." We hear these sayings in our heads, and they reinforce the easier decision to keep the status quo—especially if we've found some success. "Don't risk losing that success," your brain tells you, "You worked so hard to achieve it in the first place!"

But moving your career to the next level always involves risk. That's a fact. You cannot propel yourself to a higher rung without risk.

Who Knew?

When you think of taking a risk, you probably think of stepping outside your comfort zone and auditioning for a part outside of your type. But Kevin Spacey's risk-taking behavior was slightly more devious. As part of the University of Buffalo's 2016 Distinguished Speaker Series, Spacey told the crowd that his pivotal, risk-taking moment involved snatching an after-party invitation from the purse of a woman sleeping next to him at a lecture by acclaimed English theater director, Dr. Jonathan Miller. "The little angel on my right shoulder is telling me, 'Just ignore it,'" Spacey said. "But the little devil on my left shoulder was making a pretty good case." He explained that he knew the choice was to either take the risk or "fall into obscurity in the relentless theater business."[1]

You don't want to fall into obscurity in the business of theater, and you're likely willing to take some calculated risks to prevent that from happening. Here's a look at some topics we'll cover in this chapter:

- Creating a theater group and incorporating media with theater
- How to make conscious decisions to step outside the norm in your work
- Getting acting work in corporate entertainment—what to expect and how you can position yourself to be desirable to a booking agent
- Creating theater for social change and collaborating with likeminded artists
- Writing roles for yourself and making your own opportunities
- How to think about building a life in the theater

We'll begin with an interview with Big Art Group, a lesson in creating your own opportunities and stepping outside the traditional conventions of theater.

CREATING A CONTEMPORARY LANGUAGE FOR THE STAGE

An Interview With Caden Manson and Jemma Nelson

▸ By Emeline Jouve

Big Art Group is a New York-based theater company founded in 1999 by Caden Manson and Jemma Nelson. If you're unfamiliar with their work, the best way to describe it is *performance art.* Or perhaps you may be familiar with the term *inter-mediality*—the blending of live stage performance and digital video, which allows audience members to see multiple versions of a performance simultaneously. We also refer to this as *transmedia storytelling*, telling the same story in multiple platforms.

Caden Manson and Jemma Nelson
Photo courtesy of the artists

Manson and Nelson describe their work as aggressively attacking "the boundaries of performance through experimentation with structure, medium, and process." Experimentation defines the company, which experiments not only on stage to create a new language that translates our contemporary lives but also off stage to promote and communicate about their work.

I had the opportunity to speak with Manson and Nelson about the origins of their theater, how they developed an audience, and how they use social media to expand their following. As the success of Big Art Group notably lies on Manson and Nelson's ability to innovate, I was particularly interested in their take on innovation in theater and how actors and performers can tap into their creative wells to move forward in their careers.

Would you say that artists are, by definition, innovative?

Caden: Yes, I think people who are working in contemporary performance are. They thrive on innovation, but at the same time they have the pitfalls of the "new." So they need to be careful.

What do you mean by "contemporary performance"?

Caden: I mean work that involves a mixture of different disciplines and the idea of performativity outside of the representational theater. I'm thinking of people who are working with concepts of theater and dance and visual arts and intermediality. Inside contemporary performance, I think innovation is very important. Not just technology but techniques and ideas. Ideas are the most important.

Was innovation important when you started working together? Was it the reason you founded Big Art Group?

Jemma: We came to the innovation through a different goal actually, which was trying to make a contemporary language for the stage. We just wanted to talk about our lives and things as they were, and we then sort of said, "Well, the old models aren't working for us, so we need to look for new solutions to the old models." That's how we arrived at working with new forms and new technologies.

What was your first experimentation?

Caden: The first piece we ever made was in 1997, called, "Pangea Days." Big Art Group was just Jemma and I for about two years, and we were working on very small projects. We didn't have any money or space or any kind of support, so we made a series of monologues with beepers—there were no cellphones in 1997. No cellphones! So people had beepers. In New York, you would have a phone service, and you would have a beeper. If someone called you and left a message, you would call that phone service, your beeper would glow, and then you would go to a payphone to call it and find out. So we would leave messages on our outgoing call service, and then people could call in and listen to new chapters. We made it like a radio piece on the concept of messages. That was kind of the first piece. It was about contemporary constructs, contemporary stories, and also the tools we use to communicate. Beepers were one of the tools we used to communicate with at the time. So then we turned it on its head and used it to tell stories.

So the experimentation with beepers in 1997 marked the beginning of your collaboration, but Big Art Group really started in 1999 with the Real-Time Film technique. How did that idea come about?

Caden: Right. I was living in a loft on Avenue D. One of my roommates was a fashion stylist, and she came out one day and told me the story about how they were shooting an ad for blue jeans and they had a $5,000 frock, and the model who showed up was obviously a heroin addict. She was very, very late—a mess, and she had scabbed and hairy legs, just awful. She walked in sick, but they just took the frock, did her face, put makeup on her arms and hands, and then they duct-taped the back of the jeans, and they took the photo. My roommate described the photo as this "box of light," and you can see the constructed image of "commerce." But underneath, there was this woman's scabbed hairy body . . . a real body, right? So I was thinking about the theatrical system for that, where we can show the frame and the outside of the frame and the construction of an image, and I just sat down with Jemma and drew it out. We came up with the screen and the shot marks. It was the beginning of Big Art Group. I took a credit card and bought the equipment at B&H video. We tried it out, and it worked.

Real-Time Film

Big Art Group defines Real-Time Film as a technique "of live projection and split second-choreography" where the actors perform actions that are simultaneously projected onto screens. The spectators not only watch the action on screens but also the live performance. After their early experiments, the company developed and perfected their technique in three successive productions: *Shelf Life* (2000), *Flicker* (2002), and *House of No More* (2004).

The Real-Time Film technique was hailed as innovative and was one of the things that brought Big Art Group national and international recognition, right?

Caden: That really had to do with timing of that kind of work. Real-Time Film for us was about construction in a way, whereas if you look at the American avant-garde before that, there was *de*construction. They were tearing apart this construct to look into political underlinings, but they had torn it apart so much there was nothing left. Ours is coming out from a queer space, and we were saying, "What are these new identities that can come out of what has been ripped apart?" So it happened because we came with a new proposal. The American avant-garde had one proposal, which was tearing things apart, and we had a new one, which was "we're making Frankenstein—we're making these new identities," and *Flicker* really does embody that.

To create the Real-Time Film technique, did you work with technology specialists?

Jemma: No, we were the technology people, so we had to learn how to use the tools that we wanted to use.

Caden: All the technology behind the work, all the technique of Big Art Group, was consumer goods.

Jemma: The real technology, the performed technology, is the actor.

How did you work with actors?

Jemma: It was all about working together and working over and over again. It's like choreography for the actors that they have to learn to create the screen images. So that was quite a long process—it took two years, something like that.

It's challenging for the actors. Have you developed an "acting method"?

Caden: Yes, we methodized it after we figured it out. Once we made *Shelf Life*, we had a technique, and we were breaking it down so we could teach new actors how to do it.

Jemma: We're actually working on a book that summarizes that and takes it further. It's called *Frameworks*. It's a sort of a system preparing an actor for the kind of . . .

Caden: . . . *intermedial* work. It's this idea of the digital into the real, because we're always making things digital. But how does the digital influence us, and how do we pull stuff out of the network and pull it back into reality, and how does it transform us? So that's what *Frameworks* is.

Since you train the actors, do you have to also "train" the spectators to help them understand your work so they can fully appreciate it?

Caden: Well, a lot of our work is about showing how we're making it. You have to let the audience know that looking at how we're making it is part of the show.

So a lot of the directing choices in the beginnings of the Real-Time Film pieces are sort of allowing the audience to understand how this machine functions—so then if it's a game, they have the rules.

Jemma: What the work is trying to do is get the audience to have an active role in understanding that they're editing, or not editing, what they're seeing and their complicity in creating the narrative—whether it's a narrative piece, images, or an abstract piece.

Would you say that the involvement of the audience in the creation of the show is political?

Caden: Yes, there are politics in the viewing. One of the goals of Real-Time Film was to short-circuit the way the audience looks and thinks about looking, so that they begin to question a lot of images—who makes the image, who is paying for the image, what is outside that image, how is the image constructed, how all images are lies—which is all political, I think. And in 1999 up to 2005, it was a pretty radical idea—talking about how audiences have facility with the making and understanding of the moving image.

Jemma: Sometimes, in the press, you could see very bad reactions—"Why are they talking about this? They shouldn't be discussing this. They shouldn't be putting this on stage. It's worthless." And you know, that was one of the major points of Real-Time Film. If we're voracious image eaters, and we're consuming-consuming-consuming all these images, but we're told at the same time by the same culture that these images are garbage, don't pay attention—well, what does that do to you? And we know that these images are still very powerful and they're affecting you. So one of the things Real-Time Film did was to say, "Wait a second. What exactly does this image mean?"

How does the criticism affect you? How are you able to process criticism and stay confident in the work you're doing?

Caden: You make work. You just have to make the work!

Can you describe how you measure success?

Caden: It depends on the day. Success for me is that you can continue making work. But at the same time, I'll make work anywhere. If someone isn't helping to make the work, I'll make it in my living room. That's a very American perspective, because a lot of people have to make their work in their living rooms.

How do you regenerate yourself? What's the secret to remaining innovative?

Caden: There's a lot of reading. I also get inspired by other people's work. It's weird because since we're established in a way now, I feel like my relationship to other artists is different. I used to be competitive, but now I'm appreciative, more collaborative. That's why we made the Contemporary Performance website. We want to help people be positioned to create their work. But it's a combination of seeing work as much as possible and reading. We like to read theory, but it can also be a pitfall. You need to be careful, because you might get stuck in your head. And then you have to get in the rehearsal room and get people together. That's really where the work begins.

> ## Contemporary Performance Network
> http://contemporaryperformance.org/

Many people say that New York is the place to be for artists or art students. Do you share this view? Do you think that you owe part of your success to the city?

Caden: The New York City of 1997 when we started is not New York City now.

Jemma: For us, it was downtown New York that was an interesting place, where you had a lot of people who were making things. You just had that feeling that you could come here and meet people who were doing something similar. But that was New York in the East Village at that time, and since then it has moved out to Brooklyn or Bushwick, spaces like that. It's always changing, and it has to do with the cities and how they're planning their economies.

Caden: I actually tell people not to move to New York City. I think you can find interesting cultures or artists all over the country—in Detroit, Pittsburgh, LA, Portland, Seattle, Austin. The problem is that for people who want to tour in Europe, the Europeans don't actually go there. They only come to New York and sometimes LA.

Jemma: And that's something that really endangers cultural exchange. In the US, Americans were taking their work and showing it around throughout the '60s and '70s and '80s. The importance of that exchange diminished in our society and for our government. Still, there's nothing that really replaces going to another city or asking the artist to perform there or having those encounters.

Manson and Nelson remain connected to academia. They collaborate with scholars, write articles, and teach in universities. Nelson is the author of several articles about contemporary performance, and Manson is the graduate directing option coordinator of the John Wells Directing Program at Carnegie Mellon University.

You mentioned the government. Do you get public funding to produce your works?

Caden: There are some very small state grants. I would say there are four or five grants in the country that are quite large. You can get anywhere from $20,000–$40,000. There's commissioning, and you have to look for different kinds of grant or partnership.

Would you say that to be a successful artist in the US you need to be a good businessperson?

Caden: I think an artist needs a businessperson. It needs to be someone in the company who can understand it.

Jemma: In the US, you have commercial theaters and nonprofit theaters. But still, the nonprofit art world is very close to a commercial model, and it does benefit the artist to have a business partner or their own understanding of business—to take ownership themselves and be their own entrepreneur.

Caden: It's problematic to say "entrepreneur." A lot of artists get really upset, "How dare you say I'm an entrepreneur? Don't essentialize me like that. I'm not part of that machine!" But at the same time, we founded a company that hired all of these people, a company that toured all over the world. That *is* kind of an entrepreneur, even though you aren't thinking that way. You're an entrepreneur towards an artistic goal.

It seems that a good "entrepreneur" is a person who is not only good at looking for financial support but also at promoting the artwork. Big Art Group communicates with a website, Twitter account, and Facebook page. Do you think these platforms are important to reach an audience?

Caden: Yes, definitely! I think more and more audiences want to be engaged in the process. So a lot of it is communicating from the rehearsal room. People want to be there. They feel more invested in the work and in the ideas of the work.

What advice would you give to young artists who want to make it on the experimental scene?

Caden: The main thing is that the work has to be good. It's really the most important thing. Your work has to be good, and you have to make relationships. A lot of people get freaked out about the idea of networking, but you have to understand that networking really is just finding people who you have the same affiliations with. You should also do your research on presenters and know what they do so that you're not going to presenters who wouldn't be interested in your work. Presenters are individuals, and you should be able to talk to them about their work.

Jemma: However you define *success*, it's good to set goals and say, "I want to do this kind of project or I want to go here." But there are many different ways to get there.

Caden: And say "yes" as much as possible. When we started Big Art Group, if anyone asked us to do something, we would say "yes."

EMELINE JOUVE is Assistant Professor of American Literature and Culture at Champollion University and Toulouse Jean-Jaurès University in France. She is the chair of the English department at Champollion University. She has given papers at international conferences in France, Spain, and the US on Susan Glaspell, Eugene O'Neill, Gertrude Stein, Paula Vogel, the Wooster Group, and Big Art Group, and she has published articles in European and American journals and anthologies. She edited the issue on "Staging Mobility in the United States" for the peer-reviewed journal *Miranda*. She is the author of Susan Glaspell's *Poetics and Politics of Rebellion*, and she co-edited Susan Glaspell's *Trifles and "A Jury of Her Peers": Centennial Essays, Interviews, and Adaptations* with Martha C. Carpentier (forthcoming). Jouve is also the editor of "Ariel's Corner: theatre" for *Miranda*. Apart from her academic work, Jouve is also involved in the practice of theater.

Emeline Jouve

WORKING IN CORPORATE ENTERTAINMENT

▶ An Interview With Lisa Kovach

Lisa Kovach is a talent and event management specialist who has been booking talent for corporate entertainment, charitable organizations, and special events for more than twenty-five years. At Walt Disney Entertainment, she created high-profile themed events that featured celebrities and integrated multicultural talent, international dignitaries, and top-level corporate executives. She's now a senior vice president for Key Artist Group, a talent and event production company based out of Orlando. Kovach books and works with actors on a daily basis.

Lisa Kovach

Can you tell me a little about what you do and how you find work for actors?

Sure. I don't specifically find work for actors. I hire actors. Our bread and butter is the corporate market, so it's my job to service my existing clients, and that could be anybody from a destination management company or a corporate producer, even a meeting planner from a corporation. I work with them and help them figure out what entertainment they would like when they come to town or wherever they happen to be going. We work worldwide. For corporate, in particular, they might come in and want a welcome reception, so we have atmospheric entertainment, musical entertainment, animals, etc. And then they might have a general session, and this is probably where I would use more of my actors. We might do an opener, maybe a skit, to open up some of their sessions.

What is a general session?

A general session for a corporate event is when everybody coming to the conference gets into a room, and they hear the messages from the corporate headquarters—whatever messages the corporation wants conveyed through their conference to their sales team, management team, favorite vendors, etc. Usually they're larger scale, but they can range anywhere from twenty-five people to thousands.

So you'll hire actors to perform or open up this event?

Exactly. And there will be a range of needs or desires from the corporation.

How do you come across your actors?

I've been in this town for twenty-five years now, and I've developed relationships with a lot of actors. I will call them and ask, "Hey, can you do this?" And then I book them.

Do these actors have agents?

I generally go to them directly. I usually don't have to go through anyone's agent. A lot of actors in town, they might sign up with several agencies in Orlando to get work on commercials or auditions for movies or print ads. My particular needs are very different from those types of agency. Sometimes I'll go to an agency if I need a bevy of models and I don't feel like sourcing them myself. But for the most part, I'll go directly to my actors. I'm a licensed talent agent—and in Florida, you need to work with a licensed talent agency.

> "Sometimes we need a narrator who's got the deep booming voice. Sometimes I need somebody who looks like a Ken doll who can give out awards, with a Barbie look-alike. Improv is also huge in corporate. But sometimes I need people who can handle memorization and script work. I often need somebody who can MC. MC skills are very marketable in my business."

Do most actors in Orlando have multiple agents? It's kosher to have multiple agents?

Well, it depends on the individual actor's deal with their agent, but most people I know are signed with multiple agencies. The actors aren't really my clients. I don't have actors signed with me. I have odd things signed with me—I have a musical comedian, a corporate dance band, an MC, and a 1980s rock guy who does keynote speeches, living statues, things like that.

How do you find new talent?

Many different ways. One of my favorite things to do is to source new talent. I'll often talk to people I know and say, "Hey, I know you don't really do this sort of thing, but do you know anyone who fits this description and skillset?" And they say, "Oh, yeah, I met so-and-so the other day. Give them a call." That's one way I find people. I also Google people for strange requests. For example, once I needed a unique way to serve wine to guests, so I discovered an acting company out of Chicago that creates the most magnificent acts, and they have a wine bicycle.

You found them by Googling? Any other marketing tactics actors could use that might help you find them?

Having a web presence is important, but I also have actors approach me all the time. They find me and submit resumés and headshots, or they write me letters. They'll say, "If you ever need somebody like me, let me know." They direct market to me. We're one of the top ten agencies in corporate entertainment in the country. We're a small agency but we're mighty.

I also belong to an organization called the International Special Events Society with the unfortunate acronym, ISES. I was president of ISES this past year, and a lot of talent will join organizations geared toward the special events industry. There's also Meeting Planners International and National Association of Catering and Events, so a lot of actors join those groups to meet people like me one on one.

What are the drawbacks to working in corporate entertainment? Why might an actor not want to work in an industrial or corporate capacity?

Well, you're most likely working on a contract or per-job basis. So if you're looking for a steady paycheck, insurance, and benefits, you usually won't get that unless you're on the payroll of a company like Event Show Productions out of Tampa, for example. They hire people as true employees who get paid whether or not they're dancing or doing whatever type of performance they're doing.

Is there an age, or a look, or a type, or a special skill that is oversaturated with competition? Or are there certain skills, looks, or ages are so rare that it's harder for you to find the talent?

With actors, it really depends. I use actors of all ages. They must be over legal drinking age to really be on the floor at a lot of corporate events, so you need to be at least 21. And that's kind of a general rule of thumb if there's alcohol being served. But it really depends on what kind of needs we have. Sometimes we need a narrator who's got the deep booming voice. Sometimes I need somebody who looks like a Ken doll who can give out awards, with a Barbie look-alike. Improv is also huge in corporate. But sometimes I need people who can handle memorization and script work. I often need somebody who can MC. MC skills are very marketable in my business.

What are you looking for in an MC?

I require a video of them doing it before I'll work with someone. For example, I'm casting for a show that's in two weeks from tonight, but I need an MC who looks like he's from *Burning Man*. It's very specific. I need a really edgy, hip, young, energetic guy who can work with people from Western Europe, can introduce acts, and can appreciate and talk to a DJ spinning electronic dance music. So it's often specific like that, my needs.

What would the pay be for that gig, the MC gig you're describing?

I might pay him $800.

For an evening?

Yeah, it might be a four-hour gig. Four hours for $800.

And is that pretty standard across the board for four hours?

Not necessarily. With the improv actors, I might pay $100 an hour to the producers who then pay their people maybe $60 or $75 an hour, probably.

But when you go straight to the talent as opposed to going to a producer, it could be anywhere from $100 to $200 an hour?

Probably $75 to $200 an hour, depending on what I'm asking of them and what kind of budget these people have. My job as a talent agent is to be on the side of the talent. I've got to get them money, make sure they're okay, but at the same time, I have to make sure my client gets good value for the money. The rates fluctuate a lot based on the corporation coming to me.

Lisa with actors Steph Carse and Michael Cochran at a corporate event in Orlando, Florida

When a corporation comes to you and they have an event, is there a standard entertainment budget?
Absolutely no standard at all. It really just depends on what they feel like budgeting toward entertainment.

I imagine that corporate acting is likely outside of most actors' highest aspirations, but if they're looking to do this on the side as they pursue theater and film or television work, what advice would you have so that they can set themselves up for success and appear professional?
The biggest thing is that I don't have time to groom people from the ground floor. People have to come to me ready to go. I'm busy, and if I get unprofessional stuff or weird packages, I can't handle it. I need professional headshots, full body shots, and a resumé that's in a format I can manipulate if I need to. I need to be able to take off their contact information, for instance. A lot of times, people send me a PDF, and it's got their home phone on there. I can't send that, so I have to fool around and get rid of it—and it's a pain in my neck. And if it's too much of a pain in the neck, I'm moving on to the next guy. That's the way it is. So headshots and full body shots, very helpful. A comp card—a composition card—is great.

Also, go to a professional place, get professional shots, different looks, and a good resumé that's well written, no typos, and preferably in an editable form. They can have a couple versions of these things, too. I have to send it on to my clients, who often send it on to another client, and so on. Also, I need people to respond to me quickly. If I reach out, I need a call right back. I need valid contact information. I don't want to wait twenty-four hours. I'll move on. Clients these days are all about video. There's a trend where they need to see everything on video, so I need video that is unbranded, meaning I need no contact information on it. Vimeo is great. YouTube is great. If they make private channels, that's even better. No contact information should be visible.

> "We need people with big personalities who can interact, be on stage, are able to speak, can product launch or deliver workshops."

And no contact information, why? Because you need the client to go through you and not directly to the talent?
That's correct.

So would you suggest that if an actor gets signed with an agent, they check to make sure it's okay to interact directly with someone like you without having the agent's contact information on the resume?
Probably a good idea. But they at least need to have a version of their resumé and headshot that I can send forward without contact information on there. But I generally try to book my talent directly. I don't want to have to book through another agency. For the most part, I'm looking to book direct.

And that's pretty common in corporate entertainment?
Yes, but I have some things that are exclusive on my roster that people have to come to me for, like my Living World Entertainment, for example. I have these amazing characters that I've had exclusively for ten years, and we're never giving them up. If you want to book them, you've got to call us.

Is everything that you do stage based? It's all live performers?
Ninety-nine percent of it is, yes.

Do you ever have a need for speakers—or speakers who are also speechwriters?

Sometimes, facilitators. We need people with big personalities who can interact, be on stage, are able to speak, can product launch or deliver workshops. I work with them on occasion, too. Most likely, a production company might work with a speechwriter to help them with a weeklong program and have everything scripted out for their executives.

That seems like another potential avenue for actors.

Oh, yeah. I once had an actor come in three different days as this really over-the-top character. She would open up before the general session got started and would mix and mingle with the people in the seats. She was a sort of wild-looking character with big hair and glasses. Another production company booked her through me. They needed somebody, and I provided her.

Final advice for the actor?

Be a professional. Professionals work with professionals, and nobody has time for sloppy—so just make sure you're ready before you put yourself out there.

SOCIALLY CONSCIOUS THEATER
Acting as a Vessel for Change
► By Christina Rodriguez de Conte

With 600 miles of road ahead, ten women piled into a rented van on the eve of the 2009 Atlanta Gay Pride Festival, driven by a simple mission: Hand out as many PR packets and sell as many DVDs as possible.

Our web series, *The Lovers & Friends Show*, followed the lives of ethnic lesbians in South Florida and had just begun streaming on the internet. Who were we? A group of women—artists, bartenders, barbers, bankers, nannies, students, and teachers. Together, we developed a website, produced our own show, and distributed our own work.

Our ingenuity was revolutionary at the time for two reasons: 1) because of the otherwise-ignored ethnic lesbian audience we were able to connect to, and 2) because of our ability to self-distribute. Almost accidentally, *Lovers & Friends* (*LNF*) became a form of socially conscious theater, both on screen and off, as it moved from merely entertainment into community outreach.

When theater expands beyond the fourth wall and into the community, it becomes an exploration beyond the intersection of the fictional and the future—a place where activism and art present possibilities for change. As we arrived in Atlanta in 2009, *LNF* found itself the vessel of that change. After a long night of meeting, greeting, and elbow rubbing, the cast appeared to sign DVDs and give a talk at a local, queer lesbian-owned bookstore.

> We did our own bookings for *LNF*, and all of the women involved contributed in various ways. I recall digging through dumpsters to find props—and better yet, marching in a gay pride festival in the pouring rain, in heels! We were all hands on deck. All egos at the stage door.

Surprisingly, the bookstore wasn't filled with masses of people or major corporate conglomerates that would launch our careers. Instead, the room was filled with local lesbians who felt their stories were finally represented. Yes, *The L Word* was groundbreaking, but it was also limiting in its representation. *LNF* connected to the population who found little resonance with mainstream entertainment.

In retrospect, I hover over this moment in my life with equal parts adoration and frustration. Considering our limited funding and womanpower, we managed to attend multiple pride fests a season, and we used social media for as much free PR as possible. The fruits of our labor ripened, and *LNF* was picked up by Wolfe Distributors—and it continues to sell as queer art within a commercialized artistic industry. Yet, I'm left unsatisfied. To fit into what we considered "success," I believe we relied on the usual media tactics that called for overtly sexualized stories. Did we leave causes behind? Did we perpetuate stereotypes? In some ways, I question my own artistic integrity.

We all need to bring in income—and as theater artists, the ultimate goal, it seems, is to make a living with our art. But the economic oracle that paves our path demands that we question the shackles that limit the understanding of success. Entertainment is a capitalistic endeavor, rendering a loose interpretation of artistic intention. What is theater's place within society, and how can we engage with it to find our own version of success? How can theater artists fund socially conscious work without leaning too heavily into the agendas of private investors? How can theater artists produce a space where performance can coexist with community and flourish financially?

These are the questions that theater artists intent on producing socially conscious theater must grapple with. But first, most simply, perhaps we should start with the question: What *is* socially conscious theater?

Christina Rodriguez de Conte performing the "stereotypical Dyke" in her one-woman show, *Other*

Socially Conscious Theater, an Overview

Theater and society often overlap in meaning and interpretation. Those of the Brechtian persuasion might disagree, claiming art to be autonomous, but I can't help but question how art can be without purpose. Even in the most organically contrived settings, theater cannot exist without social construction and commentary—therefore, our responsibility as artists is to use theater to do just that, to comment on society.

The definition of *community* supports that of socially conscious theater. The geeky wordsmith in me chooses to look at the etymology of the word. *Community* stems from *common* and *public*, something shared by everyone in society. We find the word *community* in Webster's full definition of the word *commune*: "to communicate *with* someone or something in a very personal or spiritual way."[2] Thus, I suggest that community itself is a spiritual experience, shared by all.

This kind of theater work has many names: "theater for social justice," "theater in human rights," "political theater," "socially conscious theater," or in a broader sense, "community cultural development." I choose the name "socially conscious theater" because it encompasses the essence of all these definitions, describing a theater focused on social issues to establish awareness and to create a movement of change within the community.

The use of performance as a means to spark debate and educate the masses is not new. Since the birth of language, we performed oral histories to preserve speakers' ideals and to explore and establish new ones. The origin of theater and community education and activism would be impossible to declare. Within theater studies, some consider German director Erwin Piscator the "father of political theater." Heavily influenced by the great world wars and the artists and thinkers these wars rendered, such as Dada and Marx, Piscator rejected the idea that theater's sole purpose was amusement. Instead, as described by Canadian theater scholar Christopher Innes, Piscator "emphasized the effect of political events" on the development of his work while developing agitprop theatrical responses to a propaganda-driven society.[3]

Bertolt Brecht, student of Piscator and one of the most influential theater practitioners of the 20th century, developed Piscator's style into what we now label "epic theater." Brecht's alienation effect led to an approach to theater that allowed for deconstruction beyond the artistic and into the core of societal issues.

Paulo Freire and Augusto Boal were two other artists whose works speak to each other and expand on Brecht's aesthetic by combining political theater with community engagement and education. Freire's look at education in relation to power manifested itself into his influential literary work, *Pedagogy of the Oppressed*. Boal built on Freire's ideas and explored how theater could be used to address the imbalance within society to create change. In his 1992 book, *Games for Actors and Non-Actors*, translated by Adrian Jackson, Boal states:

> Imagine a theatre show in which we, the artists, would present our world view in the first half, and in the second half the audience could create a new world, invent their own future by trying out their own options.[4]

This impetus to provide people with tools to create change through theater informs the discussion in these pages about theater for social change and within our respective communities. When discussing both the origins and the contributors of socially conscious theater, I propose a warning, heeded by black feminist theorist, bell hooks: "Without adequate concrete knowledge of and contact with the non-white 'Other,' white theorists may move in discursive theoretical directions that are threatening and potentially disruptive of that critical practice which would support radical liberation struggle."[5]

In other words, as theater artists, we must seek out knowledge beyond the usual canon of theorists. We must move off the page and into the streets to generate concrete change. Change often occurs rapidly—and it is difficult, if not impossible, to know everything happening within theater and community. But our responsibility as artists is to investigate who is doing what where and how we can get involved. We must talk to the people to discover what is needed. We must first listen, and the art will come.

Socially Conscious Theater, Then and Now

Within socially conscious theater, we find political demonstrations turned to theater, organizations that use theater as a tool for larger discussions, and individuals who have created work to address a specific social issue. An example of a fifty-year-old collective that has transformed from political demonstrations to theater for and by its community is El Teatro Campesino. Founded by Luis Valdez in 1965, the company focused on the struggles of the United Farmworkers Union by performing short skits called "actos." The power theater held in instigating dialogue was quickly evident and fueled the organization's professional development. Valdez's play, *Zoot Suit* (1977) is one of the most successful plays to come out of Los Angeles—not to mention, the first Latino play produced on Broadway. This organization's work continues today, most recently collaborating with the Monterey County Office of Education to develop a K-12 school curriculum.[6]

Other individuals who have deeply contributed to socially conscious theater include Robbie McCauley, playwright and performer of *Sally's Rape* and *Sugar*, and Anna Deavere Smith, playwright and performer of *Fires in the Mirror* and *Twilight*. Both African American artists serve as excellent models for actors. Although each woman has her own presence and artistic power, I join them here because of the manner in which they gather their material. They begin their artistic journey as story collectors and then transform into writers to discover profoundly insightful material rooted in experience.

In an interview with Nic Paget-Clarke in *In Motion Magazine*, McCauley expresses her approach as the "culture of telling stories, of taking time to share experiences." She says:

> There is a kind of familiarity of the story, but at the same time people want to hear it in different voices in the community over and over again. Stories are passed down. They are told by different people. And that is something that I admire. It helps me to recognize that that kind of human quality is basic to art.[7]

This approach to socially conscious theater taps deep into the experiences of each individual that shapes the communal identity. McCauley and Deavere Smith's methods inspire a safe and intimate way of addressing socially taboo subjects.

Artists and organizations today continue to contribute to theater with a social consciousness and an inclination toward art as activism. In many communities worldwide, the mothers of those persecuted by social injustices use

Theater artist and professor Robbie McCauley, best known for her plays *Sally's Rape* and *Sugar*

Photo courtesy of Artsemerson

protest as performance to spotlight their outrage against governmental violations of human rights. We see these performances from organizations such as Cuba's Las Damas de Blanco, Argentina's Madres de Plaza de Mayo, and Mexico's Nuestras Hijas de Regreso a Casa, who produced *Mujeres de Arena*, a play comprised of experiences by relatives or diary entries of women who have been abducted and continue to be missing from Ciudad Juarez, Mexico. These women use theater to educate the world about the injustices plaguing their people.

Educational outreach is pivotal to producing effective socially conscious theater. Two organizations worth noting that continue to produce theater within community to instigate dialogue are the Theatre Offensive and the Medea Project. The Theatre Offensive focuses on work with LGBTQA youth in Boston, and the Medea Project is a San Francisco-based organization for incarcerated women that explores whether an "arts-based approach" can lower the number of women returning to jail. Currently, this organization uses theater to reach out to women around the world with the purpose of breaking the silence and stigmas of HIV.[8]

Where Do You Fit In?

This is the all-consuming question when finding inspiration in artists, educators, and activists who create socially conscious theater. Community engagement is ever-changing and evolving, and so is our place as artists within it. But however complicated the world may seem, we, those who reside in it and are nurtured by it, are responsible for ensuring its well-being.

I was reminded of this at a National Civil Rights Educators' Institute held in the summer of 2015. We explored how civil rights and education are influenced by the stock stories perpetuated in our history books and how concealed stories reveal themselves through community engagement. We met Japanese Internment Camp survivor Richard Yada and two of the Little Rock Nine members, Thelma Mothershed-Wair and Minnijean Brown Trickey, and we witnessed how their concealed stories of oppression instigated a dialogue among young adults. Something Trickey said in this interview remains engrained in my psyche: "In a democracy, it is our responsibility to question, critique, and create."[9]

The first three letters in the word *ACTivism* have since grown from beyond my peripheral and into my direct line of sight—a tunnel vision of performance as activism. Our responsibility as theater artists is to ACT.

There are many avenues by which artists can ACT and create social change, and the arts are not the only way to achieve such change. But as witnessed by Boal's troupe and other performers previously mentioned, theater can bridge the gap between talk and action.

Why does one choose this type of theater as a career path? On a personal level, I enjoy performing an assortment of characters on a traditional stage. The voice lessons, dance exercises, and acting classes allow me to mold my craft and honor any character with reverence. Even still, I always found myself working an *industry* and not a *stage*. The realities of the business we call *show* are stark: You spend more time looking for the audition than it takes to actually work the gig, and there are minimal gigs out there with a rainbow of characters. Socially conscious theater allowed me to restructure my career, as well as my understanding of how I defined "success." My conclusion was that by creating work that had the ability to instigate consciousness toward change within my community, I was—and would continue to be—a success.

You're Game! Now What?

If you've made the decision to pave a path that isn't Broadway bound but instead bound to social action, the next step is to address questions about balancing money and social awareness. Socially conscious theater as a form of entertainment resonates with the non-profit organizational model, primarily in its strategic management and structure. In Sharon M. Oster's book, *Strategic Management for Nonprofit Organizations: Theory and Cases*, she refers to the "constellation of particular characteristics" that define a nonprofit organization.[10] Oster categorizes these characteristics into:

- Community engagement
- Collaboration with labor-intense volunteers
- A heavy reliance on donations and nonprofit revenue

We can emulate this model when producing socially conscious theater within the community. Some artists file for nonprofit status, but that's not always necessary or beneficial. The crucial reality, though, is that one needs money to sustain a business.

First and foremost, as theater artists, we must identify ourselves as a product within a business. Like any business, we need to brand ourselves and take the time to write contracts. There's an artist at every port with a story of woe and betrayal—one that could have been prevented with a signed contract. With that in place, we must make the choice to conduct business that is socially responsible. By applying grassroots tactics that use crowdfunding, community events, and social media to generate a following, we can create a business whose success is correlated with community enhancement as opposed to financial wealth. Moreover, we must extinguish the lines between performer, director, producer, technician, and activist. Our roles must be flexible and the artistic process extended to include all areas of theater.

A business survives on two things: product and revenue. Once you've identified yourself and your work as a product and branded it as such, the next step is to identify the community you wish to engage with so that your strategy for obtaining revenue—as well as your strategy for social engagement—is clear and focused.

> Community members' contributions to making theater art will vary. Some participate creatively, others volunteer time, and there are those who donate money. In the four years I worked on *LNF*, I solicited help from as many friends and family members as I could—no one was left unscathed. My parents' house, my aunt's house, a best friend's living room, local coffee houses and pubs, even the ally of the local community playhouse all became locations for our humbly growing show.
>
> Don't be afraid to ask for help. You'll be surprised who is willing to help and in what facet. Collective thinking, combined with collaborative efforts, spun by the hand of a creative inspiration is a force to be reckoned with!

Following Oster's constellation of characteristics, the final—and most important—aspect of any socially conscious theater is funding. There are as many ways to fund theater as there are to make it. Your organization or production needs money, and someone else has that money. You ask them for it. They give it to you.

Your success in raising funds depends on who you're asking and how you choose to approach them. Do your research. Know who funds what types of project for how much and their standard process for allocating monies.

Technology has drastically changed the process for raising money for the arts. Through different applications, programs or crowdfunding websites, such as

Kickstarter and Indiegogo, artists can now launch and manage their own fundraising campaign. Additionally, social media cost-effective ways to reach people and promote your project. Last, consider partnerships with community organizations with a 501(c)3 status whose mission backs your own. This can be another route to take when planning funding opportunities for your organization.

Theater artists can be a vessel for change, be it a shift in what society deems successful or how art can function within those parameters. Socially conscious theater is a viable professional option, one rooted in community and dialogue. This theater is for those who walk the streets and see possibility. The world is a stage for us to ACT on. I invite you to use your art to join the conscious conversation about promoting change through theater and explore how you can contribute your theatrical talents and skills to better the world and our time while we're here.

CHRISTINA RODRIGUEZ DE CONTE is a theater artist, educator, and activist. Her doctoral research at Florida State University focuses primarily on gender as performance and lesbian theater, and she received her masters in Theatre & Community from Emerson College, where she completed her training in theater of the oppressed. She studied at the prestigious New York City TOPLAB, which continues to inform her pedagogical approaches as well as her art. Most recently, de Conte wrote and performed in *Other*, a comedic one-woman show that explores gender perception and otherness. Her alter ego, King Chris Rod, has been performing as a Drag King at community events nationally.

Christina Rodriguez de Conte

THE ACTOR WHO WRITES

Another Tool for Your Toolbox

► By Robert Hedley

It's six o'clock on what has been a gleaming bright day in October. In Philadelphia, Jennifer Childs is washing dishes and singing to herself in a boozy British accent, writing song lyrics on her feet for a workshop of her new show, *I Will Not Go Gently*. Across town, Tony Lawton is fine-tuning some lyrics in his adaptation of *The Light Princess*, by George MacDonald. James Ijames is on an Amtrak train after spending a week in New York at the Lark Play Development Center working on his play *Moon Man Walk*. In Los Angeles, it's three o'clock and Shem Bitterman is putting the finishing touches on a rewrite of his new comedy, *Stranger Danger* for New York director Kareem Fahmy before hopping on his bike to pick up his son, Ezra, from middle school.

The link among these four, besides their successes as writers, is that they all trained as actors. Although performance remains an essential part of their busy lives, writing has opened doors, satisfied artistic ambitions, provided work in dry periods, brought them recognition, and otherwise rounded out committed artistic lives.

But who are they?

Jennifer Childs is the Co-Founder and Producing Artistic Director of 1812 Productions, a Philadelphia-based theater company dedicated to comedy. For 1812, she has created over twenty original works of comedic theater. Her solo show, *Why I'm Scared of Dance by Jen Childs*, has been presented at Delaware Theatre Company, Act 2 Playhouse, City Theatre in Pittsburgh, and the Kohler Arts Center in Wisconsin.

Jennifer Childs

Photo by Mark Garvin

Tony Lawton, a regular on all the major stages in Philadelphia, has adapted and performed C.S. Lewis' *The Great Divorce* and *The Screwtape Letters*, as well as creating original solo pieces.

Tony Lawton

Photo by James J. Kriegsmann Jr.

James Ijames is a three-time Barrymore Award-winning actor and playwright, and in 2011 he received the F. Otto Haas Award for an Emerging Artist.

James Ijames

Photo by Kim Carson

Shem Bitterman is an award-winning playwright and screenwriter. His plays have been developed and produced at the Mark Taper Forum, the Actor's Theatre of Louisville, Steppenwolf, Midwest Playlabs, Sundance, among others.

Because they all started as actors, let's find out why and how they became writers. Acting is almost never a nine-to-five job (who would want it to be?), and it's also irregular. Meaning that you will have "down time" even in the midst of success. Could writing be something you might like to try? Would you like to have a monologue that really suits you? How about a scene based on some of your experiences?

Shem Bitterman

Photo by Andy Romanoff

My own experience, from a career in play development that started in the mid-1960s, is that actors make terrific writers. A working knowledge of theater and an intimate knowledge of plays can jumpstart a new adventure in writing. At

Iowa, where I headed the Playwrights Workshop, we encouraged writers to act—through an informal, catch-as-catch-can weekly "Midnight Madness," literally starting at midnight and thoroughly mad. The intent was serious, however, because we wanted plays written for the stage, not the classroom. But if you are already an actor, you have a head start.

Remember, the more tools in your toolbox, the more opportunities you have. As UCLA's Coach Wooden reminds us, "When opportunity comes, it's too late to prepare."

Let's talk about how you four came to writing.

Jennifer: I started writing because I was looking for something that didn't seem to be out there, and I realized that if I really wanted to find it, I had to make it myself. My first theatrical writing was done for children actually. I was co-teaching a summer camp that needed to culminate in a performance. My partner and I searched the shelves and catalogues for plays that were age appropriate, laugh-out-loud funny, and had enough roles and equal stage time for thirty students. We couldn't find any. So we wrote our own. I don't think we had any pretensions as playwrights—we just had a deadline and no idea what else to do.

Tony: I started writing and producing my own work when I realized that no one else was going to write or produce the kind of stuff I wanted to do. Another thing that prompted me to write my own stuff was the feeling of powerlessness I often had as an actor. Directors and designers seemed to have the last word in most matters, and I wanted a feeling of authorship over at least some of my work.

James: When I was about 13, my grandmother asked me to write a "play" for our church Christmas program. I used to write little poems when I was young, and she thought it would be something I could do. So that was the first play I wrote, and it was long before I realized anyone did theater for a living. After working as an actor for several years, I think I felt a void I wanted to fill—first for myself and then for my friends. I realized there weren't a lot of playwrights who were writing for people of color. It was several years after graduate school before I even played a character that was written specifically for a person of color. So initially, I wanted to write plays that I would want to do. Over time, I discovered that playwriting was a way to engage with issues and ideas that I had a great deal of passion around. So I threw myself pretty wholehearted into writing about five years ago.

Shem: I was studying acting at Juilliard, and we were working at the time—in the late '70s—almost primarily on classical texts. I enjoyed it, and, of course, the texts spoke to "universal" truths—but at the same time, there was a lot of specialized language, arcane phrases, and words that had gone out of circulation. Also, the historical interval between many of the texts I was working on and the world in which I was living included the Industrial Revolution, Freud, Marx, Evolution, the Holocaust, and Stalin, to name a few. I wanted to write plays because I thought theater should be about contemporary concerns told in a contemporary way. There should be immediacy and accessibility. It shouldn't necessitate a specialized way of hearing or require translation or explication. Which is not to say I didn't think theater should be abstract. I just felt that it should be contemporary, and the clearest way to do contemporary theater was to write it myself. My quest for immediacy may have climaxed when I wrote a two-act play in one day and made it to the bar before it closed. I was trying to write it as fast as it would be seen!

All of you were responding to a need, but what happened next? Where did you find your material?

Tony: I was largely into doing stuff that I regarded as having a deep spiritual core, much of it influenced by—or dealing with—the Judeo-Christian paradigm. I am interested in the question of how we interface with the entity that many call God. I didn't see anyone else doing that kind of work—or if I did, I didn't think much of the writing or direction—so I took matters into my own hands. I adapted C.S. Lewis' *The Great Divorce* in 1998, his *Screwtape Letters* in 2000.

> "I wanted to write plays because I thought theater should be about contemporary concerns told in a contemporary way. There should be immediacy and accessibility."

Jennifer: When I stopped writing for summer camp and started writing for my company, I was initially attracted to writing about comedic history. I was fascinated by how comedy, like hemlines, has changed through the ages—and what we are laughing at says a great deal about where we are as a society. My first plays were curated collections of comics and comedic styles of different eras. I would immerse myself in the study of a time period and the comedy that characterized and came out of it and create these living archive shows that contained both vintage and original material. Some of my favorites were *The Big Time*, which was all about vaudeville, *Like Crazy Like Wow*, which looked at 1950s nightclub comedy and the huge political, social, and comedic change that happened during that decade, and *Always A Lady*, which traced the history of women in comedy through the 20th century. I was having so much fun, I don't think I realized what a wonderful writing education I was giving myself.

Shem: When I was starting out, Sam Shepard was the rage. He was the gold standard by which young writers measured themselves. His theater at the time was visceral, surprising, poetic, and authentic. At the same time, we wanted to overthrow Shepard. We felt he was also part of the disease of cultishness. Whenever someone stands above someone else and becomes a "standard," there is a danger of homogenization. What I wanted mainly was to write the world as I saw it, with as many of the internal complications that troubled me as I could muster.

James: History and current events. That's not particularly novel, but I think the way I interact with the material perhaps is. My plays are trying to rearrange the audiences' perceptions about the people and events laid before them. For example, my play *White* is presented as a play about visual art and property as it pertains to authorship. The style of the play is realism that becomes increasingly hyper-realistic as the play unfolds. By the end of the play, the idea of art and property is exaggerated to the point that an actual person is being bought and owned by a museum. The audience expects one set of events and is left with something completely new. History and current events allows this to work well, because the audience comes to the theater expecting to know what the play will be, and that's subverted over the evening.

How did you learn to write for the stage—and for yourself?

Shem: Acting taught me how to write for the stage. Being an actor meant I wrote for myself first, wrote the kinds of moment I would enjoy playing.

Jennifer: As an actor, a part of my training is pretending to be other people, giving myself over not only to the hearts and passions of the characters I am playing but to the rhythms, vocabulary, and structure created by the playwright. In studying all these different comedians, I was learning their rhythms, vocabulary, and structure and started to be able to write in their style. I spent a lot of time imitating other people's comedic style before I finally found my own.

Tony: My experience on stage taught me a few basic things about writing for the stage. For example, conflict and struggle are, in general, a lot more stage-worthy than narration, analysis, poetry, or just about any other kind of writing. And things are a lot more dramatic in the present than in the past, as a rule.

I learned to like language and writing from a nun when I was in the 6th grade. I learned a lot of good Strunk and White fundamentals of simplicity, clarity, force, and style when I was in a Great Books program in college. After that, the writers whose work I performed were my "training wheels." The first work I produced on my own was Shel Silverstein's *The Devil and Billy Markham*, which I had no hand in writing, but I think learning his words was a bit of an education in what kind of writing does and doesn't work on stage. I next adapted the two Lewis pieces, using as much of his language as possible (I didn't think I could improve on him), but playing a heavy role myself in the editing. *The Foocy* I adapted from my own prose, cutting and pasting large bits of the story into the script. I didn't really write anything 100 percent original for the stage till I did my autobiographical work in 2009. Up until then, I'd been leaning heavily on the work of other writers.

James: I've learned primarily from being in really great plays and working on great texts. I've had the pleasure of performing Shakespeare, Oscar Wilde, Lynn Nottage, Tony Kushner, Anton Chekhov, August Wilson, Suzan-Lori Parks, and Michael Hollinger. You don't work in these masters without learning a thing or two about how to write and how a play works. I read a lot of plays. I read plays the way most people read novels. I study plays to try to unlock their magic. This has been instrumental in my development.

> "I've had the pleasure of performing Shakespeare, Oscar Wilde, Lynn Nottage, Tony Kushner, Anton Chekhov, August Wilson, Suzan-Lori Parks, and Michael Hollinger. You don't work in these masters without learning a thing or two about how to write and how a play works."

Do you have any specific advice for a young actor who wants to write for the theater?

Jennifer: I think every actor should have to study improvisation, and it should be mandatory for any actor who wants to write. At its root, it is about saying,

"Yes and . . ." to any idea that comes along, not judging your choices or second-guessing your instincts. With this in mind, I was able to take a word or an object or a very simple idea as a starting place and allow the character and monologue to develop from there. I didn't worry about it being the best idea or the right idea, I just went with the first idea that came to my mind and edited later. It's about getting past the first sentence and into the unknown. Sometimes it's terrible—or worse, mediocre. But sometimes it's genius.

Yes, your work includes a great deal of improvisation. That was particularly true of *Why I'm Scared of Dance by Jen Childs*.

Jennifer: Being an actor/improviser also enabled me to do a good deal of writing on my feet—which I still do when I feel stuck. Instead of sitting down to write, I will often play the character, talk to myself, and improvise as the person I'm inventing. I think I do more "writing" while riding my bike or cleaning the bathroom than I do sitting at the computer.

What about the rest of you?

Tony: The sound of words can be as important as their meaning. I would urge aspiring writers to learn as much as possible about language, writing, and stage craft, and then forget all of it in the act of writing. Unless you feel that "rules" and principles are making your writing stronger, I think they are only obstacles. Learn from audiences—not so much from what they say after the show, as from how they react in the moment. Pay attention to when they fidget and cough. That's not their fault—that's the artist's fault.

Shem: Right. There is no substitute for seeing your work performed. It's only when watching an audience squirming in its seat that one realizes the true amount of cutting and shaping that must be done to make a play stage-worthy.

I strive to write actor-proof parts, but what that really means is that I try to write parts that any actor can comfortably fit themselves in. I try to allow room to breathe and soar. I want what an actor brings. I no longer feel I have to play the roles myself. I feel the same about directors and all collaborators. Some writers write with a dictatorial hand, demanding line readings and precise enunciation of every written word, with no extra to spare. I've come to appreciate eccentricity and individuality. I think ultimately audiences do, too.

James: I don't know that being an actor gives me an advantage. I do tend to think about what an actor can reasonably do in performance as I write, which

I think sometimes is a disadvantage. With that said, I consider the things that I as an actor love to do. For example, large emotional journeys are so satisfying for me. The more sweeping the better, so I try to build that into the characters. Another example is lush language as opposed to cinematic pedestrian language. I want material that transports, so I try to do that with my plays as well.

How would you describe how playwriting enhances you as a human or as an actor?

Jennifer: Writing has now become a major part of my professional life. 1812 Productions is a theater company specializing in comedy, and I create a good portion of the work we produce each year. Over the years, writing—and specifically comedic writing—has become how I make sense of the world. It's how I take on things I don't understand or things that make me angry, uncomfortable, or sad—and transform them. It's how I take the power away from things that scare me. It's how I investigate what's possible. It's how I express joy.

Shem: I started writing roles for myself only to discover that I knew actors who could play them better. I soon took pleasure in what other actors could bring to the table. I realized that actors were true collaborators and that by respecting them and their process my plays would invariably become better.

Tony: Writing is also helpful for your acting. If I don't know exactly what I'm saying, the audience will be baffled. If what I'm talking about is not of the utmost importance to me, the audience will be bored.

Jennifer: Writing comedy for me is always this beautiful blend of order and chaos. The careful architecture of comedic structure, filled with the divine messiness and unpredictability of being human. Improvisation helps me find the chaos, and studying other writers and forms helps me find the order.

Any final advice?

Jennifer: The first time I set out to write something that was wholly mine and didn't incorporate other people's material, I asked the playwright Michael Hollinger to serve as my mentor. The piece was called *Cherry Bomb*, a musical about the Cherry Sisters who were the worst act in vaudeville. It was a comfortable starting place for me as it had to do with an era of history I was familiar with, but there were no recordings of the Cherry Sisters act, there was nothing for me to imitate. Michael suggested that I start with the characters and focus on finding their distinct voices. As a starting exercise, he told me to write a monologue for each character, not as a part of the script necessarily, but just as a way of investigating the voice and point of view of each character. This was a terrific way in for me as an actor—and a place where I felt my training as an improviser was especially helpful.

Shem: Playmaking is a creative and collaborative endeavor among equals. Collaboration begins with communication, and regular writing assists in developing those skills. Creativity is what you bring to it, what makes it yours. Therefore, to me, writing is nearly as essential for an actor as acting is for a playwright. After all, as an actor, you're writing the character's story in your head. While both actor and playwright come at their roles in the collaboration from different angles, it's still important that each side can appreciate the other's struggle for meaning. So even if you don't think you can write, you might as well give it a try.

James: Write something every day. Doesn't matter what it is, just write something every day. You will never know what you're capable of unless you put pen to paper. Also, talk to writers you respect. Osmosis is real. Just being around people who are dealing in big ideas and writing will make you better and will hold you accountable to keep writing.

Thank you all. Lots of good ideas here.

Okay, so where are we now? As you see, there are as many ways of approaching writing as there are writers. For an actor, writing is a way of enriching what you do, giving you a chance to express yourself beyond someone else's ideas and living your most cherished dreams.

None of this is about reinventing your life. Acting and writing are natural partners. One enhances the other. "Getting ahead" means seeing yourself and your possibilities in a fresh way. It's the refresh button for your career. Now, what should you take away from these actor-writers' words? Your own words. Dream, imagine, write!

My final list of advice. Please peruse at your leisure . . .

- A writer is someone who writes. That's all.

- Like vocal exercises, write daily, even for a few minutes.

- Find a place to write in that feels good. Return there daily.

- Write about what you genuinely care about.

- Don't worry about beginnings or endings. Write bits and pieces. Let the work tell you what the story is.

- Don't create a plot problem simply to answer it. Write about problems that you don't know the answers to.

- Write.

- Adapt work that hasn't had good exposure.

- Get actor friends to read your material aloud.

- Listen to friends' comments, but don't believe they know better than you do. Follow your instincts.

- Tell stories from your past.

- Make things happen in your plays.

- Write.

- Create characters that are different from one another.

- See if you can write a joke.

- Make sure each character has a point of view.

- Don't talk about your work. Write it.

- Read plays.

- Read novels.

- Talk to writers.

- Carry a notebook. Use it.

- Write.

- Write and be happy.

- Write and be sad.

- But write.

ROBERT HEDLEY has long been associated with the development of new plays. A former Director of the Iowa Playwrights
Workshop, he co-founded the Philadelphia Theater Company
and West Coast Playwrights. He was a master teacher at Bay
Area Playwrights Festival, served as a playwrights' mentor at the
Mark Taper Forum in Los Angeles and has been a guest speaker
on new writing at the Lincoln Center Directors Lab. In 2012, he
was awarded a writing residency at Civitella Ranieri in Umbria,
Italy. His recent article, with wife Harriet Power, on British new
writing may be read in *American Theatre* magazine. Among
former writing students are David Rabe, Leslie Lee, Rebecca
Gilman, Naomi Wallace, Charles Smith, David Hancock, Heather

McCutchen, Clay Goss, Shem Bitterman, and Sean Clark. He   Robert Hedley
has directed professionally in Philadelphia, New York, and San
Francisco and was Artistic Director of the Iowa Shakespeare
Festival. Among his many awards, Robert has been awarded
the Barrymore Lifetime Achievement Award.

A LIFE IN THE THEATER

▶ By Harriet Power

How does an early career actor make a life in theater? Every acting class teaches us to "play our objective, not our obstacle"—yet the barriers to a professional theater career, especially in acting, seem impossible to ignore.

Canadian director/dramaturg and Simon Fraser University theater professor Don Kugler declares, "There are no jobs in theater. You have to create your job." Statistics in the United States seem to uphold the first half of his assertion. Too many members of Actors' Equity are unemployed on any given day. And most of us in theater have watched excellent actors become frustrated as the vicissitudes of casting and the actor's lack of control erode idealism and love for the art form.

Women face particular challenges, with seven to twenty times as many stage roles for men and increasingly fewer roles for mature women. In Philadelphia, where I do most of my professional work and teaching, I feel genuine heartbreak as I look at the most experienced female performers in the region agonize over lack of opportunity. Most professions reward seniority and proficiency—not ours.

There are, in short, potent reasons to choose a different field. But those in love with theater can't imagine any other career. And so: how to *create the job* that will allow *a life in theater*?

I've been lucky. As a professional director/dramaturg, the imperative to concoct my creative life, rather than wait for it to happen *to* me, has—along with good fortune—yielded countless joys as I look back on an active career and forward to continued collaborations with artists I love. Yet regrets and second-guessing often arise while making a life in theater. Sometimes I look with envy, sometimes relief, at certain of my female director friends who—unlike me (a director and full-time university professor)—are continuing to run professional theaters. Their incomes may be lower, their health insurance iffier, their nights made even more sleepless by capital campaigns, board development, grants ungranted—but their lives sometimes seem much more exciting.

I've come to understand that celebrating and regretting theater choices (sometimes simultaneously) are givens in theater lives—everyone does it. I try to learn from the ups and the downs, the jubilation and the second-guessing. And I cherish, unequivocally, the variety of people and projects that together enrich my dual professional-directing-and-teaching career. It may be a cliché, but I'm constantly amazed by how much I learn from my students. I'm grateful, too, for a degree of financial stability and job security that's all too rare in the arts.

But I do wonder from time to time . . . and then I stop, because I'm just too busy.

Since adding a full-time theater professorship to a lively freelance career in 1994, I continue to feel both exhilarated and exhausted by the constant juggling and the reality that I can't be all things to all people at all moments. Time, health, body, and soul management will challenge me until I'm gone, and so I urge my students, especially those aiming to make their careers as professional actors, to proactively anticipate, prepare for, seize, and shape every potential opportunity while taking very good care of themselves physically and emotionally. My students have all heard the mantra, "There are no jobs in theater. You have to create your job."

The best advice, though, always comes from the source. I asked eight award-winning, deeply respected professional actors, all but two of whom are Philadelphia based, to share their successes and strategies. Jessica Bedford, Carla Belver, Nancy Boykin, Peter DeLaurier, Melanye Finister, Dan Kern, Luigi Sottile, and David Whalen have made, and continue to create, a life in the theater.

Photo by Becky Thurner   Photo by Kim Carson

David Whalen, MFA Acting, UNC-Chapel Hill (left) and Luigi Sottile, BA Theater, Temple University (right)]

David and Luigi perform year round, season after season, at regional theaters around the country. David also teaches and has an active career in film and television.

Photo by Kim Carson   Photo by Lauren Sowa   Photo by Campli Photography

Carla Belver, MA Theater, Villanova University (left), Peter DeLaurier, MA Acting & Directing, Illinois State University (center), and Melanye Finister, BFA Carnegie Mellon (right)]

Carla, Peter, and Melanye are all members of People's Light, one of the few theaters nationwide that maintains a resident company. Carla is the 2014 recipient of the Barrymore Lifetime Achievement Award. Peter, who co-founded Delaware Theatre Company, also directs and writes. And all three also teach and work outside as well as within their home theater.

Jessica acts, writes, directs, teaches, dramaturgs, and serves as Associate Artistic Director of a small professional company outside Philadelphia.

Jessica Bedford, MA Theater, Villanova University

Photo by Kim Carson

Nancy and Dan began their careers as professional actors and continue to act while teaching full time. Dan, a freelance actor and director and former Head of Acting and Directing at Temple University, also directs.

Nancy Boykin, MFA Acting, UNC-Chapel Hill (left), and Dan Kern, MFA Acting, American Conservatory Theater (right)]

Among these eight, all but one are married, six are parents, and all but one own their homes. Their careers affirm the many ways one can create a life in theater while enjoying a life outside. And their nuts-and-bolts experience and advice reinforce the notion that to make a life in the theater you must develop strategies for handling disappointment and creating work for yourself.

Handling Disappointment

Heartbreak, frustration, jealousy, and aggravation are every theater professional's bedfellows at least occasionally. My own MFA training never addressed the reality that jealousy and despair would sometimes visit, and that learning to welcome (and thus, sideline) these uninvited guests would become as important as script analysis or blocking.

When I moved to Philadelphia in 1990, I quickly became a "known quantity" as a director, initially through networking and soon thanks to strong productions and reviews and a flourishing freelance atmosphere. I never had to pitch a project or hound an artistic director—the work kept coming and I often had the satisfaction of picking and choosing among offers. Who knew these halcyon years were temporary?

The theater scene changed radically with the launching of over seventy small theaters (all the work directed by the founders), while at the more established venues, changes of artistic leadership led to different director-collaborators. Although I believe I'm a more skilled director with each passing year, I now have to shake more trees and live with the reality that the hot new talent is going to get some of the work I used to get. As soon as I made relative peace with this new state of affairs, treasuring the one or two professional productions and one university production I direct yearly, the phone started ringing more often. Go figure.

> "Expect fat and lean years, and create a rich enough theater life that the ups and downs don't overtake self-worth or happiness."

I asked our actors to speak to their career disappointments and strategies for handling it.

Jessica: I realize that I can't have it all. Every opportunity also bears real sacrifice. On the positive side, it keeps me fully in the game. I'm not sitting on the sidelines—I choose to take every audition, every job, and I choose to say no to the other things. But because, as an actor, you have to hustle so much, it can feel like all that work should lead you to a place where you can make a play happen *and* go to your friend's wedding and see your nephew off to school and catch your husband's opening. But that's just not always the case.

Luigi: It's always a struggle to achieve total emotional vulnerability and let go of control. My working-class, tough upbringing in Scranton, Pennsylvania, built walls I had to demolish in order to keep an open mind—and most importantly, an open heart. Let's face it, growing up Italian, Irish, and Russian can plant a volcanic temper in a person. But the freedom of expression and creative process involved in developing a character made me fall in love with the craft. That's what sustains you through both your triumphs and disappointments. I try to give 150 percent to every character I have the honor of embodying. Every character we play teaches us something that helps us understand human nature more deeply. Every character, good or evil, has a human soul we must try to make relatable to touch an audience. Our work as actors really can—I hope—make this world a better place.

David: I don't look at this business from a place of frustration or disappointment. These are givens in this kind of career and life. But I truly believe that if you aren't getting better as an actor, you're getting bitter.

Melanye: I have been in some bombs. I played Cleopatra eons ago and it was a complete disaster—I didn't know what I was doing. And yet I learned so much about myself and my work. So when I'm feeling less than terrific about a performance, I try to remember to be grateful. Being a member of an acting company is a privilege—a luxury that means I don't have to hustle for work as most actors do. How many actors have someone who thinks of them when planning a season? This is an incredible gift.

Creating Work

These eight actors bring a collective 265 years of wisdom to their work and their lives. I asked them to respond to the notion that you have to create your own jobs in the theater, and to share their best advice and insights accumulated on and offstage. Their responses are ordered from youngest to oldest.

Luigi: Keep your heart and mind open to possibility and change. Never stop learning about your craft or anything else. A more well-rounded human being makes for a better actor. And keep in good physical condition. You never know what will be asked of you physically, so you need to develop the discipline to be able to control what you put in your body. I like to drink and have a cig occasionally, and smoke weed. But you have to know how much is enough and not let it control your life.

I also believe an actor must have the discipline to change his or her body as it fits a character. I recently played a cloned, part-human, part-android character who had to look genetically modified, lean, and manufactured. Sticking with a regimented diet and specific workout program developed with health experts, I lost twenty-three pounds in three weeks for the role. The results were staggering. So don't be afraid of hard labor or what you may be asked to do physically for a role. Many actors in superb physical condition are out there who can probably do something more skillfully than you. Competition is a real thing, and you can't pretend it doesn't exist in the world of acting.

Jessica: I love to tell stories, and initially, the only way I felt I could do that was in front of the footlights. But I've found I like being on both sides as I've aged. Having the occasional opportunity to make theater as a writer or director has proven empowering to me. Being an actor can feel like you're always at the bottom of the theatrical totem pole, always subject to decisions but never making them. Taking time on the other side of the table has provided me with balance and fresh perspective.

It can feel like this career demands that you split yourself in half—one half of you (in order to survive the business) must become calculating and critically removed while the other half of you (in order to continue to make art) must remain open, vulnerable, deeply in touch with your ability to play. It's hard for these two halves to coexist in a single person. Know that this is every actor's struggle—and the key is to seek a balance between the two. Know that you will often fail at that. Welcome to being human. Just forgive and try again. The worst thing you can do is shut down one side or allow it to overtake the other.

David: My family comes first. I try to make sure the acting work fits into my life, and I weigh it accordingly. I'm a better actor when I'm centered, and my family centers me. At the same time, keep challenging yourself. An actor always has to be ready for work. Preparation is *vital*. As Hamlet says, "The readiness is all." Be the best product you can be. When you're training as an actor, you have to train your stamina in all things—voice, body, spirit, work ethic. Finally, never lose your uniqueness.

Melanye: You *can* have it all—you just can't have it all at the same time. The notion that you have to suspend family or personal life is not true. You have to be willing to put one thing on hold and give your time and attention to the other. And it's important to expand your sense of a life in the theater—event planner, teacher, audience services manager—you have to be willing to transfer your acting skills to other places. At People's Light, most of us are required to wear many hats. I've done development, house management, and interfaced with the community and other artists as a producer. It's all theater.

Peter: Experience life. We make art out of it and if you don't know much of life, how can you contribute? Read history. Read novels. Learn about people's lives. Read lots of plays—especially good ones. Watch good actors. Work with them if you can. Find good directors and make yourself indispensable to them. Don't hold back. Make sure you're willing to share what hurts your soul and gives it joy. That's what they're paying you for. It's a hard but fulfilling life. If you can think of anything else you can do and be happy, do it. If you can't, go with God.

Nancy: It's important to know yourself and be realistic about who you are. Then find a way to bring that unique quality—yourself—to the work. Trust that that is enough.

Dan: Enjoy what you do! And remember *why* it brings you joy.

Carla: Take advantage of the best training you can find. Be open to all methods, but if you find a method that doesn't work for you, move on. Learn as many different skills as you can—singing, dancing, juggling, dialects, anything! Never settle for doing what you already do. Stretch yourself whenever and wherever you can. Be a good team player, generous to your fellow actors—what goes around comes around.

As I marvel at the wisdom of these eight respected professionals, I am particularly struck by how strongly they endorse self-knowledge and readiness. These qualities can elude anyone. As a director, I have seen too many women over 35 audition with a Juliet monologue. It's hard to suppress the urge to say, "Celebrate your maturity! Find material you love that showcases who you are *now*."

A particularly poignant memory: Many years ago, I was casting a professional production of *Measure for Measure*, and a recent Villanova alumna auditioned. Her initial monologue was weak, but I wanted the artistic director to see what she was capable of, so I gave her the callback sides. She did not prepare optimally and was glued to the script rather than listening and responding to her fellow actors. She came to see me afterward about why she wasn't cast and got angry when I told her that too many other young women had so fully digested the character's words that they could freely focus on what was important: the moment-to-moment give and take with other characters. "I am too busy to memorize every side for every callback!" she countered. But as many of the eight actors in this chapter assert, there will always be others who've made themselves ready for the roles you want—so preparation is crucial.

Remembering what got you into this crazy world of acting can also boost morale during the inevitable dry spells that challenge every theater life. Peter told me that he often recalls the twist of fate that led him to theater:

I was a cellist when I was 15. I had a scholarship to a music conservatory arranged by my teacher, the principal cellist with the local orchestra, and thought that was what I was supposed to do with my life. I had for some years also been acting in school plays and taking acting classes at the university. One night my parents took me to see Pirandello's *Enrico IV*, a performance so deeply moving that I hitchhiked back to the theater the next night to see the play again. I can't fully describe what compelled me, but it was suddenly clear that this was my life's work. Within a year I had dropped the cello, left high school, started studying acting at the university, and done my first professional theater season. From forty-seven years in the profession, I know that I do this work because of the unique power actors have to live honestly in the same space and time with the audience, giving each viewer the immediate sense they are simultaneously completely the same and utterly different from the characters whose lives they are sharing. I believe this shared perspective makes the world a little better.

Peter's thoughts remind me that revisiting what got us into theater can reignite energy and purpose and ideals. Because rejections often outnumber the roles actors get to play, we must keep finding ways to recharge and move forward.

One way to do this is to lean on our mentors. In thirty-five years of theater making, I've never met a professional who didn't cite the life-changing influence of mentors. As Melanye said of her Carnegie Mellon professor, Victoria Santa

Cruz, "I still hear her voice: 'Be HERE!' She would frequently say, 'Everybody has fear, but *don't let it eat you.*'" And as Dan said of his ACT professor and mentor, William Ball:

> He was a very strong influence on my early work. His passion for 'positation,' as he referred to it, remains a brilliant tool for the arts. For him, the act of creating art is a realization of *positive energy.* Surrounding yourself with positive, life-affirming values leads to art that is equally life affirming.

At the 1990 University of Iowa Theater graduation ceremony, Professor Robert Hedley, Director of the Iowa Playwrights Workshop (also my husband) spoke to the parents of the newly crowned MFA and BA in Theater grads. He told these assembled parents that he understood their anxiety—after all, they had just footed the bill for a theater education and were wondering whether their child would ever make money, have security, own a home, have a family. "But here's the marvelous news," he said . . .

> If they remain in theater, they will have packed scores of lifetimes into their one life—they will have lived in every era, in many countries, as French maids, Danish kings, ancient Greek warriors, Brooklyn housewives, African queens, connivers and lovers and doctors and salesmen and servants and spouses. Be happy today, parents, because with theater, your child has chosen the best life in the world. They will live 100 lives and touch thousands of viewers along the way.

> "Be happy today, parents, because with theater, your child has chosen the best life in the world. They will, along the way, live 100 lives and touch thousands of viewers."

His words brought down the house—and triggered tears. And they affirm that idealism is a key exercise for actors, a trait to cultivate through the highs and lows of theater work. Idealism may be the professional actor's most important quality. It attracts directors and producers; it enhances the working atmosphere; it fosters joy; it's as important as going to the gym and getting to rehearsal on time. Idealism is the common trait among the eight actors featured here. Carla,

Dan, Dave, Jess, Luigi, Mel, Nancy, and Peter exude optimism and graciousness, which, along with fitness, ongoing training, imagination, flexibility, optimism, and support of loved ones, affirm that one can make *a life in theater.*

Harriet Power

HARRIET POWER is a director, dramaturg, artistic director, and playwright. She served as Artistic Director of Venture Theatre, Philadelphia's multiracial professional theater, and as Associate Artistic Director of Act II Playhouse in Ambler, PA, directing the world premiere of Bruce Graham's *Any Given Monday* and several regional premieres including Sebastian Barry's *The Pride of Parnell Street*. A three-time Barrymore Award "Best Director" nominee, she won for her direction of Tony Kushner's *Angels in American: Perestroika*. Freelance directing includes *Dinner With Friends* (Teatro L'Arciliuto, Rome, Italy; *Trova Roma*'s "Best of Rome" award), *Three Sisters* (Pittsburgh Irish & Classical Theatre, "Best Theatre Experience of the Season" award), world premieres of Jen Childs's *Why I'm Scared of Dance* and *I Will Not Go Gently* (1812 Productions, Philadelphia), and Seth Rozin's *Missing Link* and *Reinventing Eden* (InterAct Theatre, Philadelphia). She has worked with new plays and playwrights at New Dramatists, PlayPenn, Bay Area Playwrights Festival, West Coast Playwrights, and Iowa Playwrights Festival. Her article on British play development, *"Over There,"* with Robert Hedley, was recently published in *American Theatre*. A Professor of Theatre and head of Graduate Directing at Villanova, she is currently co-writing a musical *Dizzy* with Jeff Thomas.

Notes

1 Grossman, Jordan. "Kevin Spacey rounds of UB's Distinguished Speakers Series," The Spectrum, April 28, 2016, accessed May 1, 2016, http://www.ubspectrum.com/article/ 2016/04/kevin-spacey-rounds-out-ubs-distinguished-speakers-series.

2 "Commune," Merriam-Webster.com, accessed July 27, 2015, http://www.merriam-webster.com/dictionary/commune.

3 Innes, Christopher. 1972. *Erwin Piscator's Political Theatre: The Development of Modern German Drama.* Cambridge: Cambridge University Press, 1972.

4 Boal, Augusto. 1992. *Games for Actors and Non-Actors*, trans. Adrian Jackson. London: Routledge, 1992.

5 hooks, bell. 1990. "Postmodern Blackness," in *Yearning: Race, Gender, and Cultural Politics.* Boston, MA: South End Press, 1990.

6 *El Teatro Campesino*, accessed August 10, 2015, http://www.elteatrocampesino.com/About/ missionhistory.html.

7 McCauley, Robbie. 2015. Interview by Nic Paget-Clarke, *In Motion Magazine*,

October 10, 2000, accessed August 10, 2015, http://www.inmotionmagazine.com/rmccaul1.html.

8 The Medea Project, accessed August 10, 2015, http://themedeaproject.weebly.com.

9 Trickey, Minnijean Brown. Interview by Spirit Trickey, July 25, 2015.

10 Oster, Sharon M. 1995. *Strategic Management for Nonprofit Organizations: Theory and Cases*. Oxford: Oxford University Press, 1995.

CHAPTER 5

STARTING AGAIN

"What's so fascinating and frustrating and great
about life is that you're constantly starting over,
all the time, and I love that."

Billy Crystal

You're familiar with the sorrow that goes hand in hand with completing a show. Closing night is always followed by the morning after, which is inevitably filled with emotion.

What comes next?

That's the question you'll ask yourself when it's time to begin again, whether that need is due to the end of a run, a botched audition, a show that closed early due to bad reviews, or a recognition that you've aged into a new "type."

There is no such thing as a working actor who hasn't faced the task of starting anew. Actors will take time away to try a career in a new industry. Or they'll take breaks to start a family. And they might return to acting five or ten years later, because they discover that the bug never left them.

As you read about in the last chapter, there's no one way, right way, best way, or appropriate way to live your life as an actor. There are any number of valid approaches to having a career in the theater. And though there are few definitives in the business of acting, one thing we can say with certainty is that nothing ever plays out exactly as you envisioned it. An actor's career is filled with great surprises—much like the journeys of the greatest characters in theater.

Who Knew?

The late Alan Rickman got his start when he was well into his 30s, and he spent ten years in the theater before landing his role opposite Bruce Willis in *Die Hard*. He was 46 at the time. Judi Dench was an accomplished television and theater actor in the UK before landing her role in *Golden Eye* (1995), which propelled her to stardom at the age of 61. Check out her IMDb page to see the extensive list of nominations and awards she's received since the mid-1990s.

Here's what you're going to read about in our final chapter of this book:

- How to find, respect, and engage with your audience
- How to sustain an acting career over many decades
- Bouncing back after lean years
- Handling rejection, disappointment, and setbacks
- Redefining success as your career moves forward
- Rethinking your career and possible new directions
- Transitioning into teaching and mentorship roles
- Using your acting skills to better the world at large
- The intersection between theater and therapy

We'll start with understanding your audience, and we'll end with examining a broader view of what it means to be an actor. Can you envision a life as an actor and not box yourself into the traditional roles? Can you conceive of how your being an actor can influence and even transform people's lives?

But let's first take a closer look at the audience. The audience is the reason you're on stage to begin with—so how can you be sure you're accepting, embracing, and engaging an ever-changing audience?

UNDERSTANDING YOUR AUDIENCE

▶ By Kirsty Sedgman

In July 2015, during a Broadway performance of *Hand to God*, an audience member climbed onstage and plugged his cellphone into a fake electrical outlet—a prop, part of the set. Cue the usual social media uproar. In a Facebook post, a fellow audience member described how "[t]he crew had to stop the pre-show music, remove the cellphone, and make an announcement as to why you can't do that. Truly. [. . .] Has theatre etiquette—heck, common sense—really fallen that far??"[1] Practically before the ushers finished their reprimand, this individual act had already been sucked into an ongoing campaign to condemn theatergoers for poor behavior.

Audiences, we're told, are increasingly rude. They lack decency and respect. They don't understand the unwritten rules of the stage anymore, or if they do understand, they don't care. Both within and outside the theater's walls, efforts to preserve the sanctity of live performance abound—from Kevin Spacey's in-character rebukes, to Helen Mirren's infamous march offstage commanding street musicians to "shut the f*** up," to the United Kingdom's Theatre Charter, which sets out acceptable behavior when watching a play.

Whispering? No. Shhh-ing? Fine. Unwrap sweets and go to the loo *before* the performance begins, not during. Phones *off*, not just on silent. Leave during the interval or not at all. Oh, and ladies? Try to avoid wearing strong perfume, please.

Okay, so that last commandment isn't part of the official Charter, but it is one of many suggestions left on the website by a disgruntled patron of the arts. And beneath all this runs the idea that we can't always trust people to hold up their end of the theatrical bargain. The difficulty is that as performance makers we need audiences. They are our *raison d'être*. We want them to join us in the theater—we work to deepen participation in those who already attend and to widen participation by encouraging those who don't. In this world of falling attendance and subsidy cuts, we need audiences to be our champions. But we also mistrust them, homogenize them, complain about them, accuse them of failing to "get" a performance if they didn't like it. The British performer Chris Goode has talked vividly of this, recognizing the temptation to place participants into one of two categories: "good" audiences versus "not our audience."[2]

As an audience researcher, it's my job to find out what people get out of the things they see. What kinds of hopes, worries, or expectations do they carry with them into the theater? How do they find value in performance encounters? And how do they remember and talk about experiences afterward? This is part of the contemporary appetite for evaluating the "impact" of the arts. But instead of reducing audiences to a series of statistics that cultural agencies can target, or boiling responses down into little nuggets of advocacy—"benefits," to borrow a popular term—my approach maps audiences' engagements with theater in all their complexity, showing how pleasures and enjoyments often sit side by side with hesitations and unease.[3]

And what I've noticed is an odd tug-of-war. On one hand, we're increasingly eager to offer audiences a sense of ownership over the arts, by reminding people that it's "their theaters" that are at risk. Both the United States and the United Kingdom have witnessed a drive to draw attention to cultural inequality, noting that we tend to see far more participation from actors and theatergoers who are Caucasian, coming from middle- to higher income homes and communities, than any other groups. Examples range from Neil Patrick Harris's opening joke at the 2015 Oscars ("Tonight we honor Hollywood's best and whitest—sorry, I mean brightest") to the recent report "Equality and Diversity within the Arts and Cultural Sector in England."[4] There's a lot of debate now about how to spark in culturally under-represented groups the sensation that *this is my culture, too.* But on the other hand, we frequently hear complaints that after crossing the

Audience post-show discussion at Auburn University Theatre. Scenic Design: A. Lynn Lockrow

Photo courtesy of Auburn University College of Liberal Arts

theater's threshold, attendees should be made aware that they are in *our* space now, subject to *our* rules.

You're probably aware that the modern definition of "good" theater behavior is relatively new. Much has been made of the liveliness of Shakespeare's audience, who used to interact, boo and cheer, and even climb onstage. But what many people don't realize is that the change from active to passive spectatorship was brought about as part of a deliberate, collective effort to stop the "wrong" (mass, populist, working-class) audience from attending high arts. As Lawrence Levine explains in his excellent book *Highbrow/Lowbrow*, these cultural boundaries are not natural and timeless, as they often seem, but the subject of social construction.[5]

By the end of the nineteenth century, venues had begun displaying posters telling people how to behave, and directors would stop the performance until offending audience members left. Audiences had to be trained. The issue we now face is how they can be *retrained*—to love theater and participate respectfully, yes, but also fully and joyfully.

It's far too easy to dismiss first-time theatergoers as the ones who cause problems—they "don't know how to obey the rules." But actually, people unfamiliar with the arts, who lack what I call "cultural confidence," often talk about feeling anxious simply walking into arts buildings because of the sensation these places are not built for them. Theater, sadly, is still not for everyone. But *it could be*—and if we don't take this seriously we'll just keep haemorrhaging audiences, losing them to other media and to only the very safest, spectacularized forms of live entertainment, until soon there might be no room in the world for the stage at all. For the actor who strives to begin again, it's therefore imperative to understand how you, too, can help make theater accessible for all.

Breaking Down Barriers

Research into audiences—and particularly young people—has found that while things like music tend to be rooted in our world, helping us to shape a sense of who we are as people, theater tends to be thought of as archaic and alien, separate from daily life.[6] The question is: How might we work more effectively to draw people in—to make stage performance a central part of people's lives?

Option 1

Bring the outside world into the theater. Set yourself and your audience new rules. I attended a production of *Twelfth Night* by Filter Theatre and the Royal Shakespeare Company, where halfway through the actors handed out slices of pizza. Get audiences to take part in the performance by encouraging them to throw memories written on scraps of paper onstage, or by incorporating cell-phones within the scenography—ask people to live-tweet responses and photos. See if you can't think of a way to bring the ludic element, the "play," back into your plays, in a way that feels like a natural extension of the work rather than gimmickry. Involve people in the creative process—draw on local stories when making your performances; ask people from the community to come and watch a rehearsal, offer feedback. If you're part of a cultural venue, make the building itself a communal hub. Remove obstacles, open doors, run reading groups and coffee mornings. Be less intimidating. Figure out a way to encourage people inside.

Option 2

Bring theater into the outside world. Consider adopting some of the techniques of site-specific performance, which stages encounters on the streets and in unusual spaces. Even if you're doing a scripted drama in a traditional auditorium, start to think about how the event might fruitfully spill out beyond the theater's walls. Stage micro-performances in cafes or on public transport. Take part in scratch events and open mic nights. Visit local groups and schools. Run workshops. *Talk to everyone.* Explain what you're doing. One of the most exciting theater com-panies in the United Kingdom in terms of community engagement is National Theatre Wales (NTW), with whom I worked during their 2010–11 launch year. For NTW, audience development is not a separate strategic limb—rather, it's inside everything the company does, the very bones of their work. Speaking with residents in the places NTW performed, it was clear their approach was most successful when it produced a sense of "openness." During their production of *For Mountain, Sand & Sea*, which took place in summer 2010 in the small Welsh seaside town of Barmouth, a shop owner described being pleasantly coerced into attending by the performers, who quickly slotted into the life of the place. Theater—and by extension, actors—can often seem mysterious, unapproachable, and threateningly elitist, part of a special privileged world. What persuaded this non-theatergoer to attend was the demolishment of these boundaries, the feeling that the entire creative team seemed like "a nice crowd."

These are two options. They are not mutually exclusive. The aim is to blur the line between theater and life—to make the theatrical threshold less daunting to cross. For further inspiration, check out the emerging wave of exciting contemporary performance. Are there elements of that work you could borrow? For instance, try Googling the UK-based company Lone Twin, whose "ecological" performances over the past sixteen years have repeatedly asked what it means to be alone together, individuals yet part of society, by inviting onlookers to join them in activities like line dances, carrying heavy objects, building a boat. Or look up Action Hero's *A Western*, which took place in bars and pubs. Or Blast Theory's game/theater hybrids. Or Punchdrunk's spectacular work, where exploring vast sets in found spaces is as much a performance as watching the actors. Or the one-to-one work of the late Adrian Howells and his contemporaries, whose intimate encounters boil down theater to its essential components—one performer, one audience member, alone.

Rethinking the Role of the Audience

An important part of this contemporary work has been rethinking the role of the audience. Often this begins with a name. Augusto Boal turned spectators into actors ("spect-actors"), asking them to intervene and change the shape of the drama.[7] Forced Entertainment sees its audience as "witnesses," requiring them to feel the weight of their presence in the performance, to think about what they are complicit in by taking part.[8] More recently, Lone Twin has called its audiences "invited guests," asked rather than forced to participate. This signals an important shift away from seeing audiences as passive, needing to be made active by you as performers. For Lone Twin, *not* taking part is still an active choice.[9] In this way, *all audiences are active all the time*. So what are you asking of your participants? What roles do you want them to play? And what alternative name might you use to describe them?

But whatever road you choose to go down, travel cautiously. For touring shows, you won't have time to develop a visible presence in each new place, so the performance will need to more or less stand on its own. For some attendees, encountering elements of "audience participation" can cause excruciating embarrassment and will be hugely offputting. I've heard people on the street sneer at performers for being "smug," thinking they're "something special." In its own way, this kind of unexplained performance outreach can sometimes be more intimidating, not less. Conversely, many people *like* coming to theater to sit in the dark watching strangers perform onstage, and that's fine, too. Not all these suggestions will work for you, and not all will work for the people you hope to attract.

So what's the answer?

Get to know your audiences. Who are they? Why do they attend? What's stopping them? And what might they get out of live performance?

Knowing (and Developing) Your Audience

In his seminal guide for performers, *An Actor Prepares*, Konstantin Stanislavski described the auditorium as the "awful hole beyond the footlights."[10] The temptation is to don character like armour, to keep people from seeing and judging *you as a person.*

It's not my place to add to the excellent acting advice you've gotten from your coaches, teachers, professors, and directors. But what I will say is this. *No matter what the format of the performance*—from "traditional" theater (scripted dramas within a designated theater space) to more experimental, participatory, immersive, intimate, or site-specific events—I've found that what remains reasonably constant is the desire for an "authentic" experience (this is a bit of a sticky word, so for a more academic summary of its contested meanings I recommend Helen Freshwater's 2012 article "Consuming Authenticities").[11] By this I mean that, in my experience, people talk frequently and passionately about the desire to experience something that feels *real*—to walk out of the theater with the sense they've had a genuine human encounter, with performers, with their characters, with places, with emotions, with ideas. For many participants, the true beauty of theater lies in its ability to provoke a "liminal" quality—a state of *in-between-ness*—the sensation that performers and audiences are meeting in the middle and making an experience together. *This* is what you can work to encourage. For example, instead of the usual preshow tannoy announcement, some theaters now send actors onstage to explain personally how disturbances will affect their performances. By reminding your audience that they're an important part of the event, and in developing that sense of personal connection, they will be much more likely to engage deeply—and to turn off their phones. But if you're onstage picturing the audience as a black hole, singular and unknowable, it can get in the way of achieving that connection.

Because *audiences are made up of people.* This is, I think, very easy to forget. Within every group you'll get odd ones out—that person who thinks it's okay to clamber onstage and charge the cellphone. But when we talk about "good" and "bad" audiences, "our audience" versus "the wrong audience," what we're really doing is papering over the cracks between people, pretending that individual differences don't exist.

The real problem is that while it's easy to make assumptions about how a performance went down, it's rather tricky to test those claims. I've heard actors grumble about especially quiet and unresponsive audiences, and yet I've spoken to the attendees themselves about how "spellbound" they'd felt, too caught up in the performance to move or even breathe. Equally, I've walked next to someone during a promenade event dissecting the production's faults, only to watch them approach the director afterward delivering nothing but smiling praise. What you hear, and what people are actually saying, may be two very different things.

Considering your audience development options can help with this. So whether you're an established performer or just starting out, setting up your own theater company or building on years of work, my advice is the same. You must start thinking of audience development as an integral part of your job, not limited to the role of producers and marketing execs. What follows are some practical suggestions for how you might achieve this.

Post-Show Q&A Discussions

For years, the "post-show discussion" has been a familiar staple of live performance. However, this has increasingly come under fire for being stuffy and restrictive. With little opportunity for real debate, audiences often walk out of the discussion feeling foolish, like they'd responded to the performance in the wrong way. This is partly down to the traditional post-show format, with the creative team placed on a pedestal and grilled on their "intentions." They hold the power—the "correct interpretation" is ultimately theirs, and audiences are expected to sit quietly and drink in knowledge. More recently, though, cultural organizations have sought to reverse this dynamic by positioning audiences as the experts of their own experience. This reconsiders the post-show Q&A as an opportunity for you, the actors, to ask questions of your audience, rather than the other way around—to learn from their actual responses rather than telling them what their responses should be. Alternatively, if you feel you still have wisdom to impart, think about mixing up the format by making the event more interactive. Take a leaf out of theater company Fol Espoir's book, and devise a "DVD Extras" section, inviting participants to choose from topics like the team's working relationship, the rehearsal process, or even "bloopers" and "deleted scenes."

Facilitated Talkback

Another option is to organize facilitated sessions. Make sure that anyone who was part of the performance stays away (directors, producers, designers, actors—*everybody*). Instead, get someone with no involvement to mediate. As Caroline Heim describes, rather than privileging the voice of the theater expert, this approach invites audiences to play the role of critic.[12] With no clear hierarchy, participants have equal opportunity to discuss their differing ideas and interpretations, take part in arbitrated arguments, and learn from one another's responses. This could then be expanded outward, if you like, by starting up a kind of "theater club." In his "Theatre Talks" project, prominent researcher Willmar Sauter took groups of people to a series of performances and then mediated relaxed discussion sessions over post-show drinks.[13] In this way, he encouraged audiences to attend productions they might not have chosen for themselves, and they were able to see their collective understanding of theater evolve.

Go Online

Use social media, obviously. Set up websites. But perhaps think wider than this. For researchers, one the most difficult things to reconcile is the fact that, while people are frequently happy to talk positively about theater, this hypothetical positivity does not always translate into actual attendance. Audiences often speak glowingly of the "special," indefinable benefits of participating in live events, but few are likely to regularly take part. One answer has been the swift rise in so-called "digital content," with events live-streamed into cinemas, on TV and online. It's tempting to see this as a copout, a sad surrender to modern life, where people are too lazy to leave their sofas and so everything has to be easy and on demand. But I urge you to resist condemning audiences like this—there are many reasons for reluctance, and moaning about it won't help your cause. What *might* help is to make this digital invasion work for you. Think about setting up a simple live-stream yourself (see Katie Moffat et al. 2013 for a brilliant guide).[14] There's lots of software out there you can use, and setup costs are pretty cheap. And if you're acting in a live-streamed performance, it's worth bearing in mind the many remote participants who talk about being surprised by how "live" these events actually feel.[15] Even when they're not physically present, they're still your audience—they're rooting for you, empathizing with you, even clapping and cheering in the cinema. Try to feel them there, too, on the other side of the camera lens.

Recruit Advocates Offline

Put in place a network of people who believe in what you're doing and are willing to shout about it to others. Without a doubt, to some extent this is something you're already doing—one of the great things about social media is the opportunity they offer to use online connections for information sharing. However, it's important to get offline. Get out into the community and talk to people, from shopkeepers to neighbors to local politicians. Develop human connections, and make an effort not to limit yourself to fellow artists. Create a database of contacts who you think are on your side. This can also come in handy when you need to think about evaluating the impact of your work. Ask for testimonials that you can use in marketing and funding bids. Find out what your work means to people. Harness enthusiasm.

Building Relationships

What this essay has asked you to consider is how to *build and sustain relationships* with your audiences. Importantly, this also means getting comfortable with criticism. Remember, you'll never be able to please everybody all the time, so work on being as open to listening to disappointment as you are to hearing praise. Both can be a leaping-off point for conversation—sure, they might not have liked *this* performance, but they could well *love* the next. So listen to people, be approachable, and accept that their input is just as valid as yours. Otherwise you risk confirming their worry that your kind of theater is simply not for them—and permanently scaring them away. To make it in this difficult business, actors need people behind them now more than ever—and when we dismiss criticisms as personal failures on the part of the audience, nobody wins. While it might not always feel like it, it's actually very rare to find someone who comes hoping to be disappointed. The audience, by and large, is on your side.

KIRSTY SEDGMAN is a Lecturer in Theatre at the University of Bristol (UK) and holds a PhD in theater audience research. Her book *Locating the Audience: How People Found Value in National Theatre Wales* (2016, Intellect) is the first full-length

Kirsty Sedgman

Photo by Jess Rose

study of how people develop relationships with a new theater company, drawing on more than 800 questionnaire responses and forty interviews. As a consultant researcher, she has led a number of interdisciplinary projects evaluating the impact of cultural projects, working with partners from local communities and government agencies, and she founded and Chairs the Performing Audience Research Network (www.performingaudiences.com).

BEGINNING ACTING LATER IN LIFE

An Interview With Mary Ann Thebus

▶ By Anna Hozian

Twenty years ago, I was lucky enough to meet Mary Ann Thebus, an extraordinary force in Chicago theater who has graced the stages of the Goodman, Steppenwolf, Northlight, Writers Theatre, among others for nearly forty years. As an acting teacher and coach, she assisted me and continues to assist countless others in how to be present on stage and in auditions, helping new and seasoned actors alike grow in confidence and skill. It's no wonder that she's been a lasting presence in the ever-changing world of theater.

Settling into her apartment in the Andersonville neighborhood— known for attracting artistic and literary types—surrounded by her

Mary Ann Thebus

Photo by Brian McConkey Photography

eclectic décor, representing a life of travel and the arts, from a necklace strung with Chinese gambling pieces of colored tile hanging on her bedroom wall to ten kilim rugs from Turkey and Iran that she and her family used on picnics around the world, Mary Ann and I began to talk about her life in the theater.

As I recall, you didn't begin acting until later in life. How did you get involved in the theater?

Well, it came as a surprise to me. Way back when I was choosing a profession, I became a psychiatric social worker with a master's degree in social work from the University of Michigan's Rackham Graduate School. And that was that. But then I got married, and my husband got a job teaching English as a foreign language in Izmir, Turkey. And there we met a number of people who were ex-pats involved with an English-speaking theater. And anybody who was a professional actor or director and had taken a break and wanted to see the world was there. But anyone could audition, and I thought, "I'll try that." It was a game to me essentially. And I got cast.

Was it the first time you had ever acted?
Oh, yeah. I didn't come from a theatrical or artistic family. But then I kept getting cast, and I truly knew nothing about the craft of acting—which I respect enormously, the craft of acting. I didn't know anything. I just had a flair. And that went on for fourteen years. We lived in Turkey and then Thailand and then Iran, and I was acting all the time, doing big roles and plays at these English-speaking theaters. I did a Pinter and *Streetcar*, you name it.

So after fourteen years, you came back to the States, and then what?
Once we came back to the States, I decided to try and combine my social work with my theater experience to use drama as therapy.

How old were you at this point?
I was 44.

And had you had a therapeutic practice prior to going overseas?
Oh, yes, quite extensive. I was a director at a residential treatment center for disturbed children and had a number of different jobs.

So then how did you decide to solely pursue acting?
I spoke to Anne Thurman, who was a professor at Northwestern University at the time, and we had a long talk, and she said, "I can fix you up with a terrific degree, but I can tell you still have this acting bug, so why don't you take six months, audition around town [Chicago], and then we can talk again."

Nobody knew me at all, nor did I understand the system. I'd only worked in those other countries. So I got into a class with Bella Itkin from the Goodman and found out about monologues and two-minutes pieces, and I started to audition.

After about six months, I got cast, and the rest is history. I received my Equity card with my second part, and I've lived ever since—now almost forty years—as a paid actor. And I teach acting, too. I have for about twenty years now.

What advice do you have for someone coming out of a graduate or undergraduate program, or even for someone pursuing it later in life like you did?

I'm a big believer in study. And I know those who come out of conservatories, Northwestern, Depaul, and they think, "I've done that. I don't want to do that" [acting class]—and I get that. But being in a class with professional actors, who are pursuing it as a career is a little different than when you're a student. You meet your peers. You discuss what's going on. You discuss your frustrations—and it's a very frustrating field, no question. And you need to get to know all of the business side—how things work.

Such as?

Very often, new actors put everything on their resumés that they've done in school, but you should get those off your resumé as soon as you can—within a year or two. As you get a professional job, drop one from when you were a student. You don't want to stay in that arena too long. Also, don't worry about getting an agent right away. It's not a huge crisis. Just get out and expose yourself as much as you can. Immerse yourself.

And if you want to be in film but haven't acted in film, take a class. There's a big difference in acting on the stage and acting in film. The way you approach film is different. When I first took a class on acting for film, I remember watching myself after giving a monologue, and I was stunned. I was so animated. I was almost flying out of the box. It was awful. The look on my face—you just have to tone all that down. You need to get what you think or what you feel or what you're after, and then you speak. You can't gesture like we do in life. Brian Dennehy once said, "It's always in the eyes."

There's a difference between performing and acting, and we need both. Film centers on performance, but it's through stage work that you learn what it really means to be an actor and what you need personally. You use your emotional life. You aren't so concerned with fitting the character physically on the page but rather going internally. You have to be willing to expose your deepest self and not be afraid to do so.

What else did you need to learn about film?

I was so green, and I still don't claim to be that knowledgeable about film. But the first thing on TV that I ever did was a series, and I was in episode thirteen. I can't remember the name of the series, but I remember that I was in episode thirteen. I was so excited. I had the trailer with my name on it. They sent me to hair and makeup. I felt like a movie star. And I remember in the shoot, there was this long thing hanging down, and I kept thinking, "What is that thing?" It was the microphone! And they would say, "Hit your mark," and I didn't know what that meant.

So anyway, I shot it, and I was so excited. So the series starts, and for episode thirteen, I had my family and a few friends over. There were about fifteen of us. I was to be a nurse in the episode, and I had a little scene. So as they draw up to the hospital, I said, "It'll be coming soon." Then they show the inside of the hospital, and I say, "Okay, you'll see me any second." And of course I wasn't there. They had cut the whole thing, my whole scene. I will never forget that. I was so naive. I thought if you shot it, you were in it.

But then later, I did a scene for *Ferris Bueller's Day Off*, and it was a husband and wife and our son in a car with the real estate agent, the mother of Ferris. And the boy who was playing my son, he had the bulk of the scene—and it was really quite good. And afterward, I said to him, "Listen, I don't want to rain on your parade, and I hope this goes, for all of us, but it may get cut." He didn't think that was possible—and of course, it was cut. They shoot way more than they need, and if it doesn't really fit the storyline, they cut it.

> "There's a difference between performing and acting, and we need both. Film centers on performance, but it's through stage work that you learn what it really means to be an actor and what you need personally . . . You have to be willing to expose your deepest self and not be afraid to do so."

You said this is a very frustrating career. How so?

I'm in my 80s, and I've had a long career and I'm still working, and I'm thankful for that. But there are so many disappointments along the way. You study, you prepare, you audition, they tell you you're great, and you are—you are great—but you don't get it. Somebody else gets it. And you think, "Why?" But the actor rarely knows why. And that happens over and over and over again.

How do you pick yourself up from that and go again?

If you want it badly enough, you pick yourself up. I started in an odd way—as I said, I was older, but I wanted it. I realized somewhere along the way that this is what I was meant to do with my life. So you keep at it. You don't get paid well. Even now, you don't get paid well. My neighbor is a landscape architect, and she's successful, and I'm a successful actor. But the difference between what she gets paid and what I get paid is unbelievable. And when you start, before you're Equity, you may not get paid at all. I was lucky—my husband worked, supported us.

Which leads me to another question. How do you balance a family with being an actor?

That's another demand. They need you, and you need them, and you're gone a lot. And the kids don't like it. You do the best you can. There are pulls on you, especially if you're a stage actor. You have to weigh if you want it enough and if you can manage it.

What keeps you going all of these years, four decades?

Back in the days when I didn't get roles, I had the same frustrations, but I just really felt it was right for me. And I felt so lucky to have found the career that was right for me. And I truly believed it, so I kept coming back.

What was the longest stretch you went without landing a role?

In the beginning, I remember after I received my Equity card from the old St. Nicholas Theatre, I was Mrs. Frank in *The Diary of Anne Frank*. And interestingly, Laurie Metcalf was in it, John Mahoney, Jeff Perry, John Reeger—all these actors. And I didn't know any of them. I had been here maybe a year at most. So I got my Equity card, and then I didn't get work for two years. After that, I might have gone for a year without stage work. But I'd get called back or I'd get a small part in television. I was really green. I didn't know anyone, and I didn't really know what I was doing. But I was determined. There are actors who hit it right out of school, but for the most, people don't. They're not less talented. They just haven't gotten that break yet. They just have to keep at it.

So what advice do you have for those who are starting over?

Study. So what if you got your degree some years ago? Get back in. So much about acting is psychological balance—from feeling apprehension and feeling secure. You get scared. The exposure is so major when you audition. You begin to doubt yourself. The paranoia is huge. It's a personal exposure to act, and it should be if it is done right. And that's scary. A lot of people can't deal with auditioning. I had terrible stage fright that would show itself during auditions. You feel like people are judging you—and they are! It's a business. They want the people on the stage that they think are the best, or the most right.

> "We need to not be so hard on ourselves. To be an actor takes courage, a lot of courage. To be really personally truthful on stage, through a role—to let people see and judge that takes courage. And that's what I think actors do, or should do."

That stage fright. Do you still get it?

I still don't particularly like auditioning. It doesn't go away completely. Or the first audience—I'm still not comfortable with that.

What do you tell yourself to deal with stage fright?

One thing I found that helps is that usually we judge our anxiety as bad, but actually it's a life force. In our own paranoia, we try to push it away. But maybe it's a good thing. Maybe it should be welcomed. I try to embrace it. On opening night or for the first audience, I will still step away and sit in the dark and focus. And the length of time that I need to do that depends on the role. For tough roles like I'm doing right now at the Writers Theatre, Marjorie in *Marjorie Prime*, I need more time.

And working with someone ahead of your audition to get help with monologues is wise, someone you trust. It gets rid of that very first panic. And then you just say, "Hello, welcome" to that force—as it is just the spirits of energy, or life. Change your thinking about it. But that may take time.

Also, very often when you go to auditions, you see a friend and chat. That's a mistake. Go into the audition, maybe nod, but focus. You're entering a world after all. If you have a monologue, it doesn't exist in an isolated sphere. It's part of a whole, and the whole is the whole of the play, and the play is a piece of life. You're entering the world of that life, and hopefully that world taps into your own. And that takes respect. You must take it seriously.

Do you remember any plays or auditions that you felt you bombed?

Not plays, no. But auditions, oh my yes. One was for Michael Maggio, who was the Artistic Director at Northlight Theatre at the time, and I remember my hands were shaking so badly that I had to draw a chair up to put the scene down on it. It was awful. Needless to say, I did not get cast. And that stayed with me for so long, because I thought, "He'll remember that, and I'll never work there." But of course I did. I have quite a bit over the years.

I remember once going to a general audition at Northlight, and I did my two two-minute pieces, and Michael said to me, "You know, Mary Ann, you don't have to do these anymore. People know who you are now." At that point, I'd been in Chicago acting for about four years. It was a year or two after that other audition. It was really very nice to hear.

I've experienced every single thing I've seen as a teacher. I've never been surprised by how an actor is fearful or bombs. I've done it all. But time helps a lot. You just do it again and again. And eventually, you see there are bigger things, in a way. Primarily, we need to not be so hard on ourselves. To be an actor takes courage, a lot of courage. To be really personally truthful on stage, through a role—to let people see and judge that takes courage. And that's what I think actors do, or should do.

ANNA HOZIAN holds an MFA from UC Riverside-Palm Desert's low-residency program. Her scripts have won the New York Women in Film and Television Writers Lab, the Black List Lab Chicago, and the Drama Award in the Page International Screenwriting Awards. She has also been a semifinalist in the Academy Nicholl Fellowships and the Samuel Goldwyn Awards. Prior to making her 2012

Anna Hozian

Photo by Kristen Ryan Photography

short film, *The Guitar Lesson*, which was an official selection of the Illinois International Film Festival, Hozian explored the worlds of derivatives trading, teaching English as a foreign language in Ecuador, and acting onstage. She is a graduate of Northwestern University and the Neighborhood Playhouse School of the Theatre.

MANAGING REJECTION, DISAPPOINTMENT, AND SETBACKS

▶ By Carl Menninger and Lori Hammel

A True Story

At a callback for a national commercial, the actors were informed that the session could take up to three hours and they would be paid in accordance with union rules. The afternoon dragged on endlessly as casting paired up various combinations of actors in search of the right on-camera relationship. Suddenly, one of the actors announced, "I should just leave. I don't even know why I came here. I never get these anyway." She wasn't joking or trying to psych out the other actors. The pressure of the situation brought out overwhelming feelings of discouragement, and she finally voiced her internal thoughts. She had heard many "yeses" to get her to that callback. Her agent, casting, and production decided she deserved to be there. She was even being paid. The only "no" she heard was the one she told herself when she decided she wouldn't be hired.

Staying motivated in the face of frustration and disappointment is an ongoing and crucial task for actors. Inherent in that task is managing rejection. Even when you've signed a contract to star in a Broadway show or when you've landed a job as a TV series regular, that contract will one day end and you'll again be looking for a job.

As an actor and freelancer, you're always seeking work, no matter where you are in your career. No actor books every job. Most actors experience dry spells where the work seems to evaporate. Every working actor we've ever known has at one time or another had the fleeting thought that they may never work again.

We've been in the business of acting and directing for theater for a combined forty-plus years. And over the course of those years, we've seen actors throw away their careers, crawling into a pit of self-loathing and doubt—and on the other side of the equation, we've worked with actors who accepted the unpredictable nature of the career and implemented constructive habits and routines to deal with those challenges.

In this essay, we'll share with you some of these habits and routines. Our acting colleagues who have nurtured these strategies have weathered the acting storms over the years, embracing the idea that to succeed in this business is to accept the challenge of beginning again, and again, and again . . .

> "Sometimes, it simply isn't 'your turn.' I remind myself, I'll get the next one, or something better suited to me is on its way."
>
> —Dee Hoty, three Tony nominations for Best Actress in a Broadway Musical

First, let's look at some personal strategies you can develop to deal with the emotional rollercoaster of acting.

Personal Strategies

Put It in Perspective

It's normal to feel disappointed when you don't get what you want. It can feel devastating when the actions you've taken don't yield results. Most actors know the pain of being called back multiple times and not landing the role. And in those moments, it can be irritating to hear someone say, "Cheer up!" Platitudes are hollow and condescending and definitely don't help when you're in the throws of an emotional upset.

You can't control how you feel, but you can control the way you deal with and act on those feelings. Don't try to reason your feelings away. Give yourself permission to feel what you feel. The key is to experience the lousy feelings and then *move on*. You usually won't know why an audition didn't result in a job, and since you don't have all the information, it can be easy to gravitate toward destructive thoughts and assumptions. But why fill in the blanks with thoughts that make you feel bad about yourself?

> "I think age and perspective have been two of my greatest weapons in dealing with rejection and disappointment. When I started out, rejection stung each time, and it was hard not to take it personally. It is not personal. The older I get, the more I realize all I can control is how prepared I am and how I present myself. Taste is subjective."
>
> ——Nicholas Rodriguez, performed on and off Broadway, at Carnegie Hall, and in regional theaters; also starred in *Days of Our Lives*

Just remember that you are the person who needs to have the most faith in you. You get to decide where to concentrate your energy and attention. When you're frustrated with your current situation, focus on your successes and acknowledge your progress. Ask yourself:

- Where was I five years ago? Ten years ago?
- What are my professional accomplishments since then?
- What do I know now that I didn't know back then?
- What experiences have made me feel artistically fulfilled?
- What positive feedback have I received about my work?

Force yourself to put things into perspective. This is a deliberate process. It won't just happen.

"Most times when you don't get a job, it's because of something that's out of your control—your height, your age, your resemblance to the director's ex-wife. That can help put things in perspective. Prepare well for your auditions—you'll be less nervous if you do—then let yourself off the hook afterwards."

—Carolee Carmello, three-time Tony nominee and five-time Drama Desk nominee, winning the 1999 Drama Desk Award for Outstanding Actress in a Musical for her role in *Parade*

Create a Support Network

Think of your acting career as a business and yourself as the CEO. Every business owner needs a team of trusted advisors invested in the business's success.

Choose your support network wisely. You don't want bad advice. Be discerning. Not every friend or family member is qualified for the job—especially when you're feeling vulnerable. Just because you enjoy spending time with someone doesn't mean they should be part of your support network. While it's important to include industry professionals on your team, not all fellow actors fit the bill.

List the people in your current support network, and ask yourself if they pass the four Cs Test: Are they competent, communicative, compassionate, and consistent?

- **Competent:** Is this person actively engaged in her personal and professional pursuits? Is she motivated and driven to achieve success and fulfillment? Is she a smart, disciplined industry professional? Do you respect her work ethic?
- **Communicative:** Is he articulate? Can he respectfully and easily express thoughts, feeling, and ideas? Is he insightful? Can he draw conclusions and see things that may not be obvious to you? Is he a good listener? Does he interrupt while you're talking? Is he more interested in dispensing advice than in understanding your situation and feelings?

- **Compassionate:** Think emotional intelligence. What is this person's capacity for empathy? Is she willing to see things from your perspective? Does she affirm and acknowledge your feelings, or does she dismissively tell you to lighten up? Is she cynical, pessimistic, or jaded? (Cynics can be toxic. Their "advice and support" can do more harm than good.)
- **Consistent:** Can you count on this person all the time, or do you have to catch him on a good day? Is what he says on Tuesday the same thing he says on Friday? Is he moody? Does he behave erratically? Does he follow through on commitments? Can you rely on this person to show up for you? Do you find that he competes with you? (Competition can arise not only when two actors audition for the same roles but also because of the way someone feels about your success.)

If you're in need of support, then you should be able to provide it for others as well. Now that you've completed the litmus test for your support network, rate yourself on the way you support others. Remember, it's not always about you. Showing up for someone who needs your support might make you feel better.

Reach Out and Ask for What You Need

Be specific and clear when you ask for support, otherwise you may find yourself frustrated by someone's response. Ask for what you need. For example:

- I need five minutes to vent and then you have to stop me.
- I need to brainstorm ten things I can do to move forward.
- What would you do if you were in this situation?
- I feel terrible. Can we see a movie and not talk about it right now?

The intention is to process or validate your feelings, invite a different perspective, and then move on.

Avoid the "Negators"

Long stretches between jobs and constant rejection can lead an actor to feelings of futility or even despair. When you tell yourself, "Why do I keep doing this when I have nothing to show for it?" you put yourself on a slippery slope toward hopelessness.

You are in charge of how you view yourself and your circumstances. Choose to steer clear of people who may adversely affect your self-esteem or the way you feel about your accomplishments.

"The two things I have learned that I feel most important are: 1) Show up/say yes—ask questions later. You never know who you will meet, or on what path a new experience will lead you. 2) Try to be positive. There is so much negativity and bitchiness in this business and in the world. Try and only put out good energy. It will be most welcomed."

—Bryan Batt, Broadway veteran, Drama Desk nominee, and two-time Screen Actors Guild Award winner

In our book *Minding the Edge*, we describe what we mean by the term *Negator*. Negators are needy, unhappy individuals who believe "misery loves company." By avoiding them or dealing with them effectively, you can keep yourself from a vortex of negativity and cynicism that can lead to doubt and harsh self-criticism. Here are few ways to cope with Negators:

- Avoid getting pulled into negative conversations.
- Don't reveal sensitive information.
- Compliment Negators. Maybe they will change the subject or leave.
- Say nothing. Your silence will send a clear, simple message.
- Excuse yourself from the conversation.

"If you let every 'no' feel like rejection, then you're holding on to a lot of negativity and that's going to follow you into the room. I try to remember that if I'm wrong for one thing, it just means I'm right for something else."

—Kevin Munhall, performed on Broadway and in national tours and regional theaters

Be of Service

One of the best ways to feel better is by shifting your focus away from your problems and onto the needs of others. Being of service often means volunteering time to a worthy cause, but we suggest that you broaden that definition. Think of it as helping to make someone's day better. Simply being gracious and friendly infuses positive energy and can make you feel better. This may seem simplistic, but when we enter a zone of negativity, it's amazing how we can close ourselves off to the possibility of constructive behavior.

Consider helping another actor who wants some professional advice. It can be rewarding to mentor and encourage a colleague, and the experience may remind you just how much you know and have accomplished. Contact your high school or college and ask to speak to students who want to be where you are right now. You will feel affirmed, empowered, and positive. It's hard to help others and not feel good about it.

Now, let's examine some actions you can take that will move you forward to a place of empowerment.

Taking Action

Create Strategies to Generate Work

It takes work to get work. Be proactive. Waiting for your phone to ring isn't the key to success. If you aren't satisfied with your current acting prospects, you may have to reassess the strategies you're using. As Einstein said, the definition of insanity is "doing the same thing over and over again and expecting different results." Here are a few questions to ask yourself:

- What am I doing to generate work?
- How am I pursuing current opportunities?
- Am I keeping track of and following up with industry professionals?
- Are my marketing materials accurate and do they reflect who I am today?
- How are my efforts paying off? How have they paid off in the past?

Don't just *think* about these strategies. Commit the time and energy to reflect on them. Then discuss your plans with someone in your support network.

"Never think because you don't get cast that it wasn't a worthwhile audition. I auditioned six times for *Spamalot*. They thought I was funny but not the right kind of British funny. But the casting director liked me, and a year later after only one audition, I was cast in the Chicago production of *Jersey Boys*, then graduated to the tour, and eventually the Broadway production. You just never know who has you in mind for what. Keep your chin up and keep at it. Dreams come true."

—Jared Thomas Bradshaw, performed on Broadway, Carnegie Hall soloist, and four-time NATS winner (National Association of Teachers of Singing)

Actors consistently seek work while working. Non-actors generally do just the opposite. They tend to get jobs and stay in them long term. But as an actor, you seek work, go to an audition, get a callback, book the job, do the work, and follow up with a self-assessment.

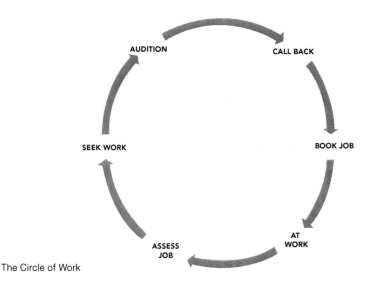

The Circle of Work

This might sound simple, but it's complicated by the fact that you can be in multiple places in the circle process at the same time—performing in a play at night while auditioning by day. Understanding, accepting, and embracing this paradigm can empower you to more easily cope with and manage your day-to-day life as an actor.

Keep Up With Your Professional Development

Sometimes actors feel defeated because they aren't exercising their artistic muscles. If you're not working on a creative project, how are you going to grow as an artist?

Our first suggestion is to take a class or workshop. The response is often, "I'm unemployed. I can't afford to take a class." Sometimes it's not possible, but if you make it a priority, you'll find that the money is there. Taking a class is an excellent way to build relationships. Meeting other artists can stimulate you creatively and potentially open windows to future opportunities. It isn't uncommon for an acting teacher or workshop instructor to recommend an actor to a casting director, agent, or director.

If taking a class isn't in your immediate future, here's a list of low-cost or free professional activities that will allow you to continue to develop as an artist:

- Teach yourself a new skill. Learn to edit your reel, play the guitar, or improve your ability with dialects. The internet is filled with free instructional videos.
- Research your industry. Stay current.
- Read a play.
- Organize a play reading with friends.
- Read the autobiography of an actor you admire. Take tips from people who have found success.
- Read the paper. Watch the news. Be informed. Remember: Art is a reflection of our society and the issues of the day.
- Attend a free workshop. Some schools provide workshops as a way of attracting potential students.
- Write a one-person show. You have something important to say. Everyone does.

Make Your Own Work

If you're feeling discouraged because work isn't coming, then make your own work. We lived in Chicago for several years. After working together on a few productions, we decided to create a cabaret act. Lori performed and Carl directed. It was a hybrid of standup comedy and traditional cabaret. The show played in various Chicago venues, and Lori developed a significant following. This visibility led to roles in musicals, and eventually Lori won a Joseph Jefferson Award (the Chicago equivalent of a Tony Award). Carl became a member of the Chicago Cabaret Professionals, taught workshops for cabaret artists, and consulted with and directed other cabaret performers.

Developing your own projects builds confidence. When artists discuss their work, they have an opportunity to communicate an engaging vibrancy and demonstrate their entrepreneurial spirit. Working on your own projects will keep you from feeling and appearing desperate. When you're excited about your work, you project a positive self-assurance that can make you more attractive to a potential employer.

> "There is no excuse for not self-generating work. You don't need someone's permission to work. If you are not working, then the onus of responsibility is on you. And it doesn't ever stop. You'll always have to keep proving yourself, no matter what level you're at—and that's the gift, because it means you're showing up for your dream. And nothing is greater than that, so enjoy the ride."
>
> —Adrian Martinez, actor, writer, and producer with nearly 100 film and TV credits, including *Focus*, *The Secret Life of Walter Mitty*, and *Casa de mi Padre*

Build Industry Relationships

One misconception about relationship building is that meeting someone new will result in instant employment. Relationship building is like planting seeds.

Not every seed results in new growth, but the more seeds you plant, the greater the odds of something growing.

Think of relationship building as investing in your career. Directors and producers want to hire people they like and respect. Knowing someone well enough to earn their respect requires an investment of time and effort on your part. Follow up when you meet industry professionals. They don't have to be people who are in a position to hire you. Go to opening night parties and industry events. Forge authentic, positive, professional relationships, and let go of the need to know where those relationships will lead.

Examine your relationship-building efforts by asking yourself:

* Who do I already know that I can contact?
* How am I following up with people?
* How can I reach out in a genuine manner?

All of these actions will help you move forward. Dealing with the challenges of disappointment and rejection demands your awareness, commitment, and desire to make things better. You must take action. And taking action requires discipline.

Acting isn't for the faint of heart. Frustrations are inevitable, but they don't need to be crippling. Creating strategies that help you get back on track is the key to personal empowerment and fulfillment—and ultimately, success.

> "I remind myself the right project always finds me in the end. If I didn't book a gig, something else is right around the corner. It's helpful to remember that this is a team effort. Your setback made someone else's dream come true. And even though it may be hard to see, that is something worth celebrating."
>
> —Margo Seibert, performed on and off Broadway and at Carnegie Hall; nominated for a Drama Desk Award, appeared in an HBO series, national commercials, and in regional theaters

CARL MENNINGER and **LORI HAMMEL** are the authors of *Minding the Edge: Strategies for a Fulfilling Successful Career as an Actor* (Waveland Press, 2011). Menninger is a writer and director and Assistant Professor of Theatre and Musical Theatre at American University in Washington, DC. He is also the Artistic Associate at The Windy City Playhouse in Chicago. Hammel made her Broadway debut in *Mamma Mia!*, and she plays conservative political pundit Leslie Hillerman on the Onion News Network series, *In the Know*. She is an award-winning actor who has appeared on and off Broadway and in national tours, feature films, and national commercials.

Carl Menninger   Lori Hammel

Photo by Michael Imbimbo

1,000+ STAGE PERFORMANCES

An Interview With 100-Year-Old Chemancheri Kunjiraman Nair

▸ By Akhila Vimal C

I was on the stage, enacting the role of Krishna in the play called Kuchelavrita. *My guru, Karunakara Menon, was acting as Kuchela, an old poor friend of Krishna. In the play, Kuchela appears at the back of the audience with a burning torch. When Krishna identifies Kuchela, he comes to the audience and shows his respect and leads him to the stage.*

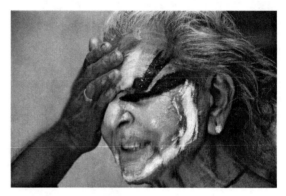

Chemancheri Kunjiraman Nair

Photo by Madhuraj

Like all other days, the performance was acquiring an affectionate tint. Kuchela was looking at Krishna with deep devotion and happiness, but his body was stiff, and it was quite difficult to lead him to the stage.

I started performing the sequence of Krishna, but Kuchela was still sitting on the stage. To complete the scene after me, he had to act out his Kuchela sequence. But the artist was not moving.

I got anxious—even angry. Singers were repeatedly calling the name Kuchela. Suddenly, he collapsed onto my hands. The play was interrupted. It was his last performance. Within a week he passed away.

Chemancheri Kunjiraman Nair is the legendary performer of Kathakali, a classical dance drama of Kerala, India. June 26, 2015, was his 100th birthday, and he proves that age has never been an obstruction for him. He has spent more than eighty years in the pastures of Kathakali enacting various roles.

Chemancheri's proficiency lies in the role of Krishna, a Hindu deity. He donned the role on more than 1,000 stages. Besides Kathakali, Chemancheri made an extensive contribution to the arena of Indian classical dances. One of the pioneers of Keralanadanam, a mixed form of two Indian classical dances, Mohiniyattam and Kathakali, he worked as a dance trainee at one of the major circus companies in Kerala. He has become a living legend, an eminent authority on the dance forms of Kerala, and he also played a leading role in the Malayalam movie, *Mukhammoodikal* (Masks).

I had the great pleasure of interviewing Chemancheri Kunjiraman Nair in the summer of 2015.

Could you tell me how you happened to be in the theater?
When I was 11, during the anniversary celebration of my school, I was watching a drama called "Wisdom of Solomon." It was the first time in my life that I witnessed a girl performing on the stage. I admired her, and I began to frequently visit a theater group near my house and watch their rehearsals. One day, when I was observing the rehearsal, the proprietor of the group asked me to join. For a year, I was part of that group. That was my first experience in acting.

What did your path look like to the genre of Kathakali?
After a year with the theater, I got an opportunity to learn Kathakali. Govinda Menon came to our group to do stage decoration for a play. After a performance, he asked us whether we wanted to learn Kathakali. I was interested, even though I didn't have any idea about the form. He asked me to get permission from my family, but my people were unwilling to send me. They warned me that during the training, Kathakali performers had to undergo rigorous massage for body fitness, which wouldn't be good for my health.

But that did nothing to dampen my enthusiasm. I joined the Radhakrishna Kathakali Yogam (1933–1940) and started learning Kathakali under the supervision of Guru Paleri Karunakara Menon.

How was the learning experience? Was it as rigorous as you had heard?
It was. The training started at 3:00 am. We would put oil on our bodies and start exercising with the body and leg in the beginning and then specialized

exercises for the eyes, face, and neck. After breakfast, Kathakali training would continue till 12:30 pm. After lunch, the guru would recite the verses and stories of Kathakali, which we had to memorize by the next day. And again by 3:00 pm, we had to be there in the classroom, and that would continue until 10:00 pm. Every year, for ninety days, massages would be arranged to suit our physique to perform Kathakali.

Can you tell me about the massage technique?
In Kathakali, along with strength and flexibility, performers need the capacity to steadily stand on the stage for a long time and to do facial and gestural acting with their heavy costumes. For this, performers need immense strength in their lower back, so the Kathakali massages are focused on the lower back. Nowadays in Kathakali, learners don't go through that ninety-day schedule. They don't study Kathakali in the traditional way, maybe because Kathakali alone can't be their source of one's livelihood. What they make as artists will be meager, but they'll want the fame that Kathakali brings.

In your early career, was it possible to survive with only Kathakali?
No, it was really difficult to survive. The entire troupe would get ten rupees for a show, and the guru would distribute that among everybody. Sometimes we wouldn't get anything. But the troupe would take care of food and accommodation. Still, we were happy to be part of Kathakali.

Did you ever think about quitting for another career?
When I started learning Kathakali, it was difficult to manage. I was even planning to run away from the school at one point. I was scared and worried about the response back home if I went. One day, I decided that I would go for the death anniversary of my father to do the rites, and my plan was to never come back. I went to the guru and asked for his permission to go, and he said that if I really loved my father I wouldn't need a particular day to remember him—I could do it every day. Even though I was disappointed, I followed his words. To this day, I keep aside a portion of my food for my beloved ones.

What did the moments of confusion and self-doubt look like for you?
After the loss of Guru Karunakara Menon, I went home and decided to involve myself in my people's farming. I was shaken, and I couldn't recover from his death. I decided to end my career, but destiny decided otherwise. One mes-

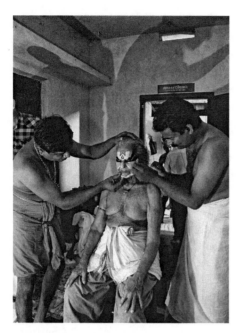

Chemancheri Kunjiraman Nair getting prepared for stage

Photo by Madhuraj

senger from Kadathanad Kuttipuram Kovilakam Kathakali Yogam (1824–1945), which was part of a royal family from North Malabar, came to my house and asked me to join their Kathakali school. I accepted the offer.

After the death of my daughter and wife Janaki, I went through the same phase again. I was in a deep, pensive state, and I couldn't surmount it. That time, Appukutti Nambiyar, owner of the Radhakrishna Kathakali School, sent me a letter with lines from *Kalyanasougadhikam* (a Kathakali play based on the Mahabharata). It was one of the lyrics that I had learned during my early years. After reading that, I got fresh energy, and I was confident that I could overcome the situation I was in. In these years, I survived and overcame severe physical injuries. It took me time, but I had little doubt about continuing my performance.

> "At all my difficult junctures, I have felt my guru talking to me in my dreams and giving me orders that it's my mission to live for art—that I have to accomplish that."

What does beginning again after all these hurdles mean to you?

For me, I believed that I could overcome these losses because of the blessings and wishes of my guru. At all my difficult junctures, I have felt my guru talking to me in my dreams and giving me orders that it's my mission to live for art—that I have to accomplish that.

Later, you worked more with classical dance forms outside Kathakali?

After the death of my guru, I was in a dilemma. It was the time when Kathakali practices of North Malabar were confronting serious problems. The popularity of Kathakali was eroding, and I couldn't stay in the field of art without shifting to other forms. The alternative would be to go to the paddy field with my uncles to earn my livelihood. At that time, though, I got an opportunity to teach dance in a school for their anniversary celebration. A freedom-fighter named Kaumudi was also teaching in that school, and she convinced me to accept the request. I took some dance movements from Kathakali and composed a piece and taught the students. From that piece, I found appreciation from a lot of people. It was during those days that I started my dance school in Thalasseri (1945).

You worked in a circus for some years as well. Could you describe that work experience?

Yes. My school was running quite well, and then one day the Fairy Circus Company owner, Ambotti, came to my school and requested that I join the troupe and teach dance to the participants. I accepted that offer and travelled all over South India with the troupe as a trainer. I met my dance teacher then and got training in classical dance for two years in Chennai under Balachandra Saraswathi Bhai.

Kathakali is extremely rigid about mixing with other dance forms. What was that shift like, moving between the two forms?

Good question. My first training was in Kathakali. But for my dance performances and dance dramas, I was using techniques of Kathakali, like sari and kummi dances and tandava (a rigorous masculine dance movement) movements. But at the same time, I was really strict when it came to bringing dance movements to Kathakali. I believed that it would kill the beauty of Kathakali. For example, I was playing the role of Parasuraman (an incarnation of Lord Vishnu of Hindu mythology) in a dance drama. From the start to the end, I used Kathakali kalasam for the movements, but I never brought the methods and techniques of dance drama into Kathakali performances.

Keralanadanam is an integrated form made by mixing two classical forms of Kerala—Kathakali and Mohiniyattam. How did you get in to the field of Keralanadanam?

When guru Gopinath choreographed Keralanadanam, he wanted me to come and perform it for the first time. The first performance, called *Kerala Vijayam*

(Victory of Kerala), was on July 1, 1949, on the formation day of Kerala as a state merging Travancore and Kochi, two independent provinces. But performance of this combined form of Kathakali and Mohiniyattam had been around for some time, called *Kathakali dance*. But it didn't receive recognition. Kathakali is one of the most difficult forms and is highly stylized and very hard to understand because of the codifications. This type of dance was performed to attract common audiences to the field of Kathakali, and Keralanadanam was an effective step toward this.

What is your opinion about integrating forms and styles?
I think when you're integrating two forms and styles, it will be enjoyable for more people. But at same time, it will reduce the aesthetic experience of the higher form. As I have said, I never bring dance movements to Kathakali, but I do take Kathakali techniques to my dance.

Chemancheri Kunjiraman Nair on stage

Photo by Madhuraj

Can you describe what inspired you to be part of Kathakali all these years, even when you've had other options?
I think I've always been a Kathakali person. If my guru were there, I would not have meandered to other fields. I always wanted to stay in the field of Kathakali. For many years, I collected Kathakali costumes to start a Kathakali school and troupe. When I was ready with all the materials, I decided to start a school in my ancestral property. I wanted to make sure that a total art form like Kathakali would get more meaning in the region of North Malabar through this school. It was my intention to bring back the lost tradition and the decorum of Kathakali in my region.

You've played the same character in more than 1,000 performances. When was your first performance as Krishna?

Initially, I performed female characters. Later, I played Kuchela, Keechaka (a villain character) and Nala (the hero of the play *Nalacharitha*, based on the stories from epic Mahabharata) on several stages. But I got appreciation for my Krishna Vesham. Shortly after, my guru decided to give me the role of Krishna. It is one of the Kuttitharam Vesham of Kathakali. I don't remember when I did it for the first time, but people from different places came for my Krishna Vesham, and they said that while watching me they experienced the presence of the real Krishna. I even had experiences of people coming on the stage and falling at my feet, chanting the names of Krishna. I find it difficult to have words to express my love and devotion to Lord Krishna.

> "I think that when you're climbing steps, you should turn back and see what you've left behind. If you do so, you'll be humble enough to see the world differently."

Can you describe how you perform Krishna?

I enter into a trance during the performance and don't remember what I am doing on stage. Even after the performance, people are scared to come near me for a long time because of my temper.

You've been performing on stage for a long time now. How have you reimagined yourself as a performer over the years?

I think that when you're climbing steps, you should turn back and see what you've left behind. If you do so, you'll be humble enough to see the world differently. I am satisfied as a performer and as a teacher. I am lucky enough to have learned under great teachers, and I have tried to give that back to the next generation.

You acted in a movie recently. How would you describe the difference between acting on stage and onscreen?

I was 93 when I acted in that movie. The story was about a Kathakali performer, one who lived his life for his art and how his passion toward Kathakali destroyed his family. On stage, we are performing for an audience right in front of us. When we're doing that for screen, we're doing that for camera. I prefer the first.

Why didn't you continue in movies?

I was disappointed, because in the climax of the film, the protagonist burns his costumes and walks toward the sea. I requested to change the climax, because burning Kathakali costume would give a wrong message. My aim was to share a good message about Kathakali. I discussed my problems with the crew. They accepted my corrections and told me that they would change it, but that did not happen. I couldn't do anything to impose the alteration I wanted. I couldn't accept the moral of that film, or the approach of the film industry.

What do you think about your achievements, and what is your ambition?

I want to teach my students, and I want to continue to perform—even at this age. I am happy to be here in the field of Kathakali. I have lived the entirety of my life for the art, and I wish to continue doing that.

AKHILA VIMAL C is PhD research scholar of Department of Theatre and Performance Studies, School of Arts and Aesthetics, Jawaharlal Nehru University, New Delhi. Her main research interests are disfiguration and staging of relationalities of disability, gender, and caste in Indian performance and textual practices. She is a trained dancer in Kathakali, Mohiniyattam, and Bharatanatyam and has completed schooling in Mohiniyattam and Bharatanatyam from Kerala Kala Mandalam.

Akhila Vimal

SUCCESS AND THE RESET BUTTON

A Moving Target

▸ By Deric McNish

A teacher I work with makes his students write a five-year plan. It's pretty hard for young actors to do, but most of them end up reading the same—move to New York City or Los Angeles, get an agent, get some good auditions, book some work, make mom proud. Of course, by now you know it's not that simple. More of your time will go toward surviving than thriving.

But why should that impact the dream?

I won't ask you to think ten or twenty years out. It's unfair for a 20-year-old to make decisions or set standards for her 30- or 40-year-old self. They are two very different people.

When you graduate and throw yourself into a market saturated with an endless sea of fresh faces that all share the same dream—yes, you may find instant success. But most of us are in this for the long haul. Let's assume you've committed to this career with all its joys and sorrows. Success may come suddenly at any age, but what if it's destined to come decades later? Will you have the patience to plod on and wait for your moment? Will you be ready to grasp that moment when it comes?

Things change over time. Your type, for example, may evolve from office assistant to office manager or from ingénue to wicked stepmother. The herds of actors thin, and competition gets a bit less fierce. Your goals will change. Your definition of success will be informed by your personal experiences. You'll reinvent yourself as a performer again and again.

As a case study, let's look at a troupe of young actors, ranging from 20 to 32 years of age that went out on a national tour in the year 2000. Among that troupe of eight was a bright-eyed younger version of myself that skipped a college class one day, drove to an audition in New York City, booked the job, and then took a semester off from college to perform.

The Bourgeois Gentleman tour, National Theatre of the Performing Arts, spring 2000

It was a paid gig, and I got to rehearse in the big city, work with professionals, see the country, and perform every day. It was educational theater for student audiences—but nonetheless, we all took the show and our professionalism very seriously. For many of us, as young artists close to the starting line, it was a defining artistic experience. Work begets work, they say, so surely when we returned to New York City bursting with stories of crowded cafetoriums from Memphis to Philly, agents like Bernard Telsey would be very interested to hear about us. Right?

It wasn't the ultimate goal. It wasn't Broadway. But for all of us, at that time, it felt like success. It's been a long and unpredictable ride since then. Everyone involved in that tour continues to enjoy success in the arts today, but only because our definitions of success have grown along with us.

Diane Chernansky

Diane Chernansky's words are informed by her long career that has recently gained momentum fifteen years after the tour. She just booked a recurring role on an HBO series called *Silicon Valley*, she booked an independent film earlier this year, and she leveraged that success to get a new agent. She's been auditioning consistently, and while she still has her day job, she says, "In the past year, I've felt more like an actor than ever before."

Diane Chernansky
Photo by jeff e photo

The 2000 tour was Diane's first year as an actor. The gig was her first real job in the industry, as it was for many of us in that van. And at the time it felt like success—five days a week, working with good people and nurturing our talents and skills. Seeking more momentum and commercial success, and heeding that misguided rumor that "Los Angeles loves New York actors," she moved to the West coast. With no immediate impact on her career, she found herself starting over—a scary proposition.

Starting over, however, became a theme in her career. The graph of her success isn't one of steady and consistent growth. It has wild peaks and valleys. Diane studied at a good studio in Los Angeles, developed her standup comedy, and sustained herself with a day job in corporate America. In the tour, she played a feisty maid, but throughout the rest of her career, she's played what she describes as "nice girls and professionals." Her type hasn't changed much, but she did notice the shift when she started getting called in for the "mom" or the office manager, rather than the secretary.

How does she accept and capitalize on that change? "I do casting director workshops at a place that has a fair amount of actors in their 50s and 60s. They're seasoned, and they're good. It helps to realize that not all actors are under 25 and hot."

> "There's room for all of us, at all ages, and all types."

But I'm a Professional! Right?

Diane points out that there's a distinct and important difference between getting paid for the work you do and getting paid *enough* for the work you do. Getting paid means you're a professional. Getting paid *enough*, over time, "is what allows you to focus on the work you want to do, that makes your heart sing."

Everyone's definition of success evolves over time, but one common theme is that we all want to get paid enough. How do we define *enough*? Well, it's important to consider the standard of living you're willing to accept.

While you may have artistic and commercial success right off the bat, if you find yourself swimming in artistic success but you're still unable to afford the things that let you feel like a successful person, or if you find yourself questioning whether you're truly a professional, then it may be time to hit the "reset" button.

The "Reset" Button

"An actor's life has ebbs and flows," Diane says. A good way to hit the reset button on a career that's not moving at the pace you want is to revisit your process. For instance, you might consider taking an acting class at a good studio as opposed to forking over all your hard-earned money to workshops with agents and casting directors. Be an actor by developing your technique. Doing a good scene in a class can make you feel like an actor, which can affect your confidence in auditions.

If all your time and energy is spent getting the bills paid, it can be easy to lose touch with your artistic self—with what drew you to the profession in the first place.

Actors are lifelong learners. At the end of years racing from class to class in a university, you may be burned out on education. You may feel as though you've learned enough. That will pass the moment you find yourself in a class again. As Diane says, "If you're committed to learning and growing, you'll find yourself in places where you say, 'wow, I am a beginner again.'"

Because what every actor learns somewhere along the way, is that going back to the beginning can be the best way to make it to the end.

Toby Pruett

Toby Pruett hit the pavement in New York City after completing the National Shakespeare Conservatory program. By the age of 28, he'd already completed two national tours and worked as a teacher at the National Shakespeare Conservatory and the Stella Adler Conservatory of Acting. This was his third tour, and it appealed to him in part because of the meaty role, but also because he wore two hats: actor and company manager. It fit right in with his goals at the time.

Toby Pruett

Photo by David Piggott

As he explains, each paid professional acting gig was a "stepping stone to the next tier of the profes-sional theater community." The artistic standards of the productions, the opportunity to keep improving a show day after day over many weeks, the outreach and educational nature of the production, and the chance to work with and manage a group of artists all appealed to him.

Being a Professional vs. Acting Professionally

Toby points out that those are two very separate things. It's possible to be a professional—a diligent, well-trained, talented, industrious actor—while not getting paid for your work. In the long run, however, we all need to pay our rent and take care of our loved ones and ourselves. Our shared goal as actors is to ply our craft in a way that we can help those around us and ourselves, while still making the world a better place. "Acting professionally," means getting paid a living wage for your work, and that becomes more important as time goes on.

Toby's work in the years since the tour and his New York City efforts reflect those values. He calls himself a "blue-collar actor," although he has also worked as a director, stunt performer, writer, and fight choreographer. For the past nine years, his steady and rewarding employment has included principal performer with Universal Studios Florida and Japan in the *Wizarding World of Harry Potter*, member of the Equity Acting Company at Walt Disney World in *Jack Sparrow's Private Tutorial*, almost 400 performances in fourteen different shows at Sleuth's Mystery Dinner Shows, and about 2,000 performances with Pirates Dinner Adventure. He has been seen, enjoyed, and photographed by millions of happy guests the world over.

His definition of success today aligns with the companies where he frequently performs: "creating a positive impact on guests, audience members, and fellow performers." He also places value on maintaining his skill set, doing diverse work, and earning a consistent and comfortable wage.

Learning From Success and Failure

Toby reminds us that we learn more from our failures than our successes and that we "must leap forward constantly, but attempt to do so with kindness for those around." We'll all make colossal blunders as artists and professionals, and the best strategy is to own it, accept it, and learn from it.

Although it's been a long time since Toby left New York City, he continues to thrive in a competitive, high-energy performance career that has a dramatic impact on a wide audience. I asked him if he felt successful, and I'll leave his answer intact.

> "I don't know if I am successful or not. I don't care anymore. I am very happy, though. I make my living as a career professional performance artist . . . I am not rich and I am most certainly not famous . . . I've been part of culturally significant events on a grand scale and individual level. I am also hopeful for the shows and roles to come, the artists I will get to work with, and the people I will make a difference to even for only a wonderfully fleeting moment."

Sassi

Sassi (she's always gone by her surname) is primarily a standup comedian who travels across the country working clubs and corporate venues, special events, and parties. She continues to act, mostly in commercials and television. As a single mom, she finds it difficult now to commit to the demanding and unforgiving schedule of theater work.

Asked about how she has evolved as a performer since the tour, Sassi said, "I am myself first, and then I build the role on top of that. I don't try and figure out what everyone wants me to be."

Sassi

Photo by Ella Steinbeck

That's good advice for an actor at any age. "Trust your imagination," she says, which becomes easier as you grow more confident in your craft.

She reaffirms Diane's advice, to embrace your changing type—in part because it allows you to be yourself and in part because it means less competition.

> When I hit 35, I started getting called in for a lot of mom roles. It was great. There was less competition than in my 20s, and it was easy to own it because

I *am* a mom. I didn't have to starve myself to compete with millions of perfect-looking girls like I did in my 20s.

What is success to Sassi? It's "making a living doing what I love." By that measure, she has achieved success, but she still admits that at times it's hand to mouth, and that she'd love more TV jobs so she could relax a little more with money.

Jared Reinmuth

Jared Reinmuth booked his role in the tour right after he decided to stop actively pursuing auditions. He was brought in as an emergency replacement. That's often the way things work—stop chasing success, and maybe it'll chase you. He was 32 at the time, and while he admits that he shared the typical actor's dream of awards, fame, and fortune, by that time he'd come to value artistic success as much as commercial.

Jared Reinmuth

Photo by Laura Rose

His work today reflects that value. He is a diverse, creative artist, and recent projects include classical roles and challenging innovative contemporary pieces that engage with difficult topics. He is directing new works and a production is scheduled of a play he wrote, *Monte Cristo*.

He wears many artistic hats, and his definition of success is grounded in artistic value.

> Success to me is having an audience believe a character. It's knowing that you had a great performance or completed a successful run. Success is learning new skills or accents while performing a role—adding to your range.

Since the tour I've kept in touch with most of these actors. I've performed with some of them. I've even lived with some of them. In the entire time I've known him, Jared's commitment to artist success has meant that he frequently has to make sacrifices. For him, there's no question about which has more value.

> "You have to commit to enjoying the journey, and enjoying the rewards of living the artist's life."

Saluda Camp

It was her first morning in New York City. It was her first professional audition. She arrived at the audition studio from the airport, having just completed a training program at one of the top conservatories in the United Kingdom. Her dad waited in the lobby while she nailed the audition and booked the job, a national tour that would take her from Maine to Florida, with a stop at her home state of South Carolina. At some point during those

Saluda Camp

Photo by Laura Rose

long drives from venue to venue, she began to sit more frequently next to Jared Reinmuth, the man she would eventually marry. Perhaps the business of acting wouldn't be as hard as everyone says!

Fifteen years later and single once again, she packed her bags and hailed a cab from her Harlem apartment, heading back home to South Carolina to pursue acting work in a smaller market, as well as another longtime interest—teaching. U2's "A Beautiful Day" was playing on the radio. A short time after a warm welcome in her hometown, she received a call from the Artistic Director of the Shakespeare Theatre of New Jersey, offering her a juicy role at a respected, professional Equity theater. So Saluda will soon pack her bags again.

I am living proof that you can have an artistically successful and satisfying career without living in NYC or LA. Sometimes, when you stop chasing the dream, it comes chasing after you. Sometimes you need to loosen your grip on the dream for it to take shape in its own time.

Artistic vs. Commercial Success

From the moment she began her career in New York City, Saluda enjoyed more artistic success than most actors. Innumerable national and regional tours of classic plays, a one-woman show that she performed in many different venues, gigs at regional Equity theaters, and roles in smaller New York City theaters. If experience is the measure of success, or the fulfilling work one does, or the friendships, meetings, relationships, reviews, or innumerable ovations, then hers is an unquestionable success story.

But when she began this journey, she also had another goal—commercial success. Classical roles are rewarding but not usually in the financial sense. She had dreams of Broadway, of films, of fame—as we all did at some time.

Saluda had been struggling as an actor for many years when her younger sister graduated from the North Carolina School of the Arts and booked an agent through an industry showcase in New York City. In a very short time, she booked recurring roles on *Mad Men*, *True Blood*, *The Good Wife*, and *The Mindy Project*. Notable films include *The Help*, *Pitch Perfect*, and *Pitch Perfect 2*. She made her Broadway debut in 2008 in *A Country House* and starred opposite Daniel Radcliffe in the 2008 Broadway revival of *Equus*. Saluda has cheered her sister every step of the way, but she's keenly aware of the comparisons that people make and how artistic and commercial success are valued differently.

Have I Seen You in Anything?

Well-meaning strangers and friends alike always ask the same question when you tell them you're an actor: "What are you working on?" Or sometimes it's: "Have I seen you in anything?"

Today, when I tell people I'm a teacher, the universal response is, "What subject do you teach?" Why is it that, when you identify as an actor, people don't ask, "What kind of an actor are you?" Then you might explain that you do stage work, or that you perform in educational theater or theater for social change, or that you do regional work, or that you focus on new plays.

For most actors, when asked what they're working on, the truthful answer is something about auditions, or classes, or projects in the past or on the hazy horizon. Saluda's answer at one point was, "I'm sure I'll get something soon."

She wants young artists to know that "no actor ever knows whether or not they will get something soon." Not Saluda, and not her sister. No matter where you are in your career, there will be a certain amount of insecurity that can chip away at your confidence if you let it.

The comparisons made between Saluda and her sister helped her to question her definition of *success*, and it's from that thoughtful reflection that she can give us such a clear contrast between commercial and artistic success. Saluda's artistic successes, many of which I had the pleasure to witness, are not valued as much as commercial successes. Financial reward aside, there is also a recognition and respect that goes to actors with immediately recognizable projects. People equate commercial success with talent, while anyone who has spent any amount of time in this fickle industry knows that there are many uncontrollable factors involved in commercial success.

Saluda's experiences, both good and bad, have helped her become the successful artist she is today, in part because she has allowed her definition of *success* to change. "All the thriving and sometimes just surviving have shaped who I am today . . . I'm a much tougher and humbler person than I was when I arrived in New York City."

Quitting

A recent article in *Backstage* insisted that if you're truly an actor, then you can never quit the business. My knee-jerk response was that it was a limiting and simplistic assertion. Of course you can quit. People do it all the time. If their definition of success evolves, if they get sick of the sacrifices, if they see some other career that could bring them joy, then let's allow them to quit without any shame from within our ranks.

Actors, of all people, should be understanding when actors decide to quit. And yet for the life of me, I can't think of a single actor I know who has quit. Sure, some of them have left New York City or Los Angeles. Others, like me, have shifted to other related careers like teaching or arts management. And still others spend most of their year doing work that has very little connection to the arts.

There's not one of them, myself included, who doesn't occasionally get up on stage, or on camera, or behind a microphone, and feel the blood of a theater artist still coursing through their veins. You can quit the profession, but you can't quit being an actor. Once it's taken hold, there's no shaking it.

So go and do whatever makes you happy. Try to quit. It won't work. By now you've been bitten. You're a thespian, come hell or high water. Whatever your definition of success is now—whether commercial or artistic—over time it will change, and you will change along with it. Keep hitting that reset button, over and over. Do what makes you happy, and you'll always feel successful.

DERIC MCNISH is an Assistant Professor of Theater: Acting, Voice, and Speech at Michigan State University. He earned a PhD from the University of Colorado Boulder and an MFA in Acting from Case Western Reserve University and the Cleveland Play House. McNish has performed at theaters such as the Shakespeare Theatre of New Jersey, the Porthouse Theatre, and the Ohio Shakespeare Festival, as well as on national tours and in NYC venues ranging from Shakespeare in the Park(ing Lot) to the Metropolitan Opera. His television work includes *Guiding Light* on CBS and NBC's *Third Watch*. He is a proud member of SAG-AFTRA, Actors' Equity Association, and the Voice and Speech Trainers Association (VASTA). McNish's research focuses on inclusive approaches to professional actor training, performance techniques applied to English Language Learning, and devising as a universal approach to inclusive ensemble work.

Deric McNish

Photo by Kellyn Uhl

TEACHING ACTING IN PRISONS

Lessons from the Actors' Gang Prison Project

▶ An Interview With Sabra Williams

Sabra Williams joined Tim Robbins' theater company, the Actors' Gang, in 2002. She had trained as an actor and dancer and had been working professionally for many years in the UK. Early in her career, she worked with the English Shakespeare Company, where they performed Shakespeare plays for people who were incarcerated, both in prisons and in juvenile halls.

Sabra Williams
Photo by Kenneth Dolin

The Actors' Gang was founded in 1981 with the goal of producing plays that contribute to the ongoing dialogue about society and culture, while never forgetting that theater's primary purpose is to entertain. The Actors' Gang has produced over 100 plays in Los Angeles, in forty US states, and on five continents. The Actors' Gang ensemble has included accomplished actors such as Jack Black, John Cusack, John C. Reilly, Helen Hunt, Kate Walsh, Fisher Stevens, Jeremy Piven, Ebbe Roe Smith, Jon Favreau, Brent Hinkley, Kate Mulligan, Lee Arenberg, Kyle Gass, and Tim Robbins.

How did you initially get involved with the Actors' Gang?
Every Sunday night, the company gets together to workshop. About forty people get together and improvise, using stock characters and this high emotional and physical form of theater—it's a very stylized version of European theater based

on commedia dell'arte with white face and masks. So I started workshopping on Sunday nights, and I immediately knew I'd found my people. They had this mission statement to do great change in society, so I told Tim that I wanted to be involved in the prison outreach—and he said they didn't have a program, and would I please invent one?

So we started in the California Rehabilitation Center in Norco, taking what we do in workshop into the prison. And the change was astounding, the way it affected them. We almost immediately had a waiting list of people who wanted to get into the white face and participate, which is kind of ironic in prison.

> "When I first started with this work, I remember that the effect it had was mindblowing—just to see the power of the arts on a population who's considered the dregs of society and ignored and invisible and forgotten."

Were you state funded when you first started?
No, we've only gotten funding from the state the last few years. Ten years ago when we started, all these issues were invisible. No one was funding prisons. The good side of that was that we were the only arts program in that prison, so we could measure the success, and we found out that the in-prison infractions dropped by eighty-nine percent for people doing our class. It was having this massive success in breaking down the gang culture. And it was undeniable that it was because of our workshops, because there were no other programs.

Can you describe what the workshops involve? Is it all improv based?
Right, yes, so we work with twenty or twenty-five students at a time. It's four hours with no break. It's really intensive. We start with something called *red hot sharing*, which is when you share anything that you need to get off your chest. It just goes in the center—we call it *throw it in the fire*, and we use it as fuel for the work.

Then we do a bunch of theater games that are very fast and furious, and they all lead to elements of what we call "the Style", this is the type of theater work that we do. All of our work is about holding up a mirror to ourselves. It's a safe place, and you play characters. I've known some people in there for seven or eight years. I don't know why they're in prison, and they don't know anything about me. It's just us meeting as human beings.

One of the most important things about this work is that we're not professors and they're empty vessels. We're not filling them up with knowledge. We're partners in the work, because we're also doing this work every Sunday night and on the stage, and it's really hard work. So it completely breaks the paradigm of prison, because there's no hierarchy.

So we start with these games, and we give them language training, which is very important. They have to use "I" statements—"I noticed," "I observed," "I wondered," "I remembered," rather than, "Yeah, man, that was cool," because that doesn't give anybody any information.

And then we always do a relaxation, which takes about twenty minutes. They're lying on the ground with their eyes closed, which is a big deal in prison.

Why is it a big deal?
Oh, you don't close your eyes in prison, and a lot of times people haven't had a good night's sleep for twenty, thirty, forty years. You have to always be aware of what's going on. It can be dangerous in prison. So that's why we do the relaxation, and it radically changes the energy in the room.

You said that those four hours are really hard work. What do you mean by that?
It's physically hard work because there's very little sitting down. There's no break, and a lot of the time we're moving very fast. It's also incredibly hard emotional work. We work in four emotional states: happy, angry, sad, and afraid. And we work on them to the max, so you're the happiest person in the world or the saddest person in the world—and we're doing this for four hours. It's exhausting. It takes great courage as well, because so often people in prison will say, "All my life, I thought I was just angry. Now I realize that actually I'm sad," or "I'm afraid." So they start to identify their emotions and also develop empathy.

They're also doing that work while looking in each other's eyes, so you have the White Supremacist and the Crip and the Northerner all in the room together being emotionally vulnerable. Then they take it out in the yards. They'll say hey to each other, or they'll laugh together, and the other people are like, what on earth is happening right now?

How and when does the white face come into the workshop? Are these students initially comfortable with that?

In the beginning, so many students say they won't put on the makeup, but they end up doing it. After we've done relaxation, that's when they put on the white face mask and get into a character. They can choose any character they want, and then we do a bunch of physical stuff, commedia dell'arte characters and interactions. It's all improvised. We play like that for a long time, and then we do some writing to have them look at their emotional lives and become more aware of the tools that we're giving them to make different choices emotionally.

And we always end with forty-five seconds of laughing, which sends them out on a high. And that's it—that's what the class is every week.

> "This class really gives the tools to change. Myself, I've been wanting to change for a while and a lot of guys in here want to change, but we don't have the tools. It's like we are standing on the ground wanting to find a way to get up to the roof and then here you guys come with a ladder."
>
> — Israel, class participant

When you say they choose a character, do they create their own? Or do you give them a list of characters to choose from?

We give them a little booklet with all the commedia dell'arte characters. There are male and female characters, and very often the biggest, baddest guy will choose to play a woman, which is always amazing. It's beautiful to see. They play like children. A lot of people in prison never played. They didn't have a childhood, and it's a fundamental part of development, playing. Very few of my students ever had exposure to the arts before, which is no surprise.

The Actors' Gang Prison Project workshop

Photo by Bob Turton

How many teachers are facilitating the twenty-five students?

Usually we have two lead teachers. Often that might be me and Tim, and then we usually have a first-year teacher and also a scribe, somebody who takes notes. So we have ten years of anecdotal evidence from these notes that we've taken. Sometimes we have other people who come to watch from the company or people who want to learn how to teach.

What is the training for an actor who wants to teach?

Every year there's a mandatory training by the Department of Corrections and Rehabilitation, so we all have to go to that. Then I also do a training two or three times a year here at the theater. The thing that I've learned over the ten years is that our boundaries have to be very clear when we're working in prisons, so we know how to cut off any inappropriate behavior. If our boundaries are clear, then there's a lot of love in the room and we can be free to play. If there's anything coming between the students and the work, with some of the personalities, it can go very badly wrong. So we have a lot of training and very clear boundaries.

Are there officers there during the workshopping? Or just members from the Actors' Gang?

It depends on the room. If we're in the gym, there are always officers, and there's usually a gunner somewhere, especially in a maximum-security prison. If we're in a substance abuse room, there's no officer, but we have a panic alarm in that situation. And what we've been doing the last couple of years in some situations is giving the work over to our students, student-led classes. And in those cases, they're in a room with no officers—just the staff sponsor.

How do the student-led groups work?

We have a couple of ways of working. For the prisons that are close by, we go one day a week for four hours; for the prisons that are far away, we go seven days straight, four hours a day. And at the end of those seven days, we choose leaders, and the students lead the class one day a week. Then we come back every six weeks to check up. In the student-led classes, the work has gone to a whole new level, because they have to learn extra skills like conflict resolution and leadership.

Can you tell me about your student who put on a play? I saw in your TED lecture that he started his own training sessions in prison?

This guy, we started the class with him seven years ago, and we had hardly any money, so we would go and do a session and then we'd have to go and fundraise, and it might be six months before we got back. So he wanted to continue the work in between, but we didn't even know. He trained forty people and wrote his first play. It was in rhyming couplets, the whole play! It was called *The Magnanimous Ass*, based on the Mechanicals from *A Midsummer Night's Dream*. Forty people that we hadn't trained doing "the Style" in this incredible play. It was truly an amazing experience to see.

Since then, he's written four plays, trained sixty new people, and he just left after nineteen years in prison. His dream is to start a theater company doing our work but for parolees. He's only been out three weeks now, and he's in a halfway house where we've started our reentry program. He's going to be our first hire. We're going to hire him to teach. After years of requests from our students, we've finally been able to create a program for people on the outside.

How incredible. Are you actively training new teachers as well? Do you have a lot of actors who want to do this work with you?

Yes, because we've expanded. We'll be eight prisons, reentry, and juvenile hall this year. Every day we get requests from wardens from all over the world to have a program, but it's such a highly specialized program, if you don't get training, it can go very badly wrong, because you're dealing with people's emotions. So I'm working on a book for the training now. We're not therapists—we're actors, but mental health experts who see the work will say, oh yes, this is cognitive therapy. It's dealing with trauma—it's transforming behavior and thinking. That's what it does. Our tagline is, "I'm master of my mind, not a victim of my thinking."

I'm fascinated by the fact that you're trained as an actor and not a therapist. Do you think there's an inherent tie between the two fields?

I definitely think there is. Everybody has their own approach to acting, but for me, so much of it is people watching and trying to understand the heart of humanity—what moves us, what motivates us. When I play a character, for example, Titania, I have to go on a journey to become a vessel for that character, so I have to examine my own behavior and what motivates me.

One of the main things is being able to look at myself without judgment, and being able to see the character as a person and try to embody what makes her tick. And then I have to take responsibility for my own actions and thinking. That's one of the great things about the power of the arts, because you're talking about universal things that apply to all humanity. I think that's why this work works so well on this population of non-actors, because they recognize something in it that's just human behavior.

I wonder, too, if it might be a nice escape to put on this mask and embody another character for some of these students. That they have an opportunity to put themselves aside for a few hours?
Yes. That's one of the big things. Well, that's one of the things about play as well, isn't it? For children, when they play, they get to go into an imaginary world. And what a gift that is for this population, the idea of escape. Some people think they shouldn't be allowed to escape from their punishment, even for a few hours. But especially with people who are gang affiliated and have tattoos on their faces, I notice that when they put on the white face, they can start neutral again and can forget who they were. They have a chance to play Mr. Pantalone, the old miser who's rich, or one of the young lovers, or the revolutionary servant. They get to experience a different life than they've ever experienced. And that helps them realize that there are other ways to live.

Sabra Williams teaching a group of students relaxation during a workshop

Photo by Jeff Bauer, courtesy of The Actors' Gang

It's so amazing to see it, especially people who are deeply embedded in a gang and have been since they were children. A lot of these young guys, they're nihilistic because they don't think they're going to live to 30. And one of the things I always say to them is, "But what if you do live past 30? Then what?" But there's no plan for that. They don't have a Plan B.

In our reentry program, I saw this young kid sitting outside our first day of class, just watching. And even watching, I could see something opening in him. So I told him, "You have to come. This class is for you." And he came the next week, and it's so overwhelming to them, because suddenly they're not invisible anymore. When you're in a gang, you're a soldier. Your life doesn't really mean anything. But we're like, "I see you. You're part of this group." And here they are with these big emotions that they've always squashed, and it's like an explosion happens inside of them. And sometimes they can't take it. They have to leave.

What's the percentage of those who do and don't come back?
Those are the students who do come back. They don't want to, but they can't resist. This young kid came back last week, and he was like, "I'm just here to say that I'm not coming back." So I'm like, "Okay, but right now you're in the room, so . . ." And he says, "Yeah, but I'm just here to let you know that I'm not coming back."

"So, okay, do you want to sit down for a bit and talk to me about why you're not coming back?"

"Yes, so, I'm not coming back, and I'm not wearing the makeup."

"Okay, so shall I just put the makeup on you while you're telling me?"

"Okay."

It's heartbreaking.

It's incredibly moving. Do you ever get so emotional that you fear you might cry in front of the students?
Yes, I cry a lot, but it's legitimate in our class. The students cry all the time too. People who haven't smiled, cried, felt fear—they haven't felt any of those things. But in this class, they're suddenly experiencing all of them. Other students will say, "I've known you thirty years. I've never seen you smile like you are now." That's in circle time, but when I'm teaching, it's not about me. Sometimes I'm

crying, but I'm still teaching. It's very overwhelming, especially when we go see a play and they've written a song or a poem. It's very emotional.

How would you say this theatrical path has shaped your life?
It's been the making of me. It's made me a better person. It's made me a better actor. It's made me understand what it is to be a human being. It's made me deeply understand and respect the power of the arts and the purpose of the arts. I started with a very conventional acting career—theater, film, and TV. I did the actress-in-LA thing for a while, but it was hollow, to be honest, because it was just about me. And I never thought being an artist was supposed to just be about me. I always thought it was supposed to be a privilege to enter into this world that's about humanity—and if it's just about me, then I haven't served my purpose as an actor.

I'm not saying that everybody has to actively serve a population like this, but I'm saying that we need to have an awareness that acting is more than about being pretty and winning awards. That's so disrespectful to the thousands of years that people have recognized acting for what it can be. It's not just about entertainment.

What do you say to the person who thinks this population doesn't deserve a second chance, or a chance to play and get in touch with their emotional life?
What I always say is that whether they deserve it or not has nothing to do with it. It's whether *we* deserve it as a society, that's the issue. Do we deserve to be able to have people come out better than when they went into prison, because if we do, here's an opportunity that's cost effective. It's not either/or. A lot of times you hear, "Well, my kids don't get access to the arts in school, so why should these guys?" Officers often say that, and we have school programs too, so that's a nonstarter.

But this work can help you to subsume your ego and your judgment. Even just witnessing this work. So for me, the most important thing is getting people to come into prison and watch, because when they sit in that room and see human beings in front of them who have the courage to change their lives through doing this work, through the arts, I don't need to say anything. Everyone's a convert after that, including the officers who are often very cynical.

In terms of judgment . . . do you think that actors are particularly suited for this type of work because you've trained yourself not to judge? Since part of doing your job is trying not to judge yourself?
Actors judge, we do. I worry less about the judgment and more about the experience. If I know someone's raped a child, I'm going to have judgment about

that person, and it's going to get in the way of being able to teach them. So right at the beginning, I made the rule that they're not allowed to tell us why they're there. I don't care if they're innocent or guilty—it has nothing to do with this work. I don't need to know anything about them, and they don't need to know anything about me. When that happens, the line between us is clear and we can just teach and learn. As humans, we do judge, so we take practical measures to make sure we can keep that judgment to a minimum. That's part of our work.

You've mentioned the power of the arts several times. Is there a specific language you need to use to explain this power to people? How can actors find their voice on this subject?

People might think artists are self-involved or narcissistic, spending so much time focused on their own work. But that's because we artists care about something that at this time in society isn't considered very important. It was considered very important in ancient Greek times. Artists and scientists were considered on the same level. And this is a big part of our battle, Tim and I, to get people to understand the power of the arts. This is why we work on legislation, as well, because we're advocates for the arts.

Artists have a responsibility to be able to speak to people so they can hear, so we need to use the data that exist. For instance, when kids practice the arts at school, they score higher on the things that people care about, like math and science. If that's what people care about, then we have to be able to speak to them in a way that they can hear what we're saying. When you have arts in corrections, it increases public safety and fiscal responsibility. We spend this money now, people don't come back to prison. This is the way we need to discuss the power of the arts, otherwise people think you're one of those hug-a-thug Hollywood types—and it's not about that.

What's next for you and the Prison Project? And what's next for your acting career?

I have two staff members who work with me now, and I'm trying to hand over more and more of the work so that I can do some film and TV work, which I've just started doing again. I'm in rehearsal for another play, and then a six-week European tour. It's quite an extraordinary ten years I've just gone through, and as an actor I really lost my attachment to Hollywood and the whole auditioning thing, which is another great outcome of this work. But I'm getting back to it recently without the attachment! A couple months ago, a friend called and asked if I wanted to do a day on her movie with Kristen Wiig. And then it happened three or four more times, people asking if I want to attach myself to a script that's going in for funding.

I like to think the Prison Project is like a magic box, and everybody gets what they need from it. It's the greatest feeling to be able to do this work and do theater and now and again and be able to work in film and TV and be able to teach. My life is pretty incredible, and this isn't what I ever imagined my life would be when I was in drama school.

What advice would you have for someone still in drama school?
Don't be narrow about it, because it's important to be able to receive what's actually going on rather than try to force things to be how you want them. This is a normal instinct, because we all have fear about how we should be and what we should do, but there's a whole universe out there of possibilities and things you can do. And you can invent things to do, too, like I did. You don't have to wait for someone to give you the opportunity.

Notes

1 Vaidyanathan, Rajini. 2015. "How Far Will We Go to Charge Our Phones?" http://www.bbc.co.uk/news/magazine-33295211, accessed July 9, 2015.
2 Goode, Chris. 2008. "Tone Clusters; or, The Audience is Listening . . .". http://beescope.blogspot.co.uk/2008/07/tone-clusters-or-audience-is-listening.html, accessed July 20, 2015.
3 Sedgman, Kirsty. 2016. *Locating the Audience: How People Found Value in National Theatre Wales*. Bristol: Intellect, 2016.
4 Parkinson, Andy and Jamie Buttrick. 2014. "Equality and Diversity within the Arts and Cultural Sector in England: Evidence and Literature Review Final Report." Manchester: Arts Council England and Consilium Research and Consultancy, 2014.
5 Levine, Lawrence. 1988. *Highbrow/Lowbrow*. Cambridge, MA: Harvard University Press, 1988.
6 Reason, Matthew. 2010. *The Young Audience: Exploring and Enhancing Children's Experiences of Theatre*. Stoke-on-Trent: Trentham Books Ltd, 2010.
7 Boal, Augusto. 2000. *Theater of the Oppressed*. London: Pluto Press, 2000.
8 Etchells, Tim. 1999. *Certain Fragments: Contemporary Performance and Forced Entertainment*. London: Psychology Press, 1999.
9 Lavery, Carl and David Williams. 2011. "Practising Participation: A Conversation with Lone Twin." *Performance Research* 16:4 (2011): 7–14.
10 Stanislavski, Konstantin. 1989. *An Actor Prepares*. London: Taylor & Francis, 1989.

11 Freshwater, Helen. 2012. "Consuming Authenticities: *Billy Elliot the Musical* and the Performing Child." *The Lion and the Unicorn* 36:2 (2012): 154–173.

12 Heim, Caroline.2012. "'Argue with Us!': Audience Co-creation through Post-Performance Discussions." *New Theatre Quarterly* 28:2 (2012): 189–197.

13 Sauter, Willmar. 2014. *The Theatrical Event: Dynamics of Performance and Perception.* Iowa City: University of Iowa (2014).

14 Moffat, Katie and Katherine Jewkes. 2015. "Lessons in Live Streaming from National Theatre Wales." Culture Hive. (2013) http://culturehive.co.uk/wp-content/uploads/2013/11/Lessons-in-live-streaming.pdf, accessed July 25, 2015.

15 Barker, Martin. 2012. *Live to Your Local Cinema: The Remarkable Rise of Livecasting.* Basingstoke: Palgrave Macmillan, 2012.

INDEX

Anna Weinstein is the Series Editor for PERFORM. A writer and editor with over fifteen years of experience in educational publishing, she received her MFA in Writing for the Performing Arts from the University of California at Riverside–Palm Desert and her BA in Communication Studies/Performance from the University of North Carolina at Chapel Hill. She teaches introductory and advanced screenwriting at Auburn University, and she is a frequent contributor to *Film International*, where she publishes interviews with award-winning female directors in her series "Diva Directors Around the Globe."

Chris Qualls is an Associate Professor of Theatre at Auburn University, where he teaches voiceover acting, acting for stage and screen, and introduction to theater. He received his MFA in Acting from the Alabama Shakespeare Festival and his BA in Communication Studies/Film from the University of North Carolina at Chapel Hill. He has worked as a voiceover actor for thirty years. His research and creative work focus on the integration of classical and nontraditional approaches to Shakespeare in performance, theater and media for social justice, and voice acting. He is a member of Actors' Equity Association.